Emma Ten Broeck Runk

Ten Broeck genealogy

Emma Ten Broeck Runk

Ten Broeck genealogy

ISBN/EAN: 9783337142438

Printed in Europe, USA, Canada, Australia, Japan

Cover: Foto ©Andreas Hilbeck / pixelio.de

More available books at **www.hansebooks.com**

THE TEN BROECK GENEALOGY

BEING THE RECORDS AND ANNALS OF
DIRCK WESSELSE TEN BROECK
OF ALBANY
AND HIS DESCENDANTS

COMPILED BY

EMMA TEN BROECK RUNK

❦

"Perge Carpisti"

❦

NEW YORK
PRINTED AT THE DE VINNE PRESS
1897

PREFACE.

Thus work is designed as a convenient genealogy and book of reference for the descendants of Dirck Wesselse Ten Broeck, without regard to the family name they bear to-day. From the first to the sixth generations the records are confined to those families where either one or other parent bore the surname of Ten Broeck. In the three last generations all descendants have been given, irrespective of name.

The sources of these annals are many. In addition to the wealth of material on the shelves of libraries, wills and deeds in county offices, and church and old Dutch Bible records have been collated.

Care has been taken to make a list of all authorities. The reference figures running through the narrative portion of the book are explained by the reference index which is found on the pages preceding the index to names.

The preference shown to the " Documents Relating to the Colonial History of New York," by E. B. O'Callaghan, and the " Documentary History of New York," by the same author, is on the ground that original

ii   v

State documents are indisputable. The references to the Documentary History are paged according to the quarto edition.

To Mr. Henry Brace of New York I am greatly indebted. The result of years of patient investigation of early records, and of an extensive correspondence, he has most generously placed at my disposal, grudging not in addition continuous assistance in the work.

General James Grant Wilson, President of the New York Genealogical and Biographical Society, has kindly allowed me to incorporate into this volume the data of the Ten Broeck Family which were printed in Volume XX of *The Record*.

The family tradition referred to on page eight was committed to writing by the late Judge John Sanders of Schenectady, at his daughter's request. This daughter, Mrs. Harold Wilson of Clermont, has done much toward rendering this work a great pleasure by assisting in manifold ways, and by a cheerful courage which has lightened many labors.

To all, new friends and old, who have united in deeds of cordial helpfulness I give most hearty thanks. I desire especially to acknowledge my indebtedness to all who have made it possible for me to add the valued illustrations to this work. Their names are found in the text in connection with the mention of the originals, with only two exceptions. I here express my gratification that through the kindness of Miss Margaret P. Hillhouse, the copy of the portrait and also the book-plate of her ancestor, Major John C. Ten Broeck, are given in these covers. The book-plate is reproduced from the original copper-plate which was probably executed by Maverick, now owned by Mr. Mansfield Lovell Hillhouse of New Brunswick, New Jersey.

My thanks are also due Miss E. H. B. Forman of Brooklyn, through whose courtesy some years since I made the sketch of the coat-of-arms from the valued painting still in her possession.

Mr. Berthold Fernow, sometime keeper of the historical records and documents of the State of New York, made the translation from the original Dutch of the will of Dirck Wesselse Ten Broeck.

It remains only for me to say that this subject is not exhausted, nor without omissions and errors. But if the flame of enthusiasm shall spread, and the several branches of Ten Broecks unite to bring their records to completion, the whole aim will have been accomplished.

EMMA TEN BROECK RUNK.

LAMBERTVILLE, N. J.,
   September the seventh, 1897.

LIST OF ILLUSTRATIONS.

x List of Illustrations

THE TEN BROECK GENEALOGY.

THE COLONIZATION OF
NEW NETHERLAND.

THE FIRST AND SECOND GENERATIONS.

THE events which led to the colonization of the Valley of the Hudson are of great interest to all who revert with pardonable pride to ancestors whose names are synonymous with the history of those early times. When Hendrik Hudson's discoveries of the great river which bears his name, and the Indian tribes inhabiting the region, were made known, the Holland merchants were prompt to improve the rare opportunity for trade thus opened.

On March the twenty-seventh, 1614, they obtained legalized permission from the States-General at The Hague to trade along the shores of America. They soon formed themselves into a body known as "The United New Netherland Company," and gained, in addition, the grant of exclusive privilege to trade with the coast settlements for a period of three years to begin on or before the first of January, 1615.

The first buildings erected for use were a block-house or fortress upon an island just below the present site of Albany, and a trading-post on the lower end of Manhattan Island. At the latter place they proceeded to collect furs and skins in immense numbers, ready for shipment to the Holland ports. The region discovered by these traders was soon named New Netherland, and recognized as Holland's dependency.

In the year 1617 a treaty of peace and goodwill was concluded between the Dutch traders and the chiefs or sachems of the five nations of Indians inhabiting this region, which proved of great value and of long continuance. The unsettled condition of affairs in Europe at this period led many wealthy merchant traders from Belgium to seek the shelter thus afforded to pursue their business, and as soon as opportunity offered a new company was incorporated. The charter conveyed the exclusive mercantile control of the Atlantic shores of America and Africa to the new body, under the title of The West India Trading Company. The central power was divided among five branches or chambers located in five principal cities of Holland, each with its directors, members and ships.

Peter Minuit, a French Protestant, a native of Wesel, the cosmopolitan city of Rhenish Prussia and adjacent to the Netherlands, was the first fully empowered Director General of this new Province. He arrived in the Bay of New Amsterdam early in May, 1626, and at once purchased from the Indian owners the present site of New York City, and vested the title in the Dutch West India Trading Company.

As colonization advanced Fort Orange was built on the present site of Albany, and clustered around it, for security, were the homes of the factors and servants of the Company, who carried forward the entire Indian trade throughout the vast tracts running back to the rivers of Ohio, and north to the boundary of the Canadian Province.

To stimulate interest, and promote civilization, the title of Patroon, with certain privileges, was granted any who should purchase lands from the Indian owners in this new world, and colonize fifty adult persons within the limit of four years. The Directors were the first to follow up this advantage, and slowly but steadily the work of agriculture advanced side by side with the work of trading.

The highest advantage of the trade thus opened accrued to those Holland merchants and Patroons who risked the most of means, though not always at the cost of personal sacrifice and toil — and it is well known how large the returns proved in many instances.

King Charles the Second, from his seat on England's throne, saw this wealth flowing past his shores at a time when his need for greater revenues was most pressing. As a first step he granted to his brother, James, Duke of York and Albany, the territory from the Connecticut River to Delaware Bay, including all Long Island and the River Hudson. Thus England's aggressive policy toward this child of Holland grew, until the squadron which conveyed Richard Nicolls, commissioned English Governor of New Netherland, arrived in the Bay of New Amsterdam and the demand for submission was heard.

There was little question of the wisest course. The

Dutch were assured continued possession of their real and personal property, freedom of religious worship, and all privileges of trade and intercourse with Holland. It appeared they had little to gain by resistance, and they might lose all !

It followed that on September the eighth, 1664, New Amsterdam passed under the English flag. Beverwyck submitted on the twenty-fourth of the same month, and the title of York and Albany became the new names of the two principal settlements. Holland gained the ascendancy once more in 1673, but it was for a short time only, and when peace was declared, the Duke of York received a second patent for the province of wide domain, which from this time took on the name of New York, only narrowing her boundaries as necessity demanded.

It has been said the history of any family through seven generations, however exalted or humble it may be, presents a true picture of the progress of society — it might be added, of the political world as well. It will be found in these pages how, in the spirit of toleration and with a high sense of honor natural to the sons of Holland, this and the allied families became the true and worthy servants and sons, both of England's colonies and of the "free and independent States."

The Dutch were attached to their own national Christian belief and form of worship, and care was exercised to provide the Colony with church buildings. Accordingly, a Reformed Protestant Dutch Church was erected at Beverwyck, or Albany, in 1643. It was of wood, and the size, thirty-four feet by nineteen, only admitted of nine benches for the worshipers. A few years later, it being necessary

THE SEAL OF GENERAL SAMUEL TEN BROECK (135).

to change the location, a new and larger building was called for. By 1715 the second had grown too small, and then the new one, of brick, was constructed in such a manner as to inclose the other, which was not demolished until the larger walls were completed around it. The last building was both ornate and curious, the pulpit and bell both being purchased in Holland.

The people worshiped according to the usages of their fathers, in the same language, and led by pastors who continued to receive their ordination in Holland; and one can imagine and picture the pride and joy they had in this house of God! How intimately it was interwoven with the lives of these early families may be brought out by calling to mind some of the customs and incidents of those days.

It was usual for the Dutch to carry their children to church for baptism, and this rite was often solemnized on the very day of birth; or, if deferred, it was rarely for many days. The entry, therefore, on the "Doop Bock," as the volume was called in which the record was entered by the pastor, was commonly accepted as the date of birth, unless the register contained the two dates.

The poor of all the city were cared for by the church for more than a century after the granting of the Charter. The public safety was in its keeping also, as appears from the following[1]: At a meeting of the Public Officers of Albany, on August the first, 1689, it was Resolved, "Since there is news of war between England and France y^t ye gem^n now mett at this Convention do each bring a gun, with ½ lb of Powder and Balls equivalent, to be hung up in ye church in ye space of three days, and that

ye Traders and other Inhabitants be persuaded to do y^u
same to make up ye number of fifty, to be made use of
upon occasion."

For the purpose of adding to the "church adorn-
ments," a number of its members were permitted to have
their armorial bearings upon the windows. Several, if
not all of these paintings, were made in the Fatherland.
Among the families so honored were those of Schuyler,
Van Rensselaer, Wendel, Herbertsen, and, it is generally
conceded, that of Ten Broeck also. There is in the family
an ancient oil-painting of the Ten Broeck arms, sur-
rounded by the mantling which characterizes both the
Schuyler and the Herbertsen arms, as given in books relating to the original church glass. This painting bears
no signature or date, but has descended in company with
the portraits of Johannes Ten Broeck, No. 17, and his
wife, of Albany. The latter bear the date of 1720.

Adaptations of the crest, arms, and motto have been
preserved in the various families of the Albany branch of
Ten Broecks, each separately and unknown to the others,
until the past year. In this way it is found among the
descendants of each of the sons of Dirck Wesselse Ten
Broeck as follows: The seal of General Samuel Ten
Broeck, No. 135; the silhouette made by Albertina Ten
Broeck Sanders, No. 140; the book-plate of Major John
C. Ten Broeck, No. 194, and the small silver seal of Dirck,
son of General Abraham Ten Broeck. The oil-painting
reproduced by steel-plate for these pages is, doubtless,
of earlier date than the others. The motto, " Perge Cœ-
pisti," is found in the latter seal abbreviated to the one
word " Sustineo," thereby losing, perhaps, something of

the force of the earlier words, "Continue as you have begun."

In these days, when awakened interest in events of Colonial and Revolutionary times is stirring all minds to appreciation of the characters and deeds of our forefathers, we count anew our treasures of history and tradition. It has been the aim, by the help of all available material in manuscript and in print, to trace the name and family of Ten Broeck, from the first mention of them in the chronicles of the Colony, down through the generations to the present time.

That in the search we find the name under various forms, and with different spellings, will be no surprise to any to whom has been granted the leisure and opportunity for the study of early state and family papers. It is a notorious fact that men did not always write their own names uniformly in those days. This confusing variety, it is well known, is met with in double measure in the Dutch Records: first, because frequently these Dutch names were at the mercy of an English-speaking scribe; then it was in part due to the gradual anglicizing of those foreign sounds. But it was owing, above all, to the use of patronymics in a form peculiar to the Dutch, the father's Christian name being annexed to that of the son or daughter, with the termination se, or sen, and the family or surname proper being usually omitted, or only employed when, in rare instances, the signature was of legal importance.

The custom of habitual use of the family name increased among the Dutch in New Netherland, from the time the Province was occupied by the English in 1664.

But among the Ten Broecks, it was not until the generation born under English rule in the Colony came into
public prominence that the custom became invariable.

There are many blanks in our early Colonial Records,
especially relating to the names of those coming to New
Netherland. The Records in Holland of the West India Trading Company were sold as waste-paper in
1821.[2] This wanton destruction, combined with the silence of family record on the subject, leaves us only the
honored tradition that Wessel Ten Broeck, the one ancestor of the several branches of the Ten Broeck family
in the United States, came to the Colony of New Netherland with Peter Minuit, the first Director General, in
1626. Whether he married in the Colony or in the
Fatherland, and where his children were born, is not
known; we cherish the hope that search of town and
church records in Holland may be soon made.

Wessel Ten Broeck's (1) Children are as follows:

2   ı Wessel Wesselse Ten Broeck, born in 1636; died
at Kingston, N. Y., November 25, 1704.

3   ıı Dirck Wesselse Ten Broeck, born December 18,
1638; died September 18, 1717, at his Bouwerie, Clermont, N. Y.; married at Albany in
1663 Christÿna Van Buren, born May 19, 1644,
died November 24, 1729, daughter of Cornelis
Maessen Van Buren and Catalyntje Martensen.

4   ııı Hendrick Wesselse Ten Broeck, resided in New
York City.

5   ıv Cornelia Wessels Ten Broeck, married at Albany,
October 16, 1687, Dominie Laurentius Van
den Bosch, fourth Pastor of the Kingston Dutch
Church.[3]

PERGE COEPISTI

John C. Ten Broeck

THE BOOK-PLATE OF MAJOR JOHN C. TEN BROECK (1941).

The eldest of this family of children, Wessel Wesselse is thought to be the colonist who is recorded as coming from Münster, in Westphalia, in the ship *Faith*, in December, 1659.[1] He married at the Dutch Collegiate Church, New York, on December the seventeenth, 1670, Maria Ten Eyck, daughter of Coenraedt Ten Eyck, of Amsterdam, and Marya Boelen. She died November the fifteenth, 1694, and his second wife was Laurentia Kellenaer, widow in turn of Dominie Van Gaasbeek, and of Major Thomas Chambers, Lord of the Manor of Foxhall. Shortly after his marriage, in 1670, he removed to Kingston, then Esopus, where he applied for a grant of land, which he received in 1676, and became a man of influence in the community. His descendants are known as the Kingston Ten Broecks; they erected the house now known as the "Senate House of the State of New York," in which the First Constitution of the State was adopted and proclaimed in April, 1777. The house stands in the heart of Kingston, and being now owned by the State, serves as a museum for an interesting and valuable collection of portraits, relics, and curios.

The second son, Dirck Wesselse, known as the progenitor of the Albany family of Ten Broecks, is he to whose descendants the following pages are devoted.

Hendrick Wesselse (4) married, resided in New York City and left many descendants.

Cornelia Wessels seems to have left no children.

Church records at Albany, N. Y., confirm the tradition of the relationship of those bearing the family name, as above. Positive proof of it is found in the ancient

2

Dordrecht Bible now in possession of Mrs. Abram Pells, of Kingston, New York.

The records in this Bible cover a period of one hundred years, in data relating to the Kingston Ten Broecks, the descendants of Wessel Wesselse. There is also an entry made by the son of Wessel Wesselse, where his "Uncle Hendrick Ten Broeck" is cited. And a later entry records the death of his "Uncle Dirck Wessels Ten Broeck." This affords a double confirmation, giving both the same name and the date as written by the eldest son of the latter, in his own family Bible. The Record reads according to the beautiful form in frequent use by this people: "1717, September 18th, Is my Uncle Dirck Wessels Ten Broeck in the Lord reposed." The following sketch is collated from state papers and manuscripts:

DIRCK WESSELSE TEN BROECK.

Regarding the youth of Dirck Wesselse Ten Broeck, and where the years were passed, we have no facts. His education can be said by inference to have been of an excellent order. He was a ready writer, expressing himself wisely and fluently as manifold duties required. He became master of the Indian language, a necessary and valuable acquisition for a man in public life in those times. Doubtless he acquired the most valuable part of his knowledge on the streets and in the council chambers of his own city, or in the solitary goings here and there as a public man on duty for the Colony. We can picture him also in the bands and knee-breeches of the times—and not indifferent to personal appearance, for

early Albany records note his purchase of silver breeches
buttons !

The first mention we find of his name in public life is
in connection with the affairs of Peter Van Alen, a tra-
der of Beverwyck, or Albany. And when the latter arranged to revisit Holland in 1662 he gave a power of
attorney to "his servant Dirck Wessels."[5] In a grant
of land made by Richard Nicolls (the English Governor
1664–1667) Dirck Wesselse and Peter Van Alen are
"partners."

The earliest date at which his signature appears on
the records, as now preserved, is under date June the
twenty-first, 1663. It is written "Dirck Wesselse ten
Broeck."[6] He continued to use the small "t" throughout
his life, writing his children's names in the same manner.

He seems to have devoted himself to business with
great intelligence and success. In 1663 he is spoken of
as "a free merchant" in Albany.[7] In a list of names,
bearing the date July the twenty-seventh, 1657, relating
to a shipment of skins and peltries is found this item,

"Derik Wessils 5000 beaver skins."[8]

The paper on file among the city documents is the
original entry, but the date is said to be an erroneous
one, which is argued from the name of the clerk and his
term of office. This large shipment was doubtless correct.

Dirck Wesselse Ten Broeck, in 1663, signed the con-
tract for the house and lot on the corner of State and
James street, Albany, the late residence of the famous
Anneke Jans, for which he agreed to pay the heirs one
thousand guilders in beaver skins. The deed,[9] given
after full payment had been made, was dated July $\frac{17}{27}$,

1667.   When he purchased this house in 1663, he was
planning for his own home ; the same year he was married
to Christina Van Buren, the daughter of an early colonist.

From this time, his importance in public affairs increased, his years were full and his cares varied.   In
the year 1676, the twenty-first of July, Governor Dongan appointed him Magistrate Commissary.   Following
this, he was chosen for the service of Envoy to Canada,
and on many occasions he bore the correspondence and
treaties between the English Colonial Governor and the
French agents.[10]

Failing to receive remuneration for certain services, he
petitioned the English Government on the subject.   The
following is the royal decision :

Whereas, It hath been represented unto us by the Peticiòn
of Derick Wessells, that having been sent upon the public service from New York to the Governor of Canada in the year 1683,
for wch said service there is due unto the Petitioner the sum of
seventy-four Pounds, eight shillings, of which he hath not re-
ceiv^d any part   .   .   .   you are to cause what shall appear to
be due to him, for the said service, to be paid unto him out of
our Revenue.[11]

Given at our Court at Kensington By her Majesty's Command.
                    Signed — NOTTINGHAM, Secy.

The Charter of the "ancient town of Beverwyck, or
Albany," as a city, was executed July twenty-sixth, 1686.
Dirck Wesselse Ten Broeck was named first in the list of
Aldermen for the city.[12]   The annual elections took place
on S. Michael and All Angels' Day, September the twenty-
ninth.   Following this first election, he was made Re-

corder. His signature appears on almost every page of the records for the following years.

On October twenty-sixth, the same year, the Common Council nominated and appointed Dirck Wesselse Recorder, and Robert Livingston Gent", to view the land above Schenectady, on the Mohawk River, called Tiononderoga, and other land adjoining, to the extent of one thousand acres, in order to purchase it for the city.[13]

After serving the city in the capacity of Recorder for ten years, he was appointed Mayor, in 1696, by Governor Fletcher — the fourth to fill the office since the granting of the Charter. He received the appointment for the second year. The Mayor, Recorder, and Aldermen were also Justices of the Peace. They held the Courts of Quarter Sessions at Albany, and the Courts of Oyer and Terminer. One of the Board presided.

Dirck Wesselse Ten Broeck had been elected a member of the first representative Provincial Assembly, the one seated in 1691. He was reëlected continuously to the second, third, fourth, and fifth. He was again chosen for the eighth, but was denied his seat, because of alleged non-residence in Albany.

The accession of Prince William of Orange to the English throne was a period of great anxiety and danger in the colony of New York. Jacob Leisler, a Captain of Troops in New York, resolved to assume control there in the interim preceding the appointment of a Governor by the new King. The magistrates at Albany considered that Leisler infringed and subverted the established laws, and they refused to listen to his demands for control over their city. They agreed in convention that public affairs should be managed by the Mayor and municipal officers until orders reached them from the King.

It proved impossible, however, for them to hold to their resolution. Albany was an isolated frontier town in those days, and ruin threatened the city and colony from the French and allied Indians.

It is at such times that the best there is in character and judgment is shown, and we are fortunate to be able to follow Dirck Wesselse Ten Broeck through this hour of extremity.

Jacob Milborne, Commander of the Sloops for this would-be Governor, arrived at Albany on the ninth of November, 1689, and in Leisler's name demanded admittance to the fort for himself and men. This he was refused, although the Convention proceeded to invite him to land, which he did; then, instead of addressing himself to the representative men, he turned to the curious, anxious assemblage, and endeavored to incite revolt against those chosen to be the leaders.

Taken by surprise, none of the Convention replied until, being taunted with silence, Dirck Wesselse, the Recorder, said, " Time enough yet. We are not authorized to make answer to such discourse. We have seen no Commission yet. The Convention has met to provide quarters for the men, if they have come with a good intent, and the billets are now on the table. There is no arbitrary power here." [14]

It was decided to meet the following day, which they did, it being "the Sabbath, after the second sermon. Past Meridian." Jacob Milborne then produced his commission, signed by Leisler.

Dirck Wesselse Ten Broeck quietly said, "Such a Commission, granted by a company of private men, is of no force here"; if he could "show a commission from His Majesty King William our Liege Lord," he would be willingly obeyed; but they were resolved to be quiet and in peace if possible, and they would dispute no more.

The following morning the Convention intended to go into the City Hall, but understanding there was so great a multitude of people assembled there, they remained at the residence of Dirck Wesselse Ten Broeck, "endeavoring to agree with Jacob Milborne."[15]

Two letters are preserved among the Colonial MSS., both of which set forth Leisler's personal opinion and feeling regarding our ancestor, Dirck Wesselse. They are very diverse in tone, and we quote both, so far as they are of interest on this point. He wrote the Colonial Governor at Boston, under date of October twenty-second, 1689, as follows:[16]

I am informed your honor has received a par'lar letter from a vessell then broke Wessell [Ten brook] of Albany of which I desire your honor for a copie; he is a persone who has formerly professed Popery, and recanted a Protestant; been employed for Ambassador to Canada, and understands not one word of French, for which embassador he has been well rewarded by both parties, being a mystery to many; he is recorder at Albany, in noe quality for that office, he has occasioned, fourty miles from Albany, towards the French, to build a Fort upon his land where he has sent twelve men to guard it, who must be a sacrifice if they come & the fort a nest to the enemies—&c.

Just eight months later Leisler sent the following
personal communication: [17]

NEW YORK, June 22, 1690.

SIR: The character which I have before received of you
from Albany, and now more particularly from Major Milborne,
doth invite me to render you thanks for your readinesse and
zeale in the managing and assisting the designe on foot against
the French, which I hereby desire you to persevere in, and
what encouragement I can afford you, assure yourselfe shall
not be wanting, being much satisfied with your frequent assistance in advising wth ye Commissioners to whom I have written
farther thereof.

        I am you^r affectionate friend to serve you,
                        JACOB LEISLER.

TO MR. DIRCK WESSELLS,

The charge of " Popery " has never been traced further — and this might very probably prove to be the
source, as the question of Protestantism was one of the
means by which Leisler sought to aggrandize himself.

A convincing counterproof is found in the circum-
stance that the names of all this contemporary generation of the Ten Broeck family are of frequent mention
on the books of the Reformed Dutch Church, and they
were each prominently connected with affairs relating
to its upbuilding, both in Albany and Kingston.

We now turn to the subject of Dirck Wesselse Ten
Broeck's greatest activity, as no doubt it proved his noblest service to the Colony, namely: Commissioner of
Indian Affairs, and his four times repeated appointment
as Political Agent to Canada.   This was largely a mat-

ter of business relating to the adjustment of the Indian question between the English and French.

His own account of two journeys to the French Province may prove of interest. He had been sent to the French Governor with the Truce from King James II., begging a cessation of hostilities; the report on his return was rendered to Peter Schuyler, then Mayor of Albany, and was as follows: [18]

Dirck Wessells, Recorder of the City of Albany, being examined, saith, that on the eleventh of June last, he was sent from Albany by Governour Dongan to carry the Truce or Cessation made between the Kings of England and France, to the Governour of Canada; and that the two and twentyeth following he came to Mount Royall, where he found the said Governour of Canada, and to his own hand, the same day delivered the letters of the said Cessation; and that the five and twentyeth day of July past, he was againe sent by the said Governour Dongan to carry several prisoners to Canada, and came again to Mount Royall about the seventh or eighth of August, where finding the Governour, he delivered to him his letters, with the prisoners.

. . . At the time before menconed, when he carried ye Cessation to Canada, and after the delivery thereof to the Governour there, he did every day during his stay att Mount Royall, wch was about five days, see and discourse with a certain Indian called Quetseits, who formerly lived on Hudson's River, and was well knowne to him; and that he left him there, who, as this examinant understands by the information of several of the Schathsooke Indians, was one of the eleven Indians that have lately done mischiefe in Connecticott River.

And further saith not.

Sworne ye 25 of September, 1688, before me,

PETER SCHUYLER, *Mayor.*

3

In August the following year, when the French and Indians were doing much to alarm and disturb the people, Dirck Wesselse Ten Broeck, in company with another of the Board, was sent to put the farmers of Kinderhook and Claverack on their guard against incursions. One month later they went north to Schenectady, to warn the people, and to concert measures for defense. The latter warning was notably ignored, and Dirck Wesselse was present when the Council met in Albany the tenth of February, 1690, and received the dread news of the horrible massacre at Schenectady, and the burning of the settlement.

Although the snow was " above knee deep," yet the Council resolved to "bury ye dead there, succor ye poor people, and pursue and follow after the French and Indian enemy, and use all means imaginable to rescue the prisoners." [19]

In 1691 the situation at Albany became very alarming, owing to the report of a predatory attack upon the city. It was determined to try the effect of calling out men, to send a force in command of Major Peter Schuyler to gain information regarding the enemy. The Mohawks promised to help defend the frontiers, but as these warriors did not arrive at the time arranged, Dirck Wesselse Ten Broeck was sent to their country to learn the cause. An idea of the inconvenience and exposure involved in this service may be gathered from the postscript to a letter written in regard to these affairs, bearing the date December thirtieth, 1691—"The scribe prays to be excused, the ink freezing in ye pen."

The Indians of this section of the country, known

among the Dutch as "The Five Nations," were distinct tribes, viz.: Mohawks, Oneidas, Onondagas, Cayugas, and Senecas. The French grouped them under the one appellation of Iroquois.

They proved themselves most reliable allies to the settlers at Albany. In 1671 they numbered about two thousand warriors. The English held them in interest as against the French, and sought their trade, which was a great source of profit.

Conferences were held on the requisition of either party. Albany was a midway meeting-place for this purpose, although the Indians' Council House was at Onondaga.

Dirck Wesselse was repeatedly sent to the Mohawk, Oneida and Onondaga Castles, to endeavor to confirm the fidelity and allegiance of the Indians to the colonists, as well as to consult with them in regard to proposals from the Canadian agents and the English governors. His journal of such an expedition in company with Robert Sanders shows the confidence he inspired. [20]

The same high regard was felt by the colonial authorities. This was set forth in a report to the London Lords of Trade. It read in part thus: "The persons most proper to treat with them [the Indians], being very much beloved by them, in the Provinces of New York and Albany, are Mr. Peter Schuyler, late Mayor of Albany . . . and one of the Council, Mr. Dirck Wessells, Justice of the Peace at Albany," and Rev. Dr. Dellius, the Dutch pastor. [21]

Shortly after this, Governor Fletcher published the following official act:

BENJAMIN FLETCHER,

Captain General and Governor in Chief of His Majesty's Province of New York, &c.

To PETER SCHUYLER, Esqr. Mr. GODFREY DELLIUS, Maj^r DIRCK WESSELLS *Mayor of the City of Albany, and the Mayor of the City for the time being :*

I do, by virtue of the power and authority to me given by his Maj^{ts.} Letters Patent, under the Great Seal of England, hereby impower you, or any two of you, to treat, confer, and consult, with the Five Indian Nations; . . . . and from time to time you are hereby required to give a constant and minute account of all your proceedings to me, and His Maj^{ts.} Council for the Province of New Yorke.

Given . . . this tenth day of August, 1696.

BENJAMIN FLETCHER. [22]

The Board thus named and constituted, managed the Indian affairs for two years only, because the succeeding English Governor found it to be a source of jealousy, and restored the power to all the Magistrates of Albany.

Dirck Wesselse was instructed by Lord Bellomont to negotiate with the Five Nations at a Convention to be held at Onondaga. His "Memorial" of the transaction was rendered to the Governor, and forwarded to the French Governor of Canada. He was usually present at the frequent conferences held in Albany and elsewhere, repeatedly acting as interpreter. [23]

He was despatched by Governor Fletcher to the Oneida Indians, to endeavor to obtain possession of the person of Revd Pierre Milet,[24] the French Jesuit, it being well known that when the Indians became Roman Catholics they allied themselves with the French.

Finally, on October the second, 1716, Governor Hunter gave to Dirck Wesselse Ten Broeck an honorable discharge from the Indian Board, where during thirty years he had labored for the peace and security of the Colony, and the protection and civilization of the Indians. [25]

The men of those days had need of patriotism in every form, and it is no surprise that one who dealt wisely for the people should also take up arms in their defense.

When in 1690 the French resolved to make a descent into the English Provinces, Fitz-John Winthrop was Commander-in-Chief of the Colonists, who advanced in defense of their borders. On his march in August of that year, he made the following entry in his journal:

Quartered this night at a place called Saratoga, about fifty English miles from Albany, where is a block-house, and some of the Dutch soldiers. At this place I overtook Mr. Wessells, Recorder of the Citty of Albany, and a Company of the principal gentleman Vollunteers of that citty.

From this time Dirck Wesselse Ten Broeck served as a leader of volunteers in times of danger. He was soon advanced from the position of Captain to that of Major under Colonel Peter Schuyler, who at this period commanded all the New York forces. When Governor Coote rendered the first report of the Colonial Militia, in 1700, he was cited as Field Officer in Schuyler's Regiment, and always thereafter was familiarly known as Major Wessells. [26]

According to the custom then prevailing among the

more prosperous, Dirck Wesselse Ten Broeck became a large landholder.

Under date of May thirteenth, 1686, Governor Dongan confirmed the deed for the "house and lot on the north side of Yonkhers (*State*) Street, where he built his little house that stands to the eastward of his greate house," and the deed of a "lot on which Dirck Wesselse and Jacob Sanderse Glen have built a tradeing house," and also a purchase from the Magistrates of Albany of "a piece of ground for a garden, lying behind the old Fort adjoining the King's pasture." The "token as Quit Rent" for the above was four shillings yearly. [27]

In reviewing Patents, or Grants for large tracts of land, it must be called to mind that the Dutch always held themselves bound to respect the rights of the Indians as proprietors of the soil, and purchased the title from them. As an added pledge of fair-dealing, the purchaser was required to make application to the Governor, before the sale, and received a confirmation from him, after obtaining the deed properly drawn and executed.

The first tract of uncultivated land so purchased by Dirck Wesselse Ten Broeck comprised four flats, or plains, lying on the Kinderhook Creek, "one Dutch mile from Jan Tysen Goes, with the woodland extending to the high hills." The land now is on the east and southeast of Kinderhook Lake, in the present town of Chatham. The original title-paper for this tract, dated October eighth, 1679, is a curious sheet; the strange signs and characters of the Indians' totems, and the seals, occupy much space in the document. [28] There were five, "alle Westenhoekse Wilde" who gave title. Sir Edmund Andros, Governor, confirmed it by a Patent dated April fifteenth, 1680.

The purchase and Patent of the "tract of land called Sarachtogie" was completed in 1684.[29] It included the land on both sides of the Hudson, from where Mechanicville now stands to Battenkill: twenty-two miles in extent north and south, and twelve miles east and west. The patentees numbered seven: Cornelis Van Dyck, Jan J. Bleecker, Peter P. Schuyler, Johannes Wendel, Dirck Wessells, David Schuyler, and Robert Livingston. In the spring of 1685 they made a division of the lowlands; for this purpose they chose disinterested men to parcel it, according to value and location; and one child each, of the several partners, drew a ticket out of a hat.[30] Dirck Wesselse's lot was known as Number three. This land continued in the possession of descendants of the line of the oldest son for several generations; and by a strange happening, General Abraham Ten Broeck led men to victory on this very spot, when the decisive battle of Saratoga was fought, in the days of '76.

On February sixth, 1697, a petition signed by Peter Schuyler, Dr. G. Dellius, Dirck Wessells, and Evert Bancker, was presented to the Governor and Council, asking permission to purchase a tract of land on the Mohawk River, extending about fifty miles in length and two in breadth, on each side of the river. In June permission was granted the applicants to make the purchase, "provided Judge Pinhorne be included." On July the eighth a bill of sale was signed by the chief Sachem "Rode" and seven other Mohawks.

The story of this grant, and the trouble it brought upon those deeply interested in it, is a long one, and for many reasons very sad. The deed given and signed by the Mohawks contained the following condition: "It is the true intent and meaning of this instrument that if we, or any of our posterity, shall have occasion or need of any part of said land, we or they shall have provision for our planting or occupancy." The same month the deed was presented, and a patent given. But, strangely enough, the description of the tract in the patent did not agree with that in the deed; it made no reservation for the occupancy of the Indians at the present, or for future time.

When this became known, it created great excitement; two of the Indians testified they had never intended to alienate their lands, and they desired the patent annulled. After public meetings and deliberations two patentees, viz., "Colonel Schuyler and Major Wessells, both of Albany, freely and of their own accord, resigned their respective interests therein to His Majesty." [31] The Council decided this, and other exorbitant grants, to be of "great prejudice to the City and Country, and a source of discouragement to the Indians." The remaining patentees were requested to resign, Dr. Dellius was suspended from the exercise of his ministerial functions, and the Mohawk patent was annulled.

Why the descriptions in the patent and the deed did not agree, it is difficult and impossible to answer. It is manifestly unfair to ascribe the change to any of the four original patentees; they had been, and continued to be, the best friends the Indians knew. Dr. Dellius had been highly regarded by them, and by all; he had learned the Indian language, instructed them in the faith, and baptized many of them. One of the Indians at his departure said, " I am grieved to my soul that you are going away."

In the Records we find a patent for what probably proved to be the final purchase Dirck W. Ten Broeck made of these large tracts. The Indian deed, and the stamp of the seal of the Province, attesting the sale to nine gentlemen, of whom one was Major Wessells Ten Broeck, were dated October, 1703, and April, 1704, and describe the patent known as the Westenhook. Kinderhook was the western line, and Claverack the southern of this tract, stretching east to Massachusetts and north to Rensselaerwyck.

The partition of this tract among the patentees did not take place until Dirck W. Ten Broeck and all his children had passed away.

It has been reserved until last to refer to an investment which proved the greatest satisfaction and pleasure. This was two tracts of land, the one lying on both sides of Roelof Jansen's Kil, of twelve hundred acres, and the other situated on the Hudson River, containing six hundred acres, both of them part of the finest land included in the tract that had been erected into Livingston Manor in 1686. The smaller tract commenced at a point but two thousand paces south of the Manor House.

It has been questioned why Livingston parted with this valuable tract, and whether Dirck Wesselse Ten Broeck might not have been a silent partner in the original grant. But the fact remains that " Dirck Wesselse

4

Ten Broeck, merchant of Albany," received deed from Robert Livingston for these lands on October twenty-sixth, 1694, in consideration of fifteen pounds and an annual rental of ten shillings.

The creek, or Kil, running through the larger of these tracts, is still called by the unusual name of those days, when it first gave the distinctive title to the Bouwerie, or farm, of Major Ten Broeck.   Roelof Jansen, the first husband of Anneke Jans, was Assistant Bouwmeester for the Patroon of Rensselaerwyck ; he died about 1636. The current tradition regarding the name of the stream is as follows : Owing to a very severe winter in those early times, Roelof Jansen's boat became so wedged in the ice of this Kil, that he was obliged to spend the season with the neighboring Indians, and await the warm air of spring to release him, and ever thereafter the waters bore his name.

On the banks of this Kil, on a gentle rise of ground, Dirck W. Ten Broeck had dwelling and barns erected, and his interest grew and centered here, as the years passed on.   His great-granddaughter, Albertina Ten Broeck (No. 140 who subsequently became the wife of Mr. John Sanders), was probably the last of the family born in the house then erected upon the Bouwerie.   She made a silhouette illustration of the place, which is both curious and interesting — a blending of imagination and reality.   It will recall the situation of the house to any whose good fortune it has been to visit the spot so fraught with interest, and shows the strength and force of a few lines to picture the life of the period.

While Dirck Wesselse Ten Broeck withdrew from the

SILHOUETTE OF THE TEN BROECK BOUWERIE.
As it appeared from 1698 to 1762.

more arduous cares and responsibilities of public life, he was still retained as Schepen, or Justice Magistrate, to which office Governor Dongan had appointed him many years previous.

Among other things this involved was the adjustment of differences arising in regard to the Palatines sent out by Queen Anne. Governor Hunter directed that all such should be submitted to him. [32]

Throughout the years of his residence in Albany, he served the church liberally with his best of means and time. In a list of twenty-four persons, entitled, because of their contributions, to seats in the new-made gallery of the church, the name of Dirck Wesselse is found; it being the old-time custom for the men of the congregation to occupy this place. [33] His name, with that of his wife, stand on the earliest extant list of members, and the children and grandchildren were baptized according to their faith and custom.

In 1673 he was a Deacon, and that year audited the accounts of the Treasurer. On the first of January, 1675, he assumed charge of the Book of Income and Expenditure. [34] He opened the entries by an introduction somewhat unusual: "Geft Godt allen de Eer," i. e., "Give God alone the Glory." For two consecutive years the books were kept in his handwriting, and frequently thereafter his signature shows his indorsement of the various Treasurers' accounts.

In consequence of one of their pastors preaching "heretical doctrines" from the church pulpit, on Sunday, August thirteenth, 1676, "an extraordinary court" was held, and Dirck Wesselse Ten Broeck was one of those to hear the case.[35] They passed judgment in words that carry wisdom to all generations : " Church disagreements should be consumed in the fire of love."

On the church books of 1690 stands a long letter, signed by his name, in which is set forth the "feeble and destitute condition of the church, by reason of the contemplated removal of Dr. Dellius." These two instances attest him to have been not unmindful of either her spiritual or temporal welfare.

It is a gratification to find that the private life of our ancestor was singularly happy and congenial. His wife proved a true helpmeet in all ways; the confidence he reposed in her requires the sole proof that by his last will, made when she had passed her three-score and tenth year, he intrusted to her the management of his large estate, besides placing the entire income at her disposal.

Large families were the fashion in those days, and at the hearthstone of rich and poor alike was the joyous sound of children's voices heard. This circle numbered six sons and seven daughters. Only two of these — twin sons — died in infancy ; eleven children reached maturity, and all married.

Shortly after Major Ten Broeck passed the age of three-score and ten, he withdrew from the activities of public life and residence in Albany, and the Bouwerie became his permanent home. Seeming to realize that his life drew toward the evening, he calmly inventoried all his possessions, and by his will arranged for the division of his estate.

Finally, on September the eighteenth, 1717, the end

came — a long and useful career was closed. He was laid to rest on his own place, according to the frequent custom of those times. The natural terrace, above the home where he had sought the repose and quiet the city denies its master-men, afforded a beautiful spot where, to this day, the peace and purple of the mountains, rising against the western sky, seem a continued promise of permanent security and repose. Near him, in this final resting-place, have been gathered, now and again, some of his own descendants, marking the generations for almost two centuries.

The record of his death, written in the Dordrecht family Bible by his eldest son, reads thus: " My father, Dirck Wesselse Ten Broeck, died on 18th September, 1717, aged seventy-eight years and nine months."

The will, written in Dutch, is on file with others of early date, in the office of the Clerk of the Court of Appeals, in the Albany Capitol. With a feeling akin to awe, one turns over the pages of the document and reads as follows :

IN THE NAME OF THE LORD.

On the fourth day of February, in the first year of our Sovereign King George of Great Brittain, &c., and in the year of our Lord 171$\frac{5}{6}$, I, Dirck Wesselsen ten Broeck, formerly of Albany, now of the Manor of Livingston, being sound in body and mind, having and using my memory, but considering the shortness and frailty of human life, the certainty of death, and uncertain hour thereof, have advisedly, without inducement, persuasion, or misleading by anybody, made, ordained, and concluded, this my last Will and Testament, revoking and an-

nulling hereby all and each Testament formerly by me made
and executed. This to be taken as my last Will and Testament,
as follows:

First.—I commend my immortal soul, whenever it shall leave
my body, to the gracious and charitable hands of God, my
Creator and Saviour; my body to a Christian burial in the earth,
whence it came, and there to remain until the day when my
soul and my body shall be re-united, on the day of resurrec-
tion, to share in the ineffable joy of eternal bliss, which God in
his grace has prepared and promised, through the death of
Jesus Christ, for and to all who faithfully believe in Him.

I. Concerning such worldly goods as the Lord has been
pleased to bestow on me, far above my deserts, I give and dispose of them as follows:

II. I give to my eldest son, Wessel ten Broeck, as his privi-
ledge of first-born son, the sum of three pounds current money of
New York; and I desire that he shall make no further claim
upon my estate than an equal share, as given hereafter to his
Sisters and Brothers.

III. It is further my will and desire, that after my death my
honest debts shall be paid by my heirs, in due time.

IV. I appoint my well-beloved wife, Christÿna Wesselsen
ten Broeck, executrix and administratrix of my whole estate,
real and personal; lands, houses, lots, bonds, notes, rents, gold
and silver, coined and uncoined; jewels, clothing, linen, woollen,
horses, cattle, negro slaves, and whatever else, nothing in the
world excepted nor reserved from my whole estate, here, in
England, Holland or elsewhere, wherever it may be; to administer thereon, without interference or contradiction by my children or anybody else, or that she should be held to give an
accounting or inventory during the time of her widowhood; but
with this express condition, that she shall not be allowed to sell,
alienate, or exchange any of my real estate, wherever it may be,

such as lands, houses, lots and mortgages, but only use thereof the fruit, and yearly income of which she may dispose during her widowhood. But, if she should again marry, she shall be held, before entering anew into the state of matrimony, to surrender the whole estate, according to a sworn inventory, to my sons, to wit: Wessel ten Broeck, Samuel ten Broeck, Johannes ten Broeck and Tobias ten Broeck, whom I then appoint executors of my whole estate, real and personal, to administer thereon.

They shall be held to give to my said wife one-third of the yearly revenue, during her life, and the other two-thirds, after deducting all expenses, I desire shall by them be equally divided between my eleven children, or their heirs, namely:

Wessel ten Broeck, Elsje ten Broeck, wife of Johannes Cuyler; Catalyntje ten Broeck, wife of John Lissger; Cornelia ten Broeck, wife of Johannes Wynkoop; Geertruy ten Broeck, wife of Abraham Schuyler; Christÿna ten Broeck, wife of Johannes Van Alen; Elisabeth ten Broeck, wife of Antony Costar; Lidia ten Broeck, wife of Volkert Van Vechten; Samuel ten Broeck, Johannes ten Broeck, Tobias ten Broeck, each to have one just eleventh share.

V. After the death of my wife, I give to my eldest son Wessel ten Broeck two-thirds of all my lands at Saratoga, in the County of Albany; and the other third I give to my daughter Geertruy, wife of Abraham Schuyler. Said lands being the just seventh part of the whole Saratoga patent, granted to me, Col. Peter Schuyler, and others. I give this to my said eldest son, and to my daughter Geertruy as above said, to wit: two-thirds to the said Wessel ten Broeck and his heirs forever, provided that these stretches of pasture-land shall be counted as £125, New York currency, in the share of my said son Wessel ten Broeck, in the estate which I shall have. And likewise the third part given to my said daughter Geertruy shall be counted as £75, New York currency; which said third part, I give to her, and her heirs, as equivalent to the mentioned sum, forever, after the death of my wife.

VI. Further, I give to my sons, Samuel ten Broeck and Tobias ten Broeck, all my lands in the said Manor of Livingston, according to the conveyance to me from Mr. Robert Livingston, to be divided into two equal parts, of which my son Tobias shall first choose his half, and the other half shall go to my son Samuel, and to their respective heirs forever. I also give to my two sons, Samuel and Tobias aforesaid, four horses, four cows, four sheep, four pigs; one of my negroes, to be selected by them; all farming utensils which then shall be found on my bouwery, for which I will that my said sons shall each pay to my said executors the sum of £190, New York currency, or together £380; provided that each of them may retain the full share of his inheritance from said sum. If their share should not amount to as much, then they add and pay to the administrators the difference. If their share amounts to more, then it shall be paid to them out of the estate; but they shall not be allowed to make a claim on the land here given to them, until after the death of my said wife; then they shall receive as their own the land with houses, barns, brewery, and other privileges.

VII. After my wife's death, I give to my son Johannes ten Broeck, my two houses and lots in the City of Albany; on the north side of Yonkers (*State*) street, on the west side of Yaugh (*now James*) street, on the east side of the house and lot of Antony Costar, and on the south side of said Costar, according to conveyance, to him and his heirs forever. I also give to the said Johannes all my right and title in and to land on the east side of Hudson's River, on a Kil called Kinderhoek Kil, which is not sold yet; according to the patents from Sir Edmond Andros and Colonel Thomas Dongan,— to him, his heirs and assigns forever: which houses and lots, and right and title to land on Kinderhoek Kil I value at £200, New York currency, and I will that so much shall be refunded to the estate, after deducting as much as one-eleventh part of the whole shall amount to, and the residue shall be paid to my executors for the behoof of my other heirs; and if his share is larger, then it shall be paid to him by the administrators.

VIII. It is my wish and will, and I give all my other lands, houses, and lots, excepting what as above I have given to my said sons and daughter Geertruy, and all my negro slaves, cattle, and other property of whatsoever nature it may be, after my own and my wife's death, to my said eleven children, to be sold to each, and the proceeds accumulated, which, with the sums to be paid by my sons and daughter, shall then be equally divided among my said eleven children, it being well understood that my said sons and daughter Geertruy, shall not pay more for their land, as appraised by me, than so much as it amounts to, more than their eleventh part of my whole estate.

IX. It is further my wish and will, that none of my real estate shall be sold to strangers, but it shall always remain in my family.

X. It is my wish and will, that Christina Legget, when she comes to marriageable age, shall have a good outfit.

All the above I declare to be my last Will, requesting that it may have full effect in every way.

Thus done and concluded, at my Bouwery, in the Manor of Livingston, and signed and sealed by my own hand this Fourth of February, 171½.

DIRCK WESSELSE TEN BROECK.

Signed and sealed in the presence of

JAN VOSBURGH,
WILLIAM SCOTT,
PIETER VOSBURGH.

This will was proved on the sixth of February, 1718. A few months later, on September the first, the wife of

5

Major Ten Broeck took steps to have assistance from those she trusted in executing the expressed wishes and will of her husband.   She appointed her—

Loving sons, Wessel Ten Broeck, Johannis Ten Broeck, and my son-in-law, Johannis Cuyler, all of the City of Albany, to be my true and lawful and irrevokable Attorneys, rendering account to me, when thereunto required; and after my decease, unto the heirs of the said Dirck Wesselse Ten Broeck.

(Signed)   CRISTŸNA TEN BROECK.[36]

Witnesses:

HENDRICK VAN RENSSELAER,
ANTHONY COSTAR.

She outlived her husband a little more than twelve years.   Doubtless Albany became again her home during this time, and it was her choice to return to the more familiar place, where she had known many happy years, now the residence of her son Johannes.   She died on the twenty-fourth of November, 1729, and was interred in the Dutch Church of Albany.

Her parents, Cornelis Maessen Van Buren and Cata-lyntje Martensen, came to the Colony from Guelderland, Holland, in 1631, in the ship "Arms of Rensselaer-wyck."   They were probably from Buren, near which is the castle of the Counts Buren.   They lived on the Manor of Rensselaerwyck, and died there in 1648, both being buried on the same day. [37]

The present geographical situation of the Bouwerie of Dirck W. Ten Broeck is in Columbia County, New York, in the towns (townships) of Clermont and Livingston.

Columbia County was formed largely from Albany County, in the year 1786.

Although the injunction "real estate shall always remain in the family" could not in every instance be observed, yet it is a great satisfaction to note that parts of each of these tracts are still the property of descendants.

Children of Dirck Wesselse Ten Broeck (3) and Christÿna Van Buren.

6   I WESSEL, born April 7, 1664; died May 27, 1747; married April 2, 1684, Cattryna, died January 6, 1729, aged 59 years and 5 months; daughter of Jacob Loockermans and Tryntje —.

7   II ELSJE, born ——; died June 29, 1752; married November 2, 1684, Johannes Cuyler, born in 1661, died July 20, 1740; eldest son of Hendrick Cuyler and Anna Schepmoes.

8   III CATALYNTJE, born ——; died October 10, 1725, aged 59; married at Albany, October 7, 1688, Johannes Legget of New York, probably son of Jan Legget, mariner, and Anna.

9   IV CORNELIA, born ——; died June 10, 1729, aged 60 years and 3 months; married June 9, 1696 (marriage license dated June 2, 1696), Johannes Wynkoop, son of Cornelius Wynkoop and Maria Janse Langedyk. He had married first, June 7, 1687, Judith Bloodgood; he died before September 13, 1733.

10   V GEERTRUY, born ——; died after 1738; married November 11, 1691, at Albany, Abraham Schuyler; born August 16, 1663; died July 9, 1726, son of David Pieterse Schuyler and Catalyn Verplanck.

11   vi Christina, born ——; died October 4, 1744, aged
     72 years and 5 months; married 1701, Johannes
     Van Alen, died April, 1750, son of Pieter Van
     Alen and Maria Teller.

12   vii Elizabeth, born ——; died 1757; married Decem-
     ber 15, 1698, Anthony Costar, died February,
     1753, buried at Albany, February 6, 1753, eldest
     son of Hendrick Costar and Geertje Goosense
     Van Schaick.

13   viii Lidia, born ——; died ——; buried at Albany, Au-
     gust, 1748, married August 26, 1702, Volckert
     Van Vechten, son of Gerrit Teunisse Van Vech-
     ten and Grietje Volkertse Douw.

14   ix Samuel, born 1680; died April 5, 1756, aged 75;
     married November 7, 1712, Maria, baptized in
     Albany, March 29, 1689, died July 31, 1771,
     aged 82, daughter of Hendrick Van Rensselaer
     and Catharina Van Brugh.

15   x Ephraim, ⎫ twins; born ——; baptized in Albany,
16   xi Manasse, ⎭   November 21, 1681; both died young.

17   xii Johannes, born 1683; died ——; married (first),
     June 18, 1709. Elizabeth, daughter of Johannes
     Wendell and Elizabeth Staats; married (second),
     December 29, 1714, Catryna, baptized in Al-
     bany, January 1, 1692, daughter of Hendrick
     Van Rensselaer and Catharina Van Brugh.

18   xiii Tobias, born ——; baptized at Albany, February 20,
     1689; died January 28, 1724, aged 35; married
     at Albany, October 24, 1714, Maritie Van
     Stryen; she married (second) at Kinderhook,
     August 9, 1727, Dominie Johannes Van Dries-
     sen, and died December 31, 1734.

THIRD GENERATION.

WESSEL TEN BROECK (6).

Wessel, the eldest child and son of Major Ten Broeck, married a few days before he was twenty years of age Caatje Loockermans, a maiden of fifteen, the daughter of one of the early men of Albany. They resided in what was called, in those days, the third ward of Albany, and as a merchant and citizen he was active and useful in both public and private life.

He first appears in a public capacity in that dangerous period of the change on England's throne, and the uncertainty of authority in her colonies, when, on November the fifth, 1689, "forty of ye inhabitants, principall men of ye town and county of Albany, agreed to keep the Fort and City, for the behoofe of King William and Queen Mary, . . . promising to assist, if occasion required, for the preservation of Peace and Tranquility."

Beginning with January, 1695, he audited, for two years, the deacon's books of the Dutch Church, and in

1697 he kept them, jointly, with Hendrick Van Rensselaer. [39] He was present as a church officer and also as a city magistrate, when Dr. Dellius, the pastor, owing to the misunderstanding consequent upon the granting of the famous Mohawk Patent, held his farewell interview with the Indian converts [40] in June, 1698.

He signed the petition of the Protestant subjects in the colony to King William the Third,[41] in December, 1701. As a Deputy from the city and county of Albany, he greeted Lord Cornbury on his arrival as Governor-General in 1702, and was one of those to present to him the address of allegiance and welcome.[42]

Wessel Ten Broeck was an alderman of Albany at the time his father served as mayor of the city ; he was a member of the Indian Board during the conference with the Five Nations, [43] held in 1701, and almost continuously, for twenty-five years, he stood among the men in whom the citizens reposed the public trust.

There was constant need for measures of defense in those times, and when in 1700 Lord Bellomont prepared the report of the militia, Wessel Ten Broeck was Lieutenant of a company of foot soldiers under Colonel Schuyler. [44]

He applied for a grant of land, and received the certificate in 1733. It was situated on the west side of the Hudson River, and extended from the Kaaterskill to the banks of the Hudson, about five miles south of Catskill. He mentioned this tract in his will, which was dated June the tenth, 1723, and recorded January the twenty-ninth, 1753, in the Albany County Clerk's office, Volume I., page 215.

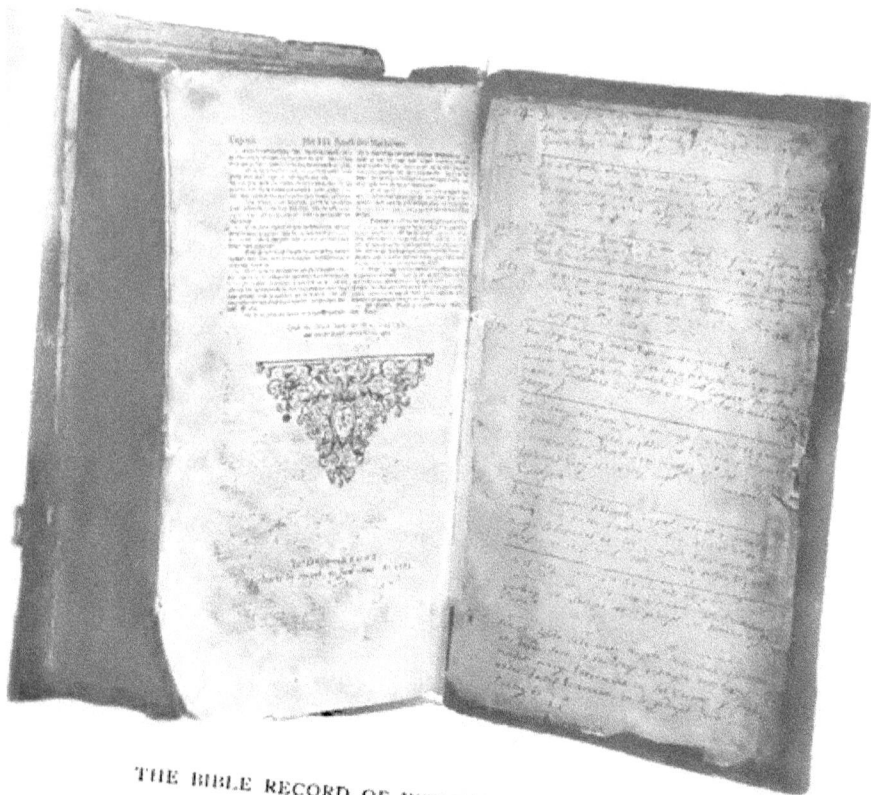

THE BIBLE RECORD OF WESSEL TEN BROECK (6).

The family Bible of Wessel Ten Broeck is of great interest; it is in Dutch, printed in 1682, at Dordrecht, Holland. This illustration, and the one on page 150, will give an idea of the size and appearance. Heavy boards, covered with tooled leather, form the binding; the corners are finished with brass pieces, and the book has clasps of the same metal. Between the Old and New Testaments are maps of Asia Minor and Egypt, and also a drawing representing Paradise.

The records are found on the boards of the covers and on the blank pages next to these, in both the front and back of the volume. The writing is in Holland Dutch, the earliest date being the marriage of Wessel to "Cattryna Locermans," on the second of April, 1684. The entries pertaining to his children and descendants are very full.

The Bible is now the property of a lineal descendant — Mr. Andrew J. Ten Broeck, of North Germantown, Columbia County, New York.

Children of Wessel Ten Broeck (6) and Caatje Loockermans.

19 I ANNA CATHARINA, born April 25, 1685; died March 6, 1743; married October 19, 1707, Antony Van Schaick, born 1681, died February, 1737, son of Sybrant Van Schaick and Elizabeth Vanderpoel.

20 II DIRCK, born December 4, 1686; died January 3, 1751; married November 26, 1714, Margarita, born October 26, 1692, died May 24, 1783, daughter of Abraham Cuyler and Caatje Bleecker.

21 III CHRISTINA, born October 16, 1689; baptized October 20, 1689; died July 16, 1690.

22   IV JACOB, born February 25, 1692; died June 25, 1693.

23   V CHRISTINA, born June 8, 1694; married April 10,
       1718, David Van Dyck, baptized at Albany,
       November 26, 1693, son of Hendrick Van Dyck
       and Maria Schuyler.

24   VI ELIZABETH, born August 18, 1696; died May 29, 1700.

25   VII MARYA, born June 23, 1698; died July 29, 1699.

26   VIII JACOB, born August 10, 1700; died September 14,
       1744; married 1st, September 29, 1725, Chris-
       tina (54) baptized April 16, 1704, died July
       28, 1753, daughter of Johannes Van Alen and
       Christina Ten Broeck; married 2nd, September
       8, 1754, Catrina, daughter of Barent Van Ben-
       thuysen.

27   IX CORNELIS, born March 6, 1706; died 1772; married
       October 11, 1733, Maria (36), baptized in New
       York, November 25, 1702, daughter of Johannes
       Cuyler and Elsje Ten Broeck.

ELSJE TEN BROECK (7).

Elsje married November 2, 1684, Johannes Cuyler,
the son of Hendrick Cuyler, who came to Albany in
1664. He was Indian Commissioner for a number of
terms, beginning with 1706, and was appointed mayor
of Albany in 1725. He was deacon in the Albany
Dutch Church in 1695 and 1700, and in later years an
elder. They always resided in Albany, and upon
Elsje's death she was accorded the honor of being interred in the church, according to the following note:
" Elsje Cuyler buried in the Albany Church July the
second, 1752."

Children of Elsje Ten Broeck (7) and Johannes Cuyler.

28   I ANNA, born November 26, 1685; died July 10, 1741; married at Albany, January 29, 1712, Anthony Van Schaick (his second wife), born June 3, 1682, died August 13, 1759, son of Anthony Van Schaick and Maria Vanderpoel.

29   II CHRISTINA, baptized September 25, 1687; died young.

30   III CHRISTINA, baptized at Albany, December 4, 1689; probably buried at Albany, November 20, 1755.

31   IV HENDRIK, baptized January 10, 1692.

32   V SARAH, baptized October 22, 1693; married at Albany, April 25, 1723, Hans Hansen, baptized in Albany, June 20, 1695, son of Hendrick Hansen and Debora Van Dam; he was Mayor of Albany, 1731–32, and from 1754 to 1756, in which year he died, being buried at the Albany Church, December 6, 1756.

33   VI ELSJE, baptized August 25, 1695, married October 25, 1724, Hendrick Roseboom, baptized August 4, 1689, died in 1754, buried at Albany, October 29, 1754; son of Johannes Roseboom and Gerritje Costar.

34   VII CORNELIS, baptized at New York, February 14, 1697, died March 14, 1765; married December 8, 1726, Catalyntje, born March 5, 1705; died February 21, 1758, daughter of Johannes Schuyler and Elizabeth Staats.

35   VIII JOHANNES A., born February 12, 1699, baptized at Albany, February 19, 1699; died October 24, 1746; married October 28, 1727, Catharine, born January 10, 1705, died April 12, 1746, daughter of Harmanus Wendel and Anna Glen.

6

36   IX Maria, baptized at New York, November 25, 1702;
        died; married in Albany, October 11, 1733,
        Cornelis Ten Broeck (27), born March 6, 1706,
        died probably in 1772, son of Wessel Ten
        Broeck and Caatje Loockermans.

37   X ELIZABETH, baptized May 13, 1705; married October
        12, 1733, Jacob Sanderse Glen, baptized at Sche-
        nectady, October 17, 1703, buried at Albany
        Church, April 16, 1746, son of Johannes Glen
        and Jannetje Bleecker.

38   XI RACHEL, baptized at Albany, September 21, 1707,
        died young.

39   XII RACHEL, baptized November 27, 1709.

CATALYNTJE TEN BROECK (8).

Catalyntje married Johannes Legget, whose family
name was also written Lissere, Lissger and Lissjer. He
was probably the son of Jan Legget, the mariner, who
was of Barbadoes, W. I., and whose will was recorded
in New York, February the second, 1680.

Children of Catalyntje Ten Broeck (8) and Johannes Legget.

40   I RACHEL, baptized in New York, July 29, 1689.

41   II Jan, baptized in New York, April 2, 1693; married
        Bata Delamater.

42   III CHRISTINA, baptized at New York, April 2, 1693.

CORNELIA TEN BROECK (9).

Cornelia married Johannes Wynkoop. The marriage
license was dated June the second, 1696.

Johannes Wynkoop took the oath of allegiance in the

colony in 1689 as from Ulster County, New York. In 1728 he was recognized as a freeholder of Kingston, and was also a major of militia. The same year, in a " List of Commanding Officers, as well military as civil," he is classed with " Old officers and old men."

His last will was dated June the ninth, 1730, and he died shortly thereafter.

Children of Cornelia Ten Broeck (9) and Johannes Wynkoop.

43   I CHRISTINA, baptized at Kingston, March 14, 1697; married May 12, 1723, Johannes De Lamater, baptized at Kingston, July 4, 1697, son of Abraham De Lamater and his second wife, Elsie Tappan.

44   II DIRCK, born November 1, 1698, died March 30, 1763, married July 3, 1725, Gertrude, baptized at Kingston, April 25, 1743, daughter of Cornelius Teunesse Kool and Jenneke Lambertse.

45   III CATHARINA, baptized at Kingston, January 19, 1701; died young.

46   IV JOHANNES, born October 7, 1702; died August 8, 1791; married December 19, 1728, Maria, born April 13, 1709, daughter of Everardus Bogardus and Tjaatje Hoffman.

47   V LYDIA, baptized at Kingston, February 21, 1714; died young.

GEERTRUY TEN BROECK (10).

Geertruy was married at Albany, November the eleventh, 1691, to Abraham Schuyler, who was for many years one of the most prominent men of that city.

He was familiar with the Indian language, and at one time resided among the Seneca tribe as agent for the government.

When, in 1709, the colony sent an expedition to England, with a view of proving to the Queen the importance of preserving the friendship of the Five Nations, he accompanied Colonel Peter Schuyler and the five Indian chiefs as their interpreter. He noted the fact in his Bible in the following entry: "1709, December 16th. I went with Colo. Schuyler to England, and returned through the Grace of God, July 26th. 1710."

He died, after a brief illness, on July the ninth, 1726, "at Sonnock's Land," where, as the name indicates, he had gone on a visit to the Seneca tribe.

Gertrude continued to reside in Albany, and outlived her husband more than twelve years.

Her son Dirck (50) was among the first of the Holland Dutch who came from the upper Hudson to East Jersey. He, with William Williamson and others, petitioned for the charter of New Brunswick, [15] which was granted in 1730.

He became a merchant in that city, and resided there until his death, in 1779. He left no descendants.

Children of Geertruy Ten Broeck (10) and Abraham Schuyler.

48   I DAVID, born November 26, 1692; married 1st, July 17, 1720, Anna Brat, buried at Albany, September 24, 1723; married 2nd, December 2, 1725, Maria, baptized April 18, 1697, daughter of Hendrick Hansen and Debora Van Dam.

49   II CHRISTINA, born July 16, 1695.

50   III DIRCK, born July 25, 1700; died 1779; married
      Anna Maria, baptized April 16, 1701, daughter
      of Abraham Santvoort and Vrouwtje Van Hoorn.

51   IV ABRAHAM, born August 24, 1704; married September
      7, 1732, Catharina, baptized December 12, 1708,
      daughter of Barent Staats and Neeltje Gerritse
      Vanderberg.

52   V JACOBUS, born March 19, 1707; married November
      12, 1735, Geertruy, baptized March 11, 1711,
      daughter of Barent Staats and Neeltje Gerritse
      Vanderberg.

CHRISTINA TEN BROECK (11).

Christina married Johannes Van Alen in 1701, and
they resided in Albany. She died on October the fourth,
1744, and was interred on the sixth. Her husband survived her almost six years, and was interred at Albany
on the twelfth of April, 1750.

Children of Christina Ten Broeck (11) and Johannes Van Alen.

53   I MARIA, baptized at Albany, February 7, 1703.

54   II CHRISTINA, baptized at Albany, April 16, 1704; died
      July 28, 1753; married September 29, 1725,
      Jacob Ten Broeck (26), baptized August 10,
      1700, died September 14, 1774, son of Wessel
      Ten Broeck and Caatje Loockermans.

55   III PIETER, baptized August 18, 1706; married probably
      Anna Van Benthuysen.

56   IV LENA, baptized September 19, 1708; died single,
      April 27, 1766, aged 57 years and 8 months.

57   v DIRCK WESSELSE, baptized October 28, 1710; married
            probably Catharina Johanna.

ELIZABETH TEN BROECK (12).

Elizabeth married on December the fifteenth, 1698,
Anthony Costar. Their residence was the property
adjoining, on the west, her paternal home on Yonkers
Street (now State Street) in Albany.

They were granted more than a half century of married life. Anthony Costar died and was buried in Albany, February the sixth, 1753; Elizabeth, his wife,
surviving him four years.

Children of Elizabeth Ten Broeck (12) and Anthony Costar.

58   I HENDRICK, baptized September 3, 1699; buried in
            the Albany Church, September 17, 1745.

59   II CHRISTINA, baptized December 15, 1700; died De-
            cember 15, 1777; married November 7, 1724,
            Pieter Van Bergen, baptized February 21, 1694,
            died at Coxsackie, Greene County, N. Y., Jan-
            uary 4, 1778, son of Marten Gerritsen Van Ber-
            gen and Neeltje Myndertse Van Iveren.

60   III GEERTRUYTJE, baptized July 28, 1706, married Kill-
            ian Winne, baptized January 13, 1706, son of
            Jacobus Winne and Marytje Brouck.

61   IV EPHRAIM, baptized September 23, 1716.

LIDIA TEN BROECK (13).

The marriage of Lidia, the youngest daughter of Major
Ten Broeck, to Volckert Van Vechten, took place on the
twenty-sixth of August, 1702.

He was a grandson of Teunis Diercksen Van Vechten, who came to the Colony in the ship "Arms of Norway," about the year 1648. His descendants had settled in Rensselaerwyck, and on the banks of the Hudson.

Lidia died in August, 1748, and was interred at Albany.

Children of Lidia Ten Broeck (13) and Volckert Van Vechten.

62   I Gerrit Teunis, baptized April 25, 1703; died March, 1747; buried at Albany, March 12, 1747; married November 6, 1739, Lena, baptized March 27, 1709, daughter of Jan Witbeck and Agnietje Brouck.

63   II Margarita, baptized March 3, 1706, married at Albany, July 15, 1729, Gerrit C. Vandenberg, baptized September 19, 1703, son of Cornelis Gysbertse Vandenberg, and Maria Van Buren, who had married first Teunisse Van Deusen.

64   III ⎰ Ephraim, baptized June 12, 1709; died at New Brunswick, N. J., December 10, 1746; married, January 3, 1744, Catharina (71), baptized at Johnstown, Columbia County, N. Y., August 5, 1722; died May 18, 1753, daughter of Samuel Ten Broeck and Maria Van Rensselaer.

[Twins.]

65   IV ⎱ Johannes, baptized June 12, 1709; died 1746; buried at Albany, December 25, 1746; married, October 29, 1734, Neeltje, baptized October 27, 1710, died 1752, buried at Albany, July 9, 1752, daughter of Johannes Martense Beekman and Eva Vinhagen.

66   v Dirck, baptized October 19, 1712.

SAMUEL TEN BROECK (54).

Samuel, through the bequest of his father Dirck Wesselse Ten Broeck, inherited his portion of the estate in
lands that were part of the bouwerie on the Roelof
Jansen Kil, in the section where the Ten Broeck family
is one of the most ancient.   It was here that he passed
the years of his life, and by his will made the twenty-
third of April, 1750, he devised the larger part of the
tract to his eldest son.

This property had formerly been divided between
Albany and Dutchess Counties, but by the Act of May
the twenty-fourth, 1717, relating to certain grants on the
south of the Roelof Jansen Kil, it was all annexed to Albany County, and remained thus until, in 1786, the lines
were once more changed, and it became part of the new
county of Columbia.

In a list of freeholders, made in 1720, "pursuant of
an order of Court," Samuel Ten Broeck is cited as " of
Claverack." [46]   He was also justice of the peace for
Albany County.

He was married on November the seventh, 1712, to
Maria Van Rensselaer, in the "two steeple " church of
Albany.

He and his younger brother Johannes married sisters,
the daughters of Hendrick Van Rensselaer and grand-
daughters of Johannes Van Brugh.   They were of notable lineage in both branches, reaching back to the
Patroons of Rensselaerwyck, and to Anneke Jans, so
famous in New York litigation suits; and through the
latter, descended from the ninth Prince of the House of

Orange,— William of Nassau, Sovereign Count of the States of Holland and Zealand. [47]

Children of Samuel Ten Broeck (14) and Maria Van Rensselaer.

67   I CHRISTINA, baptized February 7, 1714; died young.

68   II DIRCK WESSELSE, baptized May 1, 1715; married 1st, June 28, 1743, Catharina, daughter of Leendert Conyn and Jannetje Van Alen; married 2nd, previous to September, 1777, Dorothy, baptized at Kinderhook, April 20, 1735, daughter of Dirck Vosburg and Alida.

69   III HENDRICK, baptized March 24, 1717; died at Claverack, 1796; married October 14, 1743, Annatje, baptized October 22, 1722, daughter of Anthony Van Schaick and Anna Cuyler (28).

70   IV JOHANNES, baptized September 4, 1720.

71   V CATHRINA, baptized at Johnstown, Columbia County, N. Y., August 5, 1722; died May 18, 1753; married 1st, January 3, 1744, Ephraim Van Vechten (64), baptized June 12, 1709, died at New Brunswick, N. J., December 10, 1746, son of Volckert Van Vechten and Lidia Ten Broeck; married 2nd, January 29, 1752, Robert Johannes Lansing, born January 17, 1707, died March 3, 1795, son of Johannes Gerrit Lansing and Helena Sanders.

72   VI JOHANNES, baptized at Johnstown, October 18, 1724; died October 23, 1793; married December 12, 1753, Marytje Hoffman, died at Hudson, N. Y., May 10, 1805, in her 75th year.

73   VII JEREMIAS, baptized February 1, 1727; died October 24, 1802; married 1756 — marriage license June

7

10, 1756 — to Marytje, born November 20, 1733, probably daughter of Adam Van Alen and Catharine Van Alsteyn.

74   VIII CHRISTINA, born November 29, 1729; married at Claverack, September 4, 1754, Harmanus Schuyler, born at Schenectady, April 2, 1727, died September 1, 1796, son of Nicolaas Schuyler and Elsie Wendell.

JOHANNES TEN BROECK (17).

Johannes, the fifth son of Dirck Wesselse Ten Broeck and Christina Van Buren, was the son upon whom his father depended in great confidence. His name alone, among those of the family, can be found as witness to transfers of lands.[18]   To him was bequeathed the home of his parents in Albany, the storehouse there, and the title of merchant, in his father's stead.

He was married twice.   The first wife, Elizabeth Wendell, was a daughter of Johannes Wendell, and belonged to the well-known family of Albany.   She lived but a short time, and Johannes Ten Broeck married on December the twenty-ninth, 1714, Catryna, the second daughter of Hendrick Van Rensselaer, Patroon of the lower manor of Rensselaerwyck.

He was made assistant alderman in 1715, and in the list of freeholders, taken in 1720, he was of the first ward of Albany.   Three years later, in 1723, he was an alderman, and one of His Majesty's justices of the peace. [19]

On September the ninth, 1726, when Governor Burnet and the sachems of the Six Nations assembled in con-

JOHANNES TEN BROECK.
From the Oil-Painting of 1720.

ference in Albany, Johannes Ten Broeck was present on the Board of City Officers. [50]

He continued to fill his place as representative of the first ward of Albany until 1740, when he was appointed city chamberlain or treasurer, [51] which position he held for three terms.

A picture of the times, as well as of the values of the period, may be found in the following : The City Council, in August, 1737, "agreed that Johannes Ten Broeck be allowed twenty shillings to make a bridge in the Yoncker Street, on the east side of the Well, opposite Widow Livingston's."

About the time of his withdrawal from public life there was recorded a deed, in part as follows : [52] " Johannes Ten Broeck, of the city of Albany, and Catharina, his wife, sell to Luykas Wyngaert, merchant of Albany, for four hundred and twenty Pounds, two Houses and two Lotts, in the First Ward of the City, on the north side of Yonckers Street, bounded on the West and North by the house and lott of Anthony Costar, and to the East by the Lane ; the same property received by the Will of Dirck Wesselse Ten Broeck, Father of the said Johannes Ten Broeck," etc. The date of the paper is the thirtieth of October, 1743.

Tradition affirms that Johannes Ten Broeck and Catharine, his wife, came to New Brunswick, New Jersey, at this time, in company with their third son, Johannes.

Their portraits, painted in 1720, are in possession of a direct descendant in the sixth generation — Louis Barcroft Runk, Esq., of Philadelphia.

Children of Johannes Ten Broeck (17) and Catryna Van Rensselaer.

75   I DIRCK WESSELSE, baptized October 30, 1715; married at Kingston, N. Y., June 13, 1740, Catharina, baptized at Kingston, May 24, 1719, died
December 20, 1782, daughter of John Rutsen
and Catharina Beckman; she married, second,
at Kingston, June 24, 1749, Peter Ten Broeck,
born October 4, 1720, died March 5, 1777, son
of Johannes Ten Broeck of Kingston, and
Rachel Roosa.

76   II CATRYNA, baptized at Albany, January 6, 1717, was
living in 1786; she married July 5, 1738, Richard Hansen, baptized August 15, 1703, probably son of Hendrick Hansen and Debora Van
Dam; he had married 1st, Sarah Thong, on
May 14, 1727, who was buried in the Albany
Church, October 25, 1733.

77   III HENDRICK, baptized March 9, 1718.

78   IV JOHANNES, baptized September 20, 1719, died at Raritan Landing, N. J., January, 1790; married
at New Brunswick, N. J., January 30, 1746, Patience, baptized at New Brunswick, September
20, 1728, died January, 1800, daughter of William Williamson and Jannetje.

79   V EPHRAIM, baptized January 15, 1721; buried in the
Van Rensselaer family lot at Greenbush, N. Y.,
January 14, 1732.

80   VI CHRISTINA, baptized March 18, 1722; buried at Albany, February 10, 1725.

81   VII JEREMIAS, baptized January 18, 1724.

82   VIII CHRISTINA, baptized September 5, 1725.

CATRYNA VAN RENSSELAER (TEN BROECK)
From the Oil-Portrait of 1720.

83   IX CORNELIS, born May 14, 1727; baptized at Albany,
        May 22, 1727; died June 26, 1766; married
        Maria, born December 8, 1731, daughter of
        Peter Bodyn and Agnes Constance de Bruyn.

84   X PIETER, baptized at Albany, November 17, 1728.

85   XI ABRAHAM, baptized June 18, 1730, probably buried
        at Greenbush, N. Y., May 10, 1754.

86 XII MARIA, baptized November 21, 1731, died, unmar-
        ried, May 10, 1805, in her seventy-fifth year;
        buried at Claverack, N. Y.

87 XIII EPHRAIM, baptized at Albany, August 15, 1733.

TOBIAS TEN BROECK (18).

Tobias, youngest of the children of Dirck Wesselse
Ten Broeck, outlived his father only a few years.   Unfortunately, less is known of his descendants than of
those of the other sons.   ·

He was Lieutenant of the "Independent Companie
of Militia of Livingston Manor,"[53] mustered at the
manor house, November the thirtieth, 1715 — a company seeing much actual service, and maintained during
all the succeeding colonial period.

He was appointed justice magistrate for Albany
County in 1719.   The year following, his name stood at
the head of the Claverack list of freeholders.[54]

Tobias Ten Broeck was married at the Albany Church
on October the twenty-fourth, 1714, to Maritie Van
Stryen, and they resided at the bouwerie, on Roelof
Jansen's Kil.   He inherited from his father one half of
the lands in this section, the will giving him the first
choice of location.

He died at his bouwerie, on the twenty-eighth of
January, 1724, aged thirty-five years, and was buried in
the family plot. His widow, Maritie Ten Broeck, married, about three and a half years later, Dominie Johannes Van Driessen, of Albany.

Children of Tobias Ten Broeck (58) and Maritie Van Stryen.

88   I CATRYNA JOHANNA, baptized at Albany, September
26, 1715.

89   II DIRCK, baptized April 14, 1717.

90   III CHRISTINA, baptized May 17, 1719; married at Kin-
derhook, N. Y., September 30, 1737, Dirck Van
Slyck, baptized March 1, 1713, son of Teunis
Williamse Van Slyck and Jannetje Hendrickse
Van Wie.

91   IV ELIZABETH, baptized at Albany, January 8, 1721.

92   V JOHN TOBIAS, born October 17, 1722; married August 15, 1745, Elizabeth, born September 21,
1724, died January 18, 1801, daughter of Jan
Oothout of New York City, and Catalina Van
Deusen.

93   VI TOBIAS, baptized at Johnstown, Columbia County,
October 18, 1724.

THE FOURTH GENERATION.

.&

ANNA C. TEN BROECK (19).

Anna Catharina, eldest child of Wessel (6), was born in Albany, April the twenty-fifth, 1685. The baptism is recorded under the same date; the godparents being her maternal grandmother Tryntje Lookermans, and the grandfathers on both sides, Jacob Lookermans and Dirck W. Ten Broeck.

She married, at the age of twenty-two, Anthony Van Schaick, a descendant of the early colonist whose name is familiar in New York annals.

They resided in Albany. Anthony Van Schaick died in February, 1737, and was interred at Albany on the fourth of that month. His wife, Anna Catharina, survived him six years.

Children of Anna Catharina Ten Broeck (19) and Anthony Van Schaick.

94   1 SYBRANT, baptized August 1, 1708; died previous to
           1796; married at Albany, March 20, 1735,
           Anna, baptized April 21, 1706, daughter of Jo-
           hannes Roseboom and Gerritje Costar.

95   II WESSEL, baptized February 10, 1712; died previous
         to 1796; married at Albany, November 3, 1743,
         Maria Gerritse, baptized May 30, 1717, died
         January 31, 1797, daughter of Jan Gerritse and
         Marytje.

96   III CATRYNA, baptized September 27, 1713; married
         June 11, 1743, Wilson Van Slyck.

97   IV ELIZABETH, baptized September 13, 1716; buried at
         Albany, February 5, 1741.

98   V JACOB, baptized March 16, 1718; died previous to
         1796; married 1st, at Albany, September 14,
         1751, Catrina, baptized July 14, 1723, daughter
         of Hendrick Cuyler, Jr., and Margarita Van
         Deusen; married 2nd, at Albany, about 1777,
         Elizabeth Van Schaick.

99   VI LIVINUS, baptized September 4, 1720.

100   VII GOOSEN, baptized September 9, 1722; married Elsje
         ———.   He made a will under date of August 7,
         1796; it was recorded in Greene County, N. Y.
         — Volume A, page 100 — on July 7, 1807. He
         had no children.

101   VIII DIRCK, baptized April 4, 1725.

DIRCK TEN BROECK (20).

It was a fitting choice that bestowed the distinctive
christian name, now so familiar in Albany annals, upon
the eldest son of this generation.

He was a merchant, and first came into prominence
in connection with the Indian traffic, which continued to
be of great importance. The municipal officers of the

city were empowered by Common Council on March
the second, 171⅔, to encourage this trade, and to appoint
"a good and sufficient person to inspect all skins that
shall be offered for sale or shipped." Dirck Ten Broeck
received and accepted the appointment, for the revenue
of a halfpenny each skin. [55]

He was a freeholder in the third ward of Albany in
1720, and a deacon in the Dutch Church. On August
the third, that year, he, with the officers, petitioned for
an "Act of Incorporation," under the title of The Reformed Protestant Dutch Church in Albany. [56] One
week later, August the tenth, he conveyed by deed to
the church, "for perpetual use and ownership," a plot
of ground, which had been "late the occupancy of Dirck
Wesselse, and now used as a garden." This property
was situated on Pearl Street.

In July, 1722, Dirck Ten Broeck was an alderman of
Albany. He was appointed Commissioner of Indian
Affairs, and repeatedly, for fifteen years from 1728, he
heard and signed the many important petitions coming
before that Board.

On November the twenty-sixth, 1730, the intrigues
of the French with the Five Nations became so threaten-
ing that the commissioners appealed to Governor Mont-
gomerie. This paper also bears the signature of Dirck
Ten Broeck. [57]

He became recorder of the city in 1728, and was
mayor from September the twenty-ninth, 1746, for three
terms, under Governor Clinton.

He married on November the twenty-sixth, 1714,
Margarita Cuyler. The list of their children and the

8

family alliances includes names which will attract the attention of every intelligent reader.

The plate represents an "ooma," a piece of silver which belonged to Dirck and Margarita Ten Broeck. Their joint initials, in the style of marking then usual, are on the inside rim of the cover. The name was derived from the Dutch word "oom," signifying uncle, as the article was a favorite gift of an uncle to either a niece or nephew on the wedding day. It was used to sprinkle the mixed cinnamon and sugar on hot waffles. This silver is now owned by Mrs. S. Sidney Smith, of Argyle, New York, whose husband was a descendant through Catryna (102), the eldest child of the family.

Dirck Ten Broeck died on January the third, 1751, and on the seventh instant was interred in the Albany church. His wife survived him thirty-two years, living until she attained the age of ninety.

By his will, made July the first, 1748, and probated at Albany May the third, 1768, he bequeathed "the Great Dutch Bible, the Holland Gun, and the Clock" to his son Abraham, who became the future General. He appointed his sons Abraham and Dirck, the executors.

Children of Dirck Ten Broeck (20) and Margarita Cuyler.

102   1 CATRYNA, born September 1, 1715; died at Albany, April 6, 1801; married September 6, 1739, John Livingston, baptized at Albany, March 6, 1709; died at Stillwater, N. Y., in 1791, son of Robert Livingston and Margarita Schuyler.

103   11 ANNA, born June 2, 1717; interred in Albany Church, December 30, 1731.

THE OOMA OF DIRCK TEN BROECK.

104 III CHRISTINA, born December 30, 1718; died June 29,
1801; married April 14, 1740, Philip Livingston, Jr., born January 15, 1716, died at York,
Penn., June 12, 1778, son of Philip Livingston
and Catharine Brugh.

105 IV MARIA, baptized April 23, 1721; died at Beaver-
dam, Berne, Albany County, N. Y., December
22, 1805; married March 8, 1739, Gerardus
Groesbeck, baptized October 23, 1709, died
September 17, 1788, son of Stephanus Groesbeck and Elizabeth Lansing.

106 V WESSELS, baptized April 28, 1722.

107 VI SARA, baptized May 30, 1725; died February 16,
1801, aged 75.9.1?; married Johannes Hendrick Ten Eyck, baptized October 28, 1710,
died July 31, 1794, aged 83.11.10, son of Hendrick Ten Eyck and Margarita Bleecker.

108 VII MARGARITA, baptized March 26, 1727; buried at
Albany July 16, 1729.

109 VIII ABRAHAM, baptized April 6, 1729; buried at Albany
January 25, 1732.

110 IX MARGARITA, born October 10, 1731; married Gerardus Lansing, of Albany; they were both living
in 1786, according to Albany County Deeds,
Book XI., page 310.

111 X ABRAHAM, born May 13, 1734; died January 19,
1810; married November 1, 1763, Elizabeth,
born July 9, 1734, died July 4, 1813, daughter
of Stephen Van Rensselaer and Elizabeth
Groesbeck.

112 XI DIRCK, baptized May 16, 1736; buried at Albany
August 11, 1737.

113 XII DIRCK, baptized July 26, 1738; died May 29, 1780; married at Albany November 25, 1761, Ann, born March 25, 1743, died February 18, 1774, daughter of Volckert Pieter Douw and Anna De Peyster.

Children of Christina Ten Broeck (23) and David Van Dyck.

114 I HENDRICK, baptized May 3, 1719.

115 II CATHARINA, baptized March 1, 1721.

116 III MARIA, baptized February 17, 1723; married September 9 (or 28), 1742, Martin Gerritsen Van Bergen, baptized April 13, 1718, died 1788, son of Gerrit Van Bergen and Annatje De Meyer. Martin G. Van Bergen's Will was dated March 26, 1785, and proven February 9, 1789.

117 IV WESSEL, baptized October 11, 1724; married Rachel Sissum.

118 V ELIZABETH, baptized September 11, 1726.

119 VI DIRCK, baptized June 28, 1728; married Elizabeth, born December 17, 1741 (at Athens, Greene County, N. Y., according to the Athens Lutheran Church Record), daughter of Heinrich Stroop and Marytje Spikkerman.

120 VII CHRISTINA, baptized April 4, 1731; interred at Albany November 28, 1731.

121 VIII CHRISTINA, baptized September 10, 1732.

JACOB TEN BROECK (26).

The entry in the family Bible tells us that Jacob Ten Broeck was born August the tenth, 1700, and baptized, as was customary, the rite being administered in the

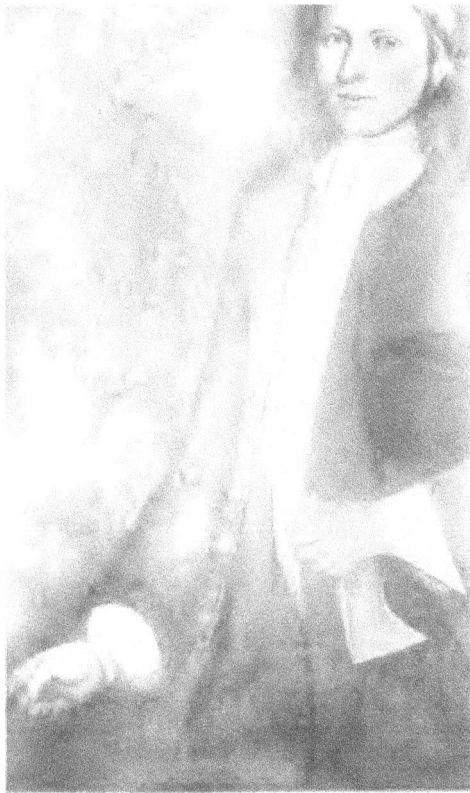

JACOB TEN BROECK (93).
From the Oil-Portrait of 1720.

Albany church by Dominic Lydius, a successor to Dr.
Godfrey Dellius. His sponsors were the maternal grandparents, Jacob and Marÿa (Tryntje) Loockermans.

He married first, on September the twenty-ninth,
1725, his cousin Christina Van Alen (54), and after her
death in 1753, took for his second wife Catrina Van
Benthuysen. The family of eleven children were by the
first marriage.

They resided upon part of the Ten Broeck Patent, on
the west side of the Hudson — land inherited from
Jacob's father, Wessel Ten Broeck (6).

The names of localities which appear in connection
with this branch of the family are unusual. The farm,
which was situated upon the Kaaterskil, was called
Lokeren — doubtless after the town by that name in
Belgium, northeast of Ghent, and brings to mind Brown-
ing's lines :

> 'T was moonset at starting; but while we drew near
> Lokeren, the cocks crew and twilight dawned clear.
> — *How They Brought the Good News to Aix.*

Kaatsbaan, the name found in the data following, is
the site of a Dutch church established about 1732, and
is seven miles south of Catskill, on the Old King's Road.

The portrait of Jacob is owned by Mr. Andrew J.
Ten Broeck, of North Germantown, N. Y., the lineal
descendant in the fifth generation. It was evidently
painted about 1720, and the similarity to the portrait of
Johannes Ten Broeck (page 50) is very striking. They
are framed alike also — in the original black-enameled

moulding of that early date. The tradition concerning
these pictures is the same — that they were executed in
Holland, although we have no record of the voyage, in
either case.

Children of Jacob Ten Broeck (26) and Christina Van Alen.

122   I CATHARINA, baptized June 4, 1727.

123   II JOHANNES, baptized February 9, 1729; died September 17, 1784; married September 27, 1769, Gerritje, baptized July 26, 1738, daughter of Hendrick Roseboom and Elsje Cuyler (33).

124   III WESSEL, baptized at Kaatsbaan March 7, 1731; died July 10, 1734.

125   IV PETRUS, ——; married March 31, 1750, Annatje, daughter of Han Jost Herchheimer and Catharine.

126   V WESSEL, baptized at Germantown 1735; died August 27, 1736.

127   VI CHRISTINA, baptized February 15, 1738; died October 22, 1739.

128   VII MARIA, baptized March 30, 1740; married Abraham J. DeLamater, born about 1730, son of Johannes DeLamater and Christina Wynkoop. He had married first, at Kingston, N. Y., December 20, 1755, Sarah, born December 21, 1729, daughter of Wessel Ten Broeck, of Kingston, and Blandina Van Gaasbeck.

129   VIII WESSEL, born February 25, 1742; died June 13, 1785; married at Kaatsbaan, February 4 (Family record gives August 21), 1764, Jannetje, born March 13, 1741, died January 7, 1831, daughter of Abraham Persen and Catharina Schoonmaker.

130 IX CHRISTINA, baptized at Germantown, N. Y., October
     12, 1743; married at Johnstown, Columbia
     County, N. Y., October 31, 1769, Rev. Gerhard
     Daniel Cock, who came to the Colony in No-
     vember, 1763. He died about 1793.

131 X JACOB, baptized at Kaatsbaan, August 22, 1745 ; died
     November 9, 1780; he married Anna Elizabeth
     Cock, sister of the Rev. G. D. Cock.

132 XI LENA (or LANY), baptized at Kaatsbaan, N. Y., April
     21, 1747; married William Schepmoes, of King-
     ston, N. Y.

CORNELIUS TEN BROECK (27).

Cornelius, the youngest child of Wessel Ten Broeck,
was a merchant, and a citizen of Albany. He married
on the eleventh of October, 1733, his first cousin, Maria
Cuyler, daughter of Elsie Ten Broeck and Johannes
Cuyler.

He was a member of the Council Board of the city,
and from 1762 till 1766 was particularly active.

In 1726 the Council had vested in the King of England's name a large tract of land in western New York,
"for the protection of free Indian Rights and Trade."
Sir Jeffrey Amherst had disregarded this, and granted
to a company of men ten thousand acres of it. The latter had followed up the opportunity to monopolize the
Indian trade.

The merchants and men of Albany determined to
resist this interference. Accordingly, a petition was resorted to, which bears date January the twenty-eighth,
1762, signed by the prominent men, begging that these

grants in western New York might be annulled. [58] Cornelius Ten Broeck's name stands on this list.

Two years later, a second petition was issued to the English Trade Commissioners, asking for the appointment of certain places or posts where the Indians could be met for traffic. Again Cornelius Ten Broeck used his influence for mutual safety and protection. [59]

He requested permission to purchase a tract of land from the Indian owners, in Albany County, on the south side of the Mohawk River. In July, 1765, Sir William Johnson signified this to be a *bona fide* purchase.

Cornelius Ten Broeck made his Will on March the thirteenth, 1771. It was recorded in Albany the twenty-ninth of April, 1773. Among its provisions he mentioned this grant, and devised it to his grandson, Cornelius Ten Broeck, Junior.

Children of Cornelius Ten Broeck (27) and Maria Cuyler.

133   I CATHARINA, baptized May 19, 1737, died September 3, 1806; married George Wray.

134   II JOHANNES, born July 27, 1740; died December 26, 1822; married June 12, 1762 (Family record gives the date January 4), to Sarah, baptized June 17, 1741, died July 20, 1811, aged 68.11.23?. daughter of Harman Gansevoort and Magdalena Douw.

DIRCK WESSELSE TEN BROECK (68).

The eldest son of Samuel Ten Broeck and Maria Van Rensselaer, was born the first of May, 1715, and named Dirck Wesselse.

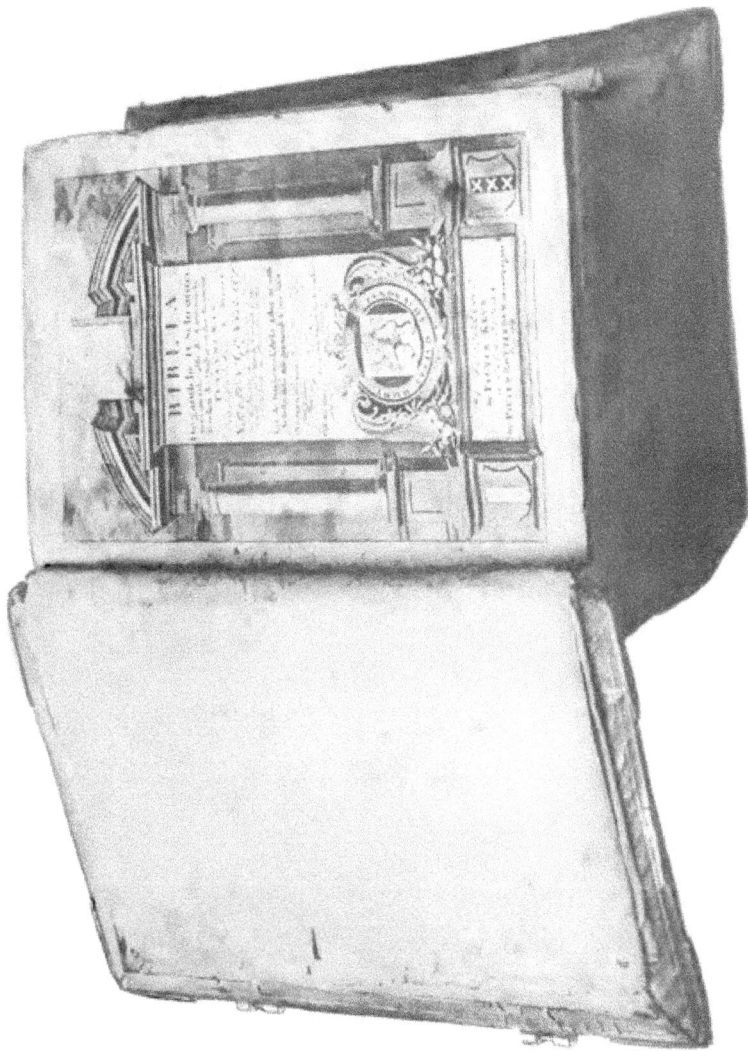

THE BIBLE OF DIRCK W. TEN BROECK 1681.
Printed at Dordrecht, Holland, 1710

He was married first, at Kinderhook, on the twenty-eighth of June, 1743, to Catharina Conyn. She was the mother of all his children. His second marriage took place when he was about sixty years of age.

Dirck W. Ten Broeck was an unyielding patriot of the Revolution, and several times represented the manor of Livingston in the Provincial Assembly. The Assembly of New York, under the first Constitution, was composed of twenty-four members. They met at Kingston, September the ninth, 1777, and the following month were dispersed by the British troops. Dirck W. Ten Broeck was a member of this session, as also of the second, which was held at Poughkeepsie the year following. He was continued the Representative [60] until 1783.

He was an intimate friend of the two Robert Livingstons, lords of the upper and lower manors.

The bouwerie of his grandfather, Dirck Wesselse, with its tract of twelve hundred acres on the Roelof Jansen Kil, became his property, partly by inheritance from his father and partly by purchase from the heirs of his uncle, Tobias Ten Broeck.

He had a new dwelling erected on this estate, but whether the old frame-house was entirely removed or was left to form the rear extension to the new one, cannot be positively known. The hipped roof and apparent antiquity of the extension suggest the latter, and it is borne out by the relative measurements. The new brick house is forty-eight feet wide, and extends back twenty-five feet to where it meets the frame portion. The latter has a width of forty feet by a depth of thirty-one.

The frontispiece represents the place as it appears to-

9

day; between the windows can be plainly seen the date of building, 1762. This plate is from a silhouette executed by Albertina (140), the daughter of Dirck W. Ten Broeck, and gives a quaint picture of the house and barns more than one hundred years ago.

This dwelling, with part of the original tract of land, is still in the possession of a lineal descendant, Mrs. Harold Wilson, of Clermont, New York.

Tradition says the bricks were brought from Holland. An ancient brass knocker adorns the door, on opening which we find the house as the period of building suggests — a wide hallway, with spacious rooms on either side. Up to the roof itself can be seen the firm, substantial material and workmanship which the passing of four generations has not impaired. The heavy timbers are of hand-hewed oak, and each piece bears the Roman number denoting its place in the structure; and strange to our modern sight are the oaken pins which hold each cross-beam and brace in position. At either end, high up toward the hipped roof, are the port-holes, which were used in the every-day emergencies of that time.

The house stands on a slight rise of ground above the banks of the clear water of the Kil. It overlooks the quiet, green meadows, or "flatts," which are an important part of the fertile and beautiful lands comprising the estate.

Dirck W. Ten Broeck died at his bouwerie, and was interred in the place of family burial. Near this was the space allotted to the slaves, and they were a goodly retinue for even those times.

On the level plateau to the north of the house, and

SILHOUETTE, REPRESENTING THE TEN BROECK BOUWERIE, ABOUT 1780.
With the Family Arms.

near the public highway, is pointed out the racecourse, where the Ten Broecks and the Livingstons found their chief recreation. None had a better eye for the points of a fine horse, and the best were sure to be found in their stables.

The records of this family are found in the Dutch Bible now owned by a descendant,— Mrs. Charles P. Sanders, of Scotia, N. Y. The plate represents the title-page.

The book was printed in Dordrecht in the year 1719. It is one of those heavy folio volumes bound in boards, covered with tooled leather, and finished with corner-pieces and clasps of brass. It contains marginal references and footnotes; numerous plates, engraved by Jonkman, illustrative of gospel scenes, are fitted, block-like, to cover full pages; each one is small,— about three inches square,— and they are both quaint and amusing.

Children of Dirck W. Ten Broeck (68) and Catharina Conyn.

135   I SAMUEL, born September 27, 1745; died May 30, 1841; married August 12, 1768, Emma Van Alsteyn, born October 11, 1749, died June 24, 1834.

136   II ELBERTJE, born at Roelof Jansen's Kil July 6, 1750; died young.

137   III LEENDERT, born November 10, 1752; died November 11, 1836; marriage license dated March 7, 1776; married Geertje, born October 23, 1756, died September 2, 1838, daughter of Jacob Schermerhorn and Magdalena.

138   IV MARIA, baptized at Germantown, N. Y., October 19, 1755; died young.

139 v Philip, baptized at Germantown, N. Y., March 19,
1758.

140 vi Albertina, born November 23, 1760; died July 23,
1840; married, 1799, John Sanders, born Octo-
ber 2, 1757, died March 30, 1834, son of Johannes Sanders and Debora Glen. He had
married 1st, February 24, 1777, his cousin
Debora, baptized February 9, 1758, died November 28, 1793, daughter of Robert Sanders
and Elizabeth Schuyler.

141 vii Maria, baptized at Claverack March 13, 1763.

HENDRICK TEN BROECK (69).

Hendrick Ten Broeck married on October the fourteenth, 1743, Annatje Van Schaick, the daughter of his
first cousin, Anna Cuyler (28). Their family records are
preserved in the Dordrecht Bible of Annatje's father —
Anthony Van Schaick. It is now in the possession of
a lineal descendant — Mrs. Robert Dunscombe Swartwout, Stamford, Conn.

Hendrick died at Claverack, in 1796, and his Will,
dated September the twentieth, 1776, and proved September the twenty-third, 1796, is recorded in the Columbia County Office, Volume A, page 362.

Children of Hendrick Ten Broeck (69) and Annatje Van Schaick.

142 i Samuel, baptized at Rhinebeck, January 27, 1745;
died young.

143 ii Samuel H., baptized at Rhinebeck, November 3,
1745; died August 23, 1800; unmarried.

144   III ANTONY, baptized at Albany, November 1, 1747;
        died young.

145   IV ANTONY, born at Claverack, June 20, 1750; died
        young.

146   V MARIA, baptized at Germantown, N. Y., November
        12, 1752; died young.

147   VI ANTJE, born May 9, 1754; died at Watervliet, N. Y.,
        May 7, 1838; married December 30, 1784, John
        Cornelise Ten Broeck (194), born at Claverack
        March 15, 1755, died August 10, 1835, son of
        Cornelis Ten Broeck and Maria Bodyn.

148   VII ANTHONY, born November 2, 1756; died October
        12, 1832; married 1st, October 13, 1782, Chris-
        tina (197), born April 4, 1761, died February 2,
        1817, daughter of Cornelis Ten Broeck and
        Maria Bodyn; married 2nd, February 3, 1823,
        Mrs. Maria Heermance, born July 28, 1756, died
        September 24, 1850.

149   VIII MARIA, baptized at Claverack June 17, 1759; died
        January, 1827; married Aaron Lane.

150   IX HENDRICK, baptized at Claverack May 10, 1761;
        died young.

151   X HENDRICK, baptized at Claverack October 26, 1766,
        died June 11, 1839; married March 23, 1797,
        Martha Comstock, died at Waterford, N. Y.,
        February 26, 1832, aged 60 years.

Child of Catharina Ten Broeck (71) and Ephraim Van Vechten.

152   I LYDIA, baptized October 19, 1744.

JOHANNES TEN BROECK (72).

Johannes Ten Broeck was born in October, 1724. He married on December the twelfth, 1753, Marytje Hoffman.

On the death of his father, Samuel Ten Broeck (14), he received his portion of the bouwerie lands from the six hundred acre tract lying on the Hudson River.

In his Will, which bears the date September the nineteenth, 1793, he writes himself "of Hudson, N. Y."

The Will was proven at that place January the seventeenth, 1795.

Children of Johannes Ten Broeck (72) and Marytje Hoffman.

153   I SAMUEL J., born June 4, 1756; died August 6, 1835; married Maria (161), baptized at Claverack January 27, 1762, died April 26, 1835, daughter of Jeremiah Ten Broeck and Marytje Van Alen.

154   II JANETJE, born 1759; baptized at Claverack, April 14, 1759; died unmarried, November 27, 1833, and interred at Claverack. Her Will was proved at Hudson March 10, 1834.

155   III MARIA, born June 17, 1761; married at Claverack, N. Y., April 7, 1782, Peter Van Rensselaer, baptized February 2, 1752, son of Hendrick Van Rensselaer and Elizabeth Van Brugh.

156   IV ANNATJE, born June 15, 1764.

157   V NICLAES, born April 5, 1767; died January 22, 1843; married 1st, January 1, 1800, Maria (173), born April 25, 1769, died March 25, 1812, daughter of Harmanus Schuyler and Christina Ten Broeck, and widow of David Van Rensse-

laer; married 2nd, at St. John's, Red Hook,
October 14, 1817, Cornelia Hoffman, born August 6, 1784, died April 13, 1830.

158   VI JEREMIAS, born January 12, 1770; died at Hudson,
N. Y., August 27, 1805; interred at Claverack.

JEREMIAH TEN BROECK (73).

The Will of Jeremiah was made at Hudson on the
fourth of February, 1801. The instrument was proved
in 1806, one of the witnesses being Abraham Ten
Broeck, Justice of the Peace in Columbia County.

Children of Jeremiah Ten Broeck (73) and Marytje Van Alen.

159   I SAMUEL J., born March 28, 1757, died April 25,
1830; married Christyntje (262), born January
8, 1765, died about 1850, daughter of Wessel
Ten Broeck and Jannetje Persen.

160   II ADAM, born July 24, 1759; died May 30, 1826; married 1st, at Claverack, May 30, 1784, Lydia
Maria, baptized at Claverack December 19,
1762, daughter of Austin Monson, Jr., M. D., of
New Haven, Conn., and Annatje Oosterhoudt;
married 2nd, January 28, 1807, Hannah Morrison, born February 1, 1780, died April 17,
1870.

161   III MARIA, born January 2, 1762; died April 26, 1835;
married Samuel J. Ten Broeck (153), born June
4, 1756, died August 6, 1835, son of Johannes
Ten Broeck and Marytje Hoffman.

162   IV JOHANNES, born July 8, 1764; married at Claverack
       December 18, 1785, Fytje (Sophia), born Sep-
       tember 1, 1765, probably daughter of Jeremias
       Müller and Sara Hogeboom, of Claverack.

163   V DIRCK WESSELSE, born December 16, 1766; married
       at Kinderhook June 25, 1796, Lena, baptized
       at Claverack August 25, 1776, probably daugh-
       ter of Abram Van Alen and Catharine Van
       Buren.

164   VI ABRAHAM, born September 4, 1769; married Lena
       Van Alen, widow of Dirck Wesselse Ten Broeck
       (163).

165   VII JEREMIAS, born August 2, 1772; died December 1,
       1826; married November 15, 1795, Jannetjen
       (265), born April 8, 1770, died October 7, 1825,
       daughter of Wessel Ten Broeck and Jannetje
       Persen.

CHRISTINA TEN BROECK (74).

Christina, the youngest child of Samuel Ten Broeck
(14) became the wife of Harmanus Schuyler on the
fourth of September, 1754.

He was at that time a jeweler in Albany, and held
the position of constable. He soon became assistant
alderman, followed, in June, 1761, by the appointment
as sheriff of Albany County. He held this office until
1770, when he removed with his family to Stillwater.

In February, 1776, he was made Assistant Deputy
Commissary-General of the Northern Department, and
was stationed at Lake George, in charge of men engaged
in building boats for the use of the Army. He finally

retired from the service, and died at Stillwater on September the first, 1796.

His wife Christina and seven children survived him. The sons followed the father's example in devoting their services to the country. The eldest, Nicholas (166) became a surgeon; the second, Samuel (167) was a clerk in the Commissary Department; and Dirck (169) became Second Lieutenant in one of the companies of the New York line.

The distinction of entertaining Washington fell to the lot of Christina's eldest daughter, Elsie. She was a woman of more than ordinary beauty of person, dignified in manner, and self-possessed.

In July, 1783, General Washington, escorted by Governor Clinton and General Schuyler, was on a tour of inspection of the battlefields of Saratoga and the Mohawk Valley. On their arrival at Stillwater they sought entertainment at the Schuyler-Ten Broeck residence.

Christina was absent from home, and upon her daughter devolved the honor of receiving the General as a guest. The party remained overnight, and when the hour for departure arrived, Washington, with his habitual courtesy, took Elsie's hand and raised it to his lips.

This was never forgotten. Nearly fifty years later, when her youngest nephew called to pay his respects, and was about to kiss her lips, she held up her hand and said: "Not my lips, George, but my hand, once kissed by Washington!"[61] Elsie Schuyler was at that time the bride of Dr. Nicholas N. Bogart, who died within a few weeks. Some years later she married Major James Van Rensselaer of Albany.

10

Children of Christina Ten Broeck (74) and Harmanus Schuyler.

166   I NICHOLAS, born June 13, 1755, died November, 1824,
       married August 13, 1782, at Lancaster, Penn.,
       Shinah Simons, born 1762. They had no
       children.

167   II SAMUEL, born November 17, 1757; died unmarried
       at Albany, January, 1832.

168   III ELSIE, born February 5, 1760; died 1838, in her
       78th year; married first at Stillwater, N. Y.,
       June 15, 1783, Nicholas N. Bogart, M. D., of
       New York, died September 26, 1783, aged
       22.6.22; married second, June 24, 1789, James
       Van Rensselaer, baptized in Albany February
       1, 1747, died at Bethlehem, N. Y., January 25,
       1827, son of Johannes Van Rensselaer and En-
       geltje Livingston.

169   IV DIRCK, born November 29, 1761; died unmarried,
       at Ballston, N. Y., June, 1811.

170   V JOHANNES HARMANUS, born July 30, 1763; died at
       Ithaca, N. Y., August 18, 1846; married first at
       Half Moon, N. Y., June 6, 1786, Hendrika,
       born June 6, 1761, daughter of Harman Fort
       and Rebecca Van Woert; married second,
       June 10, 1800, Annatje, born March 29, 1770,
       died January 12, 1851, sister to the first wife,
       Hendrika Fort.

171   VI MARIA, born February 1, 1766; died October 18,
       1767.

172   VII PHILIP, born December 12, 1767; died August 25,
       1769.

173   VIII MARIA, born April 25, 1769; died at Claverack,
       March 25, 1812; married first, at Stillwater,

November 22, 1793, David Van Rensselaer,
baptized at Claverack September 16, 1749, son
of Hendrick Van Rensselaer and Elizabeth
Van Brugh; married second, January 1, 1800,
Nicholas Ten Broeck (157), born April 5, 1767,
died January 22, 1843, son of Johannes Ten
Broeck and Marytje Hoffman.

174   IX PHILIP, born August 22, 1771; died in 1807; married
      May 22, 1797, Mary, daughter of Beriah
      Palmer, Jr., of Canaan, Conn.

DIRCK WESSELSE TEN BROECK (75).

Dirck Wesselse Ten Broeck married, on the thirteenth
of June, 1740, Catharina Rutsen, of Kingston. He lived
but a short time, and there were no children by the
marriage.

In June, 1749, his widow, Catharina, was married to
Petrus, son of John Ten Broeck and Rachel Roosa, and
grandson of Wessel Wesselse Ten Broeck (2), of Kingston.

Petrus Ten Broeck was a citizen of Rhinebeck, and
upon the opening of the Revolution at once took an
active part. He was commissioned Colonel of the Rhinebeck militia, and chosen deputy to the Provincial Congress of November, 1775. He was also Secretary of the
Committee of War, [62] and later bore the title of General.

His death occurred on March the fifth, 1777. His
wife survived him five years. Their Wills are on file in
the office of the clerk of the Court of Appeals, Albany.
There is no mention made of children.

Children of Catryna Ten Broeck (76) and Richard Hansen.

175   i Debora, born January 14, 1739; probably buried at Albany August 21, 1739.

176   ii Johannes, born May 25, 1740.

177   iii Pieter, baptized October 18, 1741.

178   iv Dirck, baptized April 24, 1743; married at Albany July 1, 1781, Lena (Helen) Low.

179   v Debora, baptized January 6, 1745; probably buried at Albany September 27, 1747.

180   vi Jeremie, baptized August 17, 1746.

181   vii Debora, born July 14, 1748.

182   viii Hendrick, born May 18, 1750.

183   ix Catryna, born September 27, 1751.

184   x Maria, baptized March 3, 1754.

JOHANNES TEN BROECK (78).

Johannes was born at Albany, September, 1719, and soon after attaining the age of manhood he came to East New Jersey.

Through the influence of the Dutch from the upper Hudson, New Brunswick had been incorporated in 1730. The Indian pathway from the Delaware River to the sea had become the king's highway, and an outlet for the commerce of the region. Three miles above the town, at the head of the sloop-navigation waters of the Raritan River, was a station known as Raritan Landing, which was described as "a market for the most plentiful wheat country of its bigness in America." Here Johannes,

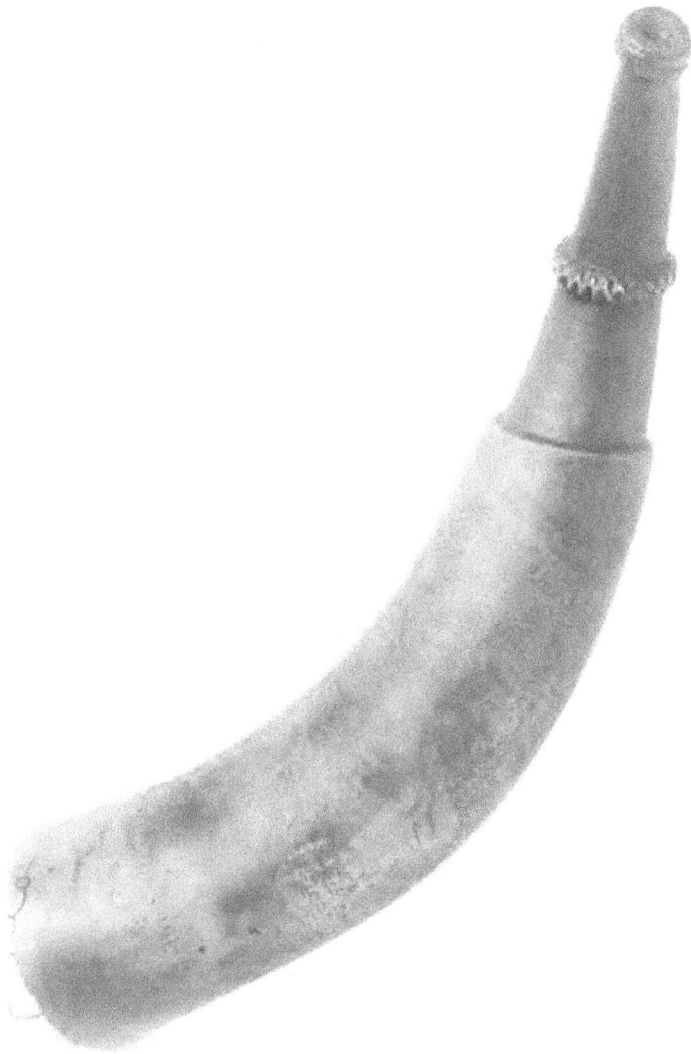

POWDER-HORN OF CAPTAIN JOHANNES TEN BROECK.

either for himself or in company with his parents, purchased a tract of land.

In 1748 lotteries were numerous in New Jersey; there was scarcely a town that did not seek to enrich itself by such means. The objects were various — to complete a church, to erect a parsonage, or to relieve distress, public or private. In this year Johannes Ten Broeck advertised a lottery at Raritan Landing, and offered his real estate as the prizes.[63] However the scheme succeeded, Johannes retained over two hundred and twenty-five acres of the land, and it became the family home for three generations.

He had married on the thirtieth of January, 1746, Patientie (Patience), the eldest child of William Williamson, who was a citizen of prominence and also a Church-master of the Dutch Church of New Brunswick. They resided on the farm at Raritan Landing.

Those were unquiet times, and the last colonial war, the one which ended the rule of France in the colonies, was declared in 1756. Between 1758 and 1761 the New Jersey Assembly increased its quota of fighting men from five hundred to one thousand. This force was detailed to "remove the enemy from the frontier." In addition to this, Johannes Ten Broeck raised a company, which consisted of sixty-one men and three officers. He was commissioned the Captain on the seventh of April, 1761.

The troops of this section were called "Jersey Blues." The name is said to be due to the fact that a certain volunteer company were furnished with "tow frocks and pantaloons dyed blue" by the patriotic women. Is it a marvel that they proved singularly efficient in the days of trial ?

The company of Johannes Ten Broeck was incorporated into Colonel Samuel Hunt's regiment of Jersey Blues, and was reserved for special garrison duty.[64]

Fort Oswego, the natural gateway between the enemy in Canada and the colonies, had been reinforced in 1755 by the erection of Fort Ontario on the east side of Onondaga River. This was built by Governor Shirley as a defense against the attacks and advances of the French and Indians.

Johannes Ten Broeck and his company "embarked" for this point on the fourth of June, 1761. They were on duty in this fort sixteen months, and doubtless continued in the service until the definite treaty was concluded at Paris in February, 1763. In accordance with the proclamation of this year (1763), Captain Ten Broeck received a grant of three thousand acres of land, in recognition of his services. The confirmation of the grant was never sought.

His pay-rolls are in the possession of Mr. Frank La Rue Ten Broeck, of Asbury Park, N. J. They each bear upon the face the date, month by month, and the names of the men comprising the company, noting the changes which occur and the amount due each one for service. On the reverse is found the signatures of the men, upon receipt of the monthly payment, and also the date at which the examining committee certified the correctness of the paper.

The powder-horn carried by Captain Ten Broeck bears the etchings which are a feature of the horns of that

period, the markings and names portraying the route of their march to the frontier. This is now owned by Mrs. Katharine M. Joralemon, of Newark. N. J.

Whether John Ten Broeck, who in the Revolutionary War was advanced from the position of Captain to that of First Major and Lieutenant-Colonel of the Fourth Hunterdon County, N. J., Regiment, is the Johannes of this colonial service, has not yet been proven. The state papers of the Revolutionary period lack the autograph, and many family papers have been destroyed and mislaid.

The Dutch Church of New Brunswick was the religious home of this family, although they continued to reside at The Landing. Johannes Ten Broeck died at the homestead, and was buried there, near the King's highway, on the east side of the river. The land passed out of the family in the third generation, and each year the husbandman encroaches, little by little, upon the space where once stood many stones inscribed with the heart history of this branch of the family.

Governor Livingston, on February the fifteenth, 1790, granted to Peter and Van Rensselaer Ten Broeck letters of administration on their father's estate.

After the death of Johannes, his wife took up her residence with their eldest son William, in New Brunswick, where she died in January, 1800. Her Will was made on January the fifteenth, 1796. It was recorded the twenty-fifth of February, 1800, and is on file at Trenton, N. J., Book 39. The following extracts from it may prove of interest to the descendants: "I will and bequeath unto my son, William Ten Broeck . . . the pictures now hanging in my room, my easy chair, and my large Bible. . . .

"I give and bequeath to my son, John Ten Broeck, six leather-bottomed chairs, and one armchair.

"I give and bequeath to my son, Peter Ten Broeck, one large folding table . . . and my tea-cups and saucers. . . ."

Her executors were her son William, and her daughter, Mary Ten Broeck.

It may not be amiss to state that Johannes Ten Broeck anglicized his entire name, writing it John Ten Brook, but only for a short time did his descendants follow his example in simplifying the spelling of the last word.

Children of Johannes Ten Broeck (78) and Patience Williamson.

185   i CATHARINE, born March 1, 1747; married Samuel H. Phillips, M. D.

186   ii WILLIAM, born January 14, 1749; died at New Brunswick, N. J., 1827; married Sarah Harvey, died October 24, 1823, aged 74.

187   iii MARY, born November 6, 1751; died September, 1806; unmarried.

188   iv JANE, born May 31, 1754; died October 1, 1777; married.

189   v JOHN, born September 10, 1757; died August 18, 1798; married Mary Ladner, born 1761, died April 5, 1832, in her 71st year. She had married first, John Webster, and she married third, John Scott, born 1765, died December 6, 1841.

190 vi PETER, born September 4, 1760; died at Readington, N. J., July 20, 1840; married first, July 4, 1781, Ame Chamberlain, born 1756, died December 5, 1805, daughter of Joseph Chamberlain and Amy. He married second, May 31, 1812, Catharine, born February 26, 1791, died October 27, 1838, daughter of Nicholas Emmons and Elizabeth Egbert.

191 vii VAN RENSSELAER, born August 11, 1763; died in New Brunswick, N. J.; married Sarah, born August 14, 1776, died August 7, 1864, daughter of John Webster and Mary Ladner (*vide* 189).

192 viii CHRISTINA, born December 7, 1765; died October 8, 1766.

193 ix SAMUEL W., born January 21, 1768; died at Shrewsbury, N. J., August 24, 1828; married June 4, 1797, Mary, born December 31, 1776, died May 7, 1826, daughter of Edmund Williams.

CORNELIS TEN BROECK (83).

Cornelis, the sixth son of Johannes Ten Broeck and Catryna Van Rensselaer, was born at Albany the fourteenth of May, 1727.

It seems not improbable that in early manhood he came to New Jersey, as he married Maria Bodyn, whose parents in both branches were Huguenots and New Jersey settlers. After their marriage they resided at Claverack and Kinderhook, and the baptisms of most of their children are recorded at the Claverack Dutch Church.

It is almost impossible for us to realize the dangers and

troubles occasioned in colonial days by the disputes over both public and private divisions of lands. History traces for us the progress of the long and bitter feud regarding the boundary between Massachusetts and New York.

In the section of country familiar to our ancestors, dissatisfaction was chiefly due to two causes, the persistence of certain men from Massachusetts who claimed parts of the Livingston manor, and to the exaction of quit rents.

These rents were the conditioned stipulations of grants of land from the Governor, an acknowledgment, so to speak, of his rights as grantor. Large tracts upon which arrears of quit rents had accumulated were sold from time to time to satisfy these claims.

Riots were the outgrowth of these grievances, and frequently the magistrates and local militia were compelled to subdue them. In such an affray, on the twenty-sixth of June, 1766, it is believed that Cornelis Ten Broeck met his death.[65]

The following record of the children's births and baptisms is in possession of Mrs. Robert Dunscombe Swartwout, Stamford, Conn.

Children of Cornelis Ten Broeck (83) and Maria Bodyn.

194   I JOHN C., born at Claverack, March 15, 1755; baptized at Readington, N. J., April 13, 1755; died August 10, 1835; married December 30, 1784, Antje (147), born at Claverack, May 9, 1754, died May 7, 1838, daughter of Hendrick Ten Broeck and Annatje Van Schaick.

195   II DIRCK WESSELSE, born August 4, 1756; baptized at Readington, N. J., August 29, 1757.

196   III PETER BODINE, born August 6, 1759; baptized at Claverack.

197   IV CHRISTINA, born April 4, 1761; baptized at Claverack May 10, 1761; died February 2, 1817; married October 13, 1782, Antony Ten Broeck (148), born November 2, 1756, died October 12, 1832, son of Hendrick Ten Broeck and Annatje Van Schaick.

198   V GABRIEL, born February 8, 1763; baptized at Claverack March 13, 1763; married Catharine Bodine.

199   VI HENDRICK, born October 20, 1765; baptized at Claverack, November 24, 1765.

Child of Christina Ten Broeck (90) and Dirck Van Slyck.

200   I TOBIAS, baptized at Kinderhook October 17, 1738; married, probably Jesyna, daughter of John Wheeler and Elizabeth.

JOHN TOBIAS TEN BROECK (92).

He was born at the bouwerie on the Roelof Jansen Kil, on the seventeenth of October, 1722. Fifteen months later his father died, and in a few years his mother had married a second time. These events, doubtless, separated the family from the Ten Broecks.

When John Tobias became of age, as the heir-at-law and devisee of his father he sold his equal one-half portion of the eighteen hundred acres of the bouwerie to his cousin Dirck W. Ten Broeck (68), for the sum of three thousand Spanish milled dollars. The papers bear the date of the seventh of December, 1743.

It is said he then removed to New Jersey. On the fifteenth of August, 1745, he married Elizabeth Oothout, of New York City. They had a family of twelve children, but the only two sons died before reaching the age of twelve years. Thus the family name in this line terminated in this generation.

Children of John Tobias Ten Broeck (92) and Elizabeth Oothout.

201   I   TOBIAS, born June 13, 1746; died July 23, 1757.

202   II   JOHN, born May 14, 1748; died December 20, 1757.

203   III   MARIA, born in New Brunswick, N. J., July 31, 1750; died at Albany, January 15, 1829; married in New York, November 15, 1770, Goosen Van Schaick, baptized September 5, 1736, died July 4, 1789, son of Sybrant Van Schaick and Alida Roseboom.

204   IV   CATELYNA, born January 16, 1752.

205   V   ELIZABETH, born February 16, 1754; died August 8, 1754.

206   VI   ELIZABETH, born June 29, 1755; died March 4, 1765.

207   VII   CATRYNA, born November 3, 1757; married David Fonda, baptized January 16, 1757, died August 3, 1805, aged 48.6.22, son of Isaac Douw Fonda and Susanna (Santje) De Forest.

208   VIII   MARAGREITA, born March 13, 1760.

209   IX   JOHANNA, born April 2, 1762.

210   X   LYDIA, born May 30, 1764; died June 10, 1765.

211   XI   ELIZABETH, born September 14, 1766; died October 10, 1766.

212   XII   ELIZABETH, born September 8, 1768; died November 27, 1771.

THE FIFTH GENERATION.

CATRYNA TEN BROECK (102).

Catryna was baptized at Albany on the fourth of September, 1715, when three days old. We are fortunate in having a copy of her portrait in childhood. The original is in the possession of Miss Katharine Livingston Smith, of Argyle, New York — a lineal descendant through her daughter, Catharine (220). In the left-hand corner of the canvas there is inscribed in red letters :

ÆTAT⁵ SUA.   One would never imagine it to be
3 YEARS.   the likeness of a child of only that
1719.   age. The description of Holmes's
"Dorothy Q" fits our little maid
wonderfully well :

Grandmother's mother : her age, I guess,
Thirteen summers, or something less ;
Girlish bust, but womanly air ;
Smooth, square forehead, with uprolled hair ;

Lips that never a lover has kissed;
Taper fingers, and slender wrist;
Hanging sleeves of stiff brocade —
So they painted the little maid.

On her hand a parrot green
Sits unmoved and broods serene.
Look not on her with eyes of scorn;
Dorothy Q was a lady born!

One thinks of her maidenhood as full of manifold and varied duties and pleasures, for she was the eldest of a family of twelve children. At the age of twenty-four she became the wife of John Livingston, of Albany, the third son of Robert Livingston and Margarita Schuyler. She shared with him the varied experiences of more than fifty years of married life.

They resided for a time in Montreal, Canada, but when the Revolution commenced they removed to Stillwater, New York. They had probably both inherited portions of the Saratoga Patent, and thus it became their permanent home from this time. On the fifth of March, 1784, Catryna received from her husband the " Power of Attorney for all Saratoga lands devised to her by her father, Dirck Ten Broeck, or her brother, Dirck Ten Broeck; and all or any claim in a patent called Lokermans." [66]

John Livingston died at Stillwater, in 1791, and his wife then returned to Albany, and found a home with her daughter, Catharine (220), the wife of Dr. Elias Willard. She was here shown every considerate kindness due the aged parent.

CATRYNA TEN BROECK (LIVINGSTON).
From the Oil-Portrait of 1719.

It is said Catryna never spoke the English language. A description of the ceremonious visits the children of the family paid their grandmother is still repeated among the descendants. On New Year's, the only day of the year on which the grandchildren were permitted to visit her apartments, they came with the greatest delight, mingled with awe. The low curtsey was made, and their greetings spoken in Dutch taught them for the occasion !

Catryna died at her daughter's house on Broadway, Albany, April the sixth, 1801.

Her ancient Dutch Bible and Psalm Book are now the property of Mrs. Israel Smith, of Williamsburg, Va. The former was purchased on the twentieth of November, 1728, according to the inscription, but it contains no records. The Psalm Book was printed in 1725, and probably belonged to her father, as on the final page is written, "Dirck Ten Broeck, syn Boock, 1732." Her own name is on the cover of the book, in this form :

CATH^E LIVINGSTON

TEN BROECK,

Albany.

Children of Catryna Ten Broeck (102) and John Livingston.

213   I ROBERT, baptized March 16, 1741 ; died unmarried, in the West Indies.

214   II MARGRIETA, baptized October 10, 1742 ; died at Albany, November 17, 1820 ; married Edward Chinn, born at Bridgewater, England, in 1732, died at Albany, August 17, 1802.

215 III DIRCK (Richard), baptized October 19, 1744; died
   March, 1784, at Stillwater; married, Elizabeth
   Rencour, of Montreal, Canada, died in 1796,
   aged fifty-five.

216 IV JAMES, born March 27, 1747; died November 29,
   1842; married Elizabeth Simpson, of Montreal,
   born October 10, 1750, died June 10, 1800.

217 V ANNATJE (Nancy), baptized at New York, May 10,
   1749; married Jacob Jordan, of Montreal.

218 VI JANET, baptized at New York July 24, 1751; died
   at Albany; married Jacob Van der Heyden,
   probably baptized at Albany March 3, 1737,
   son of David Van der Heyden and Geertruy
   Visscher.

219 VII ABRAHAM, born 1754; died at Montreal, Canada, in
   1803; married Maria Peoples.

220 VIII CATHARINE TEN BROECK, born November 2, 1755;
   died January 26, 1827; married July 8, 1778,
   Elias Willard, born at Harvard, Mass., January
   17, 1756, died March 20, 1827, son of Lemuel
   Willard and Hannah Haskell.

221 IX MARIA, born 1761; baptized at New York, April 22,
   1761; died September 22, 1839, unmarried.

CHRISTINA TEN BROECK (104).

Christina, the third child of Direk Ten Broeck, of Albany, was born on the thirtieth of December, 1718.

On the fourteenth of April, 1740, she married Philip
Livingston, who was a cousin to John Livingston, the
husband of her eldest sister.

Philip Livingston was born at Albany January the

fifteenth, 1716. He was graduated from Yale College in 1737, and after his marriage resided in New York City. He was an alderman for several years, and in 1759 was elected member of the Provincial Assembly. This was the opening of a career that was at the same time illustrious and honorable. His position in the Continental Congress and his signature to the Declaration of Independence would, of themselves, make his name widely known.

He died at York, Pennsylvania, on June the twelfth, 1778, where Congress was then assembled. Christina, his honored wife for nearly forty years, survived him, and died in Albany, June the twenty-ninth, 1801. Her will was made on April the twenty-fourth, 1800, and recorded in Albany County in November, 1801.

A portrait of Christina Ten Broeck, painted in her second year, hangs in the hallway of the Van Rensselaer mansion at Greenbush, N. Y. A second portrait was painted when growth of character and wideness of experience had changed the expression of the round baby face, and the child had become the wife of a distinguished man. This is in the possession of Mrs. Crosby, of New York City, who is also a descendant.

Children of Christina Ten Broeck (104) and Philip Livingston.

222   I PHILIP PHILIP, born at Albany, May 28, 1741; died at New York, November 2, 1787; married, at Jamaica, W. I., on June 29, 1768, Sarah Johnson, born March 23, 1749, died at New York, November 6, 1802.

223   II DIRCK, born June 6, 1743; died unmarried.

12

224   III CATHARINE, baptized August 25, 1745; died April
          17, 1810; married first at New York, January
          23, 1764, Stephen Van Rensselaer, baptized
          June 2, 1742, died 1769, son of Stephen Van
          Rensselaer and Elizabeth Groesbeck; married
          second, July 19, 1775, Dom. Eilardus Westerlo,
          died December 26, 1790, aged fifty-three years.

225   IV MARGARET, baptized at New York October 25, 1747;
          married at Kingston, N. Y., July 30, 1776,
          Thomas Jones, M. D., of New York.

226   V PIETER VAN BRUG, baptized at New York, March
          13, 1751; died at Jamaica, W. I.

227   VI SARAH, baptized at New York, December 13, 1752;
          died at New Brunswick, N. J., December 29,
          1814: married at Kingston New Church, No-
          vember 26, 1775, John H. Livingston, D. D.,
          born at Poughkeepsie, N. Y., May 30, 1746,
          died at New Brunswick, January 20, 1825, son
          of Henry Livingston and Susan Conklin.

228   VII ABRAHAM, baptized at New York, July 3, 1754; died
          at Charleston, S. C., in 1782.

229   VIII HENRY, baptized at New York, March 26, 1760; died
          unmarried.

230   IX ALIDA, died unmarried.

Children of Maria Ten Broeck (105) and Gerardus Groesbeck.

231   I ELIZABETH, baptized July 8, 1740; buried at Albany
          Church November 25, 1754.

232   II STEPHANUS, baptized May 9, 1742.

233   III MARGARITA, baptized June 10, 1744; buried at Al-
          bany Church, September 14, 1745.

234 IV MARGARITA, baptized January 10, 1746; married August 9, 1766, Nicholas Gerrit Marselis, baptized May 25, 1740, son of Gerrit G. Marselis and Margarita Bleecker.

235 V DIRCK, baptized May 29, 1748; perhaps buried at Albany, February 6, 1757.

236 VI JOHANNES, baptized February 18, 1750; buried at Albany, July 14, 1751.

237 VII ANNA, baptized December 1, 1751.

238 VIII JOHANNES, baptized November 11, 1753; probably buried at Albany, January 7, 1757.

239 IX CATRINA, baptized September 26, 1756; buried at Albany, January 26, 1757.

240 X CATARINA, baptized April 8, 1759.

Children of Sara Ten Broeck (107) and Johannes H. Ten Eyck.

241 I HENDRICK, baptized April 17, 1748; died young.

242 II HENDRICK, baptized May 28, 1749; buried at Albany June 27, 1749.

243 III HENDRICK, baptized June 23, 1754.

244 IV MARGARITA, baptized April 16, 1758.

ABRAHAM TEN BROECK (111).

This man, who performed great services for the colony and became of such note in the country, was the tenth of a family of twelve children.

He was born the thirteenth of May, 1734, and baptized when six days old, in the church of his ancestors,— the Reformed Church of America,— his sponsors being his eldest sister, Catryna (102), and his maternal

grandfather, Abraham Cuyler. His early life was passed
in Albany, his native city; he was then sent to New
York, and educated as a merchant in the counting-room
of Philip Livingston, who had married his sister Christina (104), and whose name is famous as a signer of the
Declaration of Independence.

On the completion of his mercantile education he
made a tour of the Eastern provinces, and immediately
thereafter returned to his native city to establish himself
in business.

He married the first of November, 1763, Elizabeth,
the only daughter of Stephen Van Rensselaer, Patroon
of Rensselaerwyck. At the death of the latter, Abraham Ten Broeck was chosen trustee of the estate during
the minority of the boy patroon. For sixteen years he
superintended the vast property with great ability, so
that he was enabled to deliver it into the hands of its
next proprietor in an improved condition.

His first call to public duty came when he was chosen
a member of the Colonial Assembly in 1761, where he
represented the manor of Rensselaerwyck. In this position he used his influence in favor of popular rights,[67]
until the opening of the Revolutionary struggle in 1775.

He was found among the militia at the beginning of
the war, and on March the twenty-first, 1775, was elected
by the Committee of Correspondence to represent the
city and county of Albany at the Provincial Convention
to be assembled in New York City the twentieth of
April.[68] At this Convention he was appointed a delegate to the Continental Congress, to be held in Philadelphia the following month.

GENERAL ABRAHAM TEN BROECK.
From the Oil-Painting of 1799.

A notable resolution which these delegates adopted
during the Congress of May, 1775, and which the signature of Abraham Ten Broeck indorsed, is as follows: —
" To oppose the arbitrary and oppressive measures of
the British Parliament, and to preserve Peace, Order,
and Safety." This Congress also ordered a Committee
of Safety, of which Abraham Ten Broeck was made a
member, to " report an arrangement of the Troops to be
embodyed for the defence of this Colony."

The officers for the third regiment of the first battalion of Rensselaerwyck were elected on August the
twenty-sixth, and the commissions issued October twentieth, 1775, Abraham Ten Broeck being named Colonel
Commandant.[69]

Early in the year 1776 he was made General, and in
February was ordered, with the members of his Committee, to revise the Militia Law, and to prepare a Draft
of Instructions for the Committee of War.[70] Can we not
feel the quickened pulse and see the stress of danger in
these rapidly repeated orders?

Before many months elapsed he received the position
of Brigadier-General; thus was he placed in command
of all militia in Dutchess and Ulster counties, and to the
north and west of those boundaries.

During this year he was made President of the New
York Convention of Representatives, and in December,
1776, this body decided to revive the Committee of
Safety, of which he was also chosen President.[71]

John Hancock, President of the General Congress of
Philadelphia, wrote to this Committee from Baltimore,
February the twenty-fifth, 1777, asking for militia to

reinforce General Washington's army, particularly to protect the passes in the Highlands. The following is General Ten Broeck's reply:

Mr. HANCOCK, President:

Sir:

Your favor of the 25th of February I have had the Honor of receiving and laying before the Convention. It is earnestly wished that the Army under the more immediate command of General Washington was augmented to the number intended by Congress; and that it was in the power of this State to station a competent force in the Highlands and West Chester County, to defend the Passes and protect the Inhabitants from the insults of the Enemy.

This State, Sir, has cheerfully sustained Burthens during the Summer and Winter Champaigns, far beyond her strength. Her losses of Men and Labour are severely felt, and the incessant calls upon the Militia have become a Greviance which is no longer tolerable.

The Convention flattered themselves that the large army provided for the Defence of the United States would have rendered their Services, except on very urgent and Sudden Emergencies, unnecessary, and have given Repose to the Husbandman and the Artificer. It is therefore with equal Pain and Disappointment that the Convention views the Resolution of the honorable Congress to draw all the Continental Battalions raised in this State, to the Westward, and to leave our Militia to the accumulated Charge of garrisoning the Passes and of defending the Country against the Inroads and Ravages of the Enemy, who from Fort Independence and Kings bridge continue to carry on a predatory war, to captivate and carry off our best friends, destroy their effects, and beat off the feeble Guards which we are able to maintain. No less than sixty of our Rangers, surprised by a Superior Force, fell into their Hands this week; besides the Chairman of the County Committee and several of his Friends and Family.

What, Sir, under these circumstances must be the Feelings of our Inhabitants should their Quota of the Continental Troops according to the Proposition, be drawn off from their Assistance, at a time too, when it is generally expected that a more vigorous attack will be made upon the exposed Frontiers of this State.

I am directed, Sir, to call your attention to the repeated Exertions of our Militia.

This letter is only one of an important correspondence, and Abraham Ten Broeck was as wise in active service as in deliberation.

When Burgoyne was defeated at Saratoga, in October, 1777, it is said "the bravest men of Albany County were there under General Ten Broeck"; and a second account gives the following:

General Enoch Poor, with his New Hampshire men, and General Abraham Ten Broeck with three thousand New Yorkers, faced unmoved the cannon and grape-shot with which they were greeted, as, emerging from the wood, they fell fiercely upon the British left. The dash and courage of the Americans amazed and appalled the haughty Britons. They poured a deadly fire upon each flank, then closed, and grappling hand-to-hand, the mad mass swayed to and fro for half an hour, five times taking and retaking a single gun.

In another description of the Battle of Bemis Heights we read:

Fraser fell, mortally wounded, in this assault, and swiftly
behind the half-crazy volunteers came Ten Broeck with a force
nearly double that of the whole British line. That line was now
in full retreat.[72]

General Ten Broeck was an intimate and beloved
friend of General Washington, and was selected by him
as his special companion on several important expeditions. On the evacuation of New York by the British,
he was one of the Council appointed to receive possession.

He resigned the position of Brigadier-General on
March the twenty-sixth, 1781, evidently not to retire
from the duty of a servant and leader of his people, but
that he might the more faithfully discharge his duty.[73]

Two weeks previous to this the governor, George
Clinton, had appointed him the first Judge of the Court
of Common Pleas.[74] For a term of thirteen years he
presided with great ability and distinction.

He was mayor of the city of Albany from Michael-
mas, 1779, to 1783, and again from 1796 to 1799, and a
member of the State Senate 1780 to 1783.

He was the first President of the Bank of Albany, and
held the office from 1792 till 1799, when he declined a
reëlection. At this time the directors, as a mark of
esteem, had his portrait painted for their counting-house.
It represents him in the act of signing bank bills. From
it has been reproduced the illustration here given.

The story of the original is as follows: At a sale of
the assets of the bank, Mr. Thomas Worth Olcott purchased the painting and removed it to adorn the wall of

RESIDENCE OF GENERAL ABRAHAM TEN BROECK.

Built in 1798.

the Ten Broeck mansion in Albany, which he at that time owned, and where he resided. Upon his death the portrait became the property of his son, Mr. Frederick P. Olcott. The latter presented it to the city, as an addition to the valuable collection of portraits of the mayors of Albany; it now hangs in the Council Chamber of the new City Hall.

General Ten Broeck's residence formerly stood at Broadway and Columbia streets, Albany, looking south and stretching across Broadway. It was destroyed by the great fire of 1797. In order to insure his home against future conflagrations, he purchased a tract of land quite above and outside the thickly-settled portion of the city, had bricks imported from Holland, and erected the house that is now in as good condition as when he removed to it. It stands on Ten Broeck Street, in grounds that occupy the square block; facing the east, the entrance is from Ten Broeck Place.

The view here given is of the southeast front of the mansion. High on the south end can be seen the iron figures, "1798," as the General had them placed at the time of building. On the north end are the E. A. T. B. letters (his wife's name being Elizabeth), in Colonial ornamental script. Entering the house, we find ourselves in a spacious hall, through which one passes to reach the winding stairway. A few steps further leads to the hall-door of the west entrance; here is seen a fine example of the Dutch stoop, the roof being supported by Doric columns and the sides inclosed by massive lattice.

Abraham Ten Broeck had lived and died a devout

13

and consistent member of the Dutch Church. His death occurred on the nineteenth of January, 1810. He was buried with military honors, and added to this was the greater tribute of personal affection and respect attested by the large concourse of citizens.

His will, made on the twenty-seventh of March, 1809, was recorded the third of February, 1810, at Albany.

Children of Abraham Ten Broeck (111) and Elizabeth Van Rensselaer.

245 — I DIRCK, born November 3, 1765; died December, 1832; married September 6, 1785, Cornelia, born October 21, 1768, died at Trenton, N. J., February 24, 1825, daughter of Petrus Stuyvesant and Margaret Livingston.

Twins.

246 — II ELIZABETH, born November 3, 1765; died May 5, 1767.

247   III ELIZABETH, born August 25, 1772; died April 10, 1848; married Rensselaer Schuyler, born January 29, 1773, died December 16, 1847, son of Philip Schuyler and Catrina Van Rensselaer. There were no children. They are buried at Stillwater, N. Y.

248   IV MARGARITA, born July 18, 1776; died August 6, 1812, unmarried. Her will is in Albany, Book 4, page 183.

249   V MARIA VAN RENSSELAER, born February 23, 1779; died February 2, 1784.

DIRCK TEN BROECK (113).

The youngest child of Dirck Ten Broeck (20) and Margarita Cuyler was born the twenty-sixth of July,

1738. He was named for his father, and became a merchant in his native city. He married on November the twenty-fifth, 1761, Ann Douw. There is no record of children, but Richard Ten Broeck, mentioned at the end of the seventh generation, may have been a descendant.

Dirck Ten Broeck was appointed a fire-master of Albany in 1769, and was active in the interests of the city and colony from this time until his death.[75]

When the commissions were issued on the twentieth of October, 1775, he was appointed Lieutenant-Colonel of the First Regiment of the City of Albany. He was also Commissioner of the Continental Loan Office, but was compelled to resign in the year 1779 on account of ill health.[76]

On the third of March, 1780, he resigned his position of Commander of the City Troop, and died the twenty-ninth day of May following, having only reached the age of forty-two.

His will, made in 1765, was probated in Albany June the twenty-sixth, 1780. He left all his estate, real and personal, to his wife, but in the event of her remarrying there was a reservation in favor of his own brother Abraham and sisters.

Children of Johannes Ten Broeck (123) and Gerritje Roseboom.

250   1 JACOB, born December 23, 1773; died at Catskill, March, 1833; married first, at Kaatsbaan, January 16, 1808, Catharina De Lamater; married second, Priscilla Musier, died August or September, 1834, widow of Richardson. (There were no children by either marriage.)

251   II A son, born October 10, 1777, died in earliest infancy.

252   III HENDRICK, born November 20, 1779.

PETRUS TEN BROECK (125).

Petrus, the son of Jacob Ten Broeck (26) and Christina Van Alen, married on the thirty-first of March,
1750, Annatje Herchheimer (Herkimer). Through his
marriage he was allied to the most influential Germans
in the Mohawk Valley, as his wife was a sister of General Nicholas Herkimer, of Revolutionary fame.

The residence was in Montgomery County, N. Y., as
the names and dates of baptism of several of his children
stand on the register of the church at Stone Arabia. His
name is entered as Major Petrus Ten Broeck at the
baptism of the third son, in 1771, showing his standing
in the militia at that date.

Under date of October, 1776, he is unfortunately found
associated with Johan Jost Schuyler in the following:
" Peter Ten Broeck, of the Fall Kill, joined the enemy.
He, with Han Yost Schuyler and about twelve others,
went to Oswego, hoping to meet the enemy there." [77]
A shade more light is thrown on this event by a letter
to General Schuyler, which relates how, " After a con-
sultation at Canajoharie Castle among the Indians and
Tories, they absconded to the enemy."

It is doubtful if this plan carried, as Schuyler and
others, to the number of twenty-eight, were captured.
Major Ten Broeck probably even found a way to avoid
being a refugee, as on January the tenth, 1780, he pre-

sented his youngest child for baptism at the Germantown Church, Columbia County.

These few unconnected facts regarding the life of Petrus Ten Broeck leave many unsolved problems in their wake, and trace of his children, beyond the following list, cannot be found.

Children of Petrus Ten Broeck (125) and Annatje Herkimer.

253   I ANNATJE, baptized at Kaatsbaan July 5, 1760.

254   II JACOBUS, born at Stone Arabia, December, 1761.

255   III JOHANNES, born at Stone Arabia, October 26, 1764; died young.

256   IV ANNA, baptized February 8, 1769.

257   V GERTRUDE, baptized February 8, 1769.

258   VI JOHN NICHOLAS HERKIMER, born at Stone Arabia, January 10, 1771; married Delia, daughter of Colonel Peter Billinger and Delia Catherine Herkimer.

259   VII JOHANNES, baptized at Germantown, N. Y., January 10, 1780.

Children of Maria Ten Broeck (128) and Abraham J. De Lamater.

260   I JACOB, baptized at Kingston New Church, August 24, 1773.

261   II CATHARINE, baptized at Kingston New Church, December 3, 1775.

Children of Wessel Ten Broeck (129) and Jannetje Persen.

262   I CHRISTINA, born January 8, 1765; died about 1850, married Samuel J. Ten Broeck (159), born March 28, 1757, died April 25, 1830, son of Jeremiah Ten Broeck and Marytje Van Alen.

263   II CATHARINA, born October 19, 1766; died February
       12, 1820, married December 19, 1787, William
       Van Orden, born April 4, 1765, died November
       14, 1840, son of Ignatius Van Orden and An-
       natje Oosterhoudt.

264   III JACOB, born April 6, 1768; died at Clermont May
       10, 1829; married Christina (274), born July
       3, 1775, died April 29, 1811, daughter of Will-
       iam Schepmoes and Lena Ten Broeck.

265   IV JANNETJEN, born April 8, 1770; died October 7,
       1825; married November 15, 1795, Jeremias
       Ten Broeck (165), born August 2, 1772, died
       December 1, 1826, son of Jeremiah Ten Broeck
       and Marytje Van Alen.

Children of Christina Ten Broeck (130) and Gerhard Daniel Cock.

266   I JACOB, baptized at Germantown, N. Y., September
       16, 1770.

267   II CHRISTINA, baptized October 8, 1771.

268   III ANNA, baptized October 8, 1771.

269   IV GERRIT, baptized May 15, 1774; married at St.
       John's Red Hook, November 8, 1801, Catha-
       rine Benner.

270   V DANIEL, baptized December 25, 1776; died young.

271   VI DANIEL, baptized April 23, 1780.

272   VII ABRAHAM, baptized July 21, 1782; married Annatje
       Segendorf.
       All these baptisms are recorded at Germantown, N. Y.

Child of Jacob Ten Broeck (131) and Anna Elizabeth Cock.

273   I ANNA, born April 15, 1776; died May 5, 1857; married
       November 15, 1795, James Kortz. He served
       in the War of 1812 and died November 11, 1815.

Children of Lena Ten Broeck (132) and William Schepmoes.

274   I CHRISTINA, born July 3, 1775; died April 29, 1811; married Jacob Ten Broeck (264), born April 6, 1768, died May 10, 1829, son of Wessel Ten Broeck and Jannetje Persen.

275   II ELSIE, ———; married at Kaatsbaan October 24, 1800, James Gale, of Cairo, Greene County, N. Y.

276   III MARIA, baptized at Kingston July 28, 1782; died young.

277   IV CATHARINA, baptized at Germantown, August 7, 1785.

278   V MARYTJE, baptized at Germantown, November 25, 1787; died February 13, 1830; married at Germantown, September 17, 1812, Seth Ten Broeck (339), born September 11, 1789, died July 12, 1815, son of Adam Ten Broeck and Lydia Maria Monson.

Children of Catharina Ten Broeck (133) and George Wray.

279   I JENNET, died at Albany November 16, 1789, aged 20.1.6; married at Albany, February 6, 1789, John Jacob Cuyler, born August 14, 1766, died at Albany June 5, 1804, son of Jacob Cuyler and Lydia Van Vechten.

280   II MARIA, baptized in New York December 22, 1771.

JOHANNES TEN BROECK (134).

Johannes, the only son of Cornelis Ten Broeck (27) and Maria Cuyler, was born the twenty-seventh of July, 1740. He was a merchant in Albany, and immediately upon his majority, his name appears in connection with municipal affairs.

He was a member of Common Council in 1766. In September, 1773, he was a loyal candidate for alderman from the third ward; he was elected, but owing to bitter partizanship his seat was contested. Only after a warm dispute was he allowed to occupy the position.[78]

As a magistrate of Albany he took part in the decisions, and signed the deed whereby the city gave a new title to the Indians for the Tiononderoga Patent, thus carrying out the wish and intent of his father and other merchants of Albany, as expressed by petition twenty years earlier.

The measures of defense resorted to in 1775 in preparation for the Revolution were partly under his supervision, because of his position as a public officer. In addition, he was chosen member of the "Committee of Safety," and delegated to coöperate with General Schuyler in devising and executing the most effective measures for repelling the enemy on the northern and western frontiers.[79] His faithfulness as a member of this committee is attested by his constant attendance on all the numerous meetings of the organization. He was a delegate to the third and fourth Provincial Congresses. He served Albany County as sheriff in 1781 and 1786, and was a member of the House of Assembly in 1792.[80]

He had married, on the twelfth of June, 1762, Sara Gansevoort, of Albany. To them were born eleven children, eight of whom died unmarried, some in childhood and others in middle age. His wife died in 1811, and his death occurred on the twenty-sixth of December, 1822.

The Fifth Generation. 105

Children of Johannes Ten Broeck (134) and Sara Gansevoort.

281   i CORNELIS, born February 23, 1763; died November 30, 1814; unmarried.

282   ii MAGDALENA, born May 8, 1765; died March, 1845; married Theodorus Van Wyck Graham.

283   iii HARMAN, born March 25, 1767; died September 14, 1787.

284   iv MARIA, born November 11, 1768; died February 10, 1790; unmarried.

285   v JOHANNES, born March 26, 1771; died March 15, 1796; unmarried.

286   vi PETRUS, born May 1, 1773; died November 18, 1783.

287   vii LEENDERT, born January 21, 1775; died June 25, 1812; married at Kingston November 10, 1802, Sarah, baptized at Kingston October 17, 1776, died at Napanock, N. Y., September, 1819, daughter of Dom. George Leonhard Doll and Susanna Christina Deerker.

288 viii SARA, born February 2, 1778; died September 25, 1838; unmarried.

289   ix CATHARINA, born November 20, 1779; died February 15, 1835; married at Half Moon, N. Y., May, 1815, Isaac Bailey, born in Dutchess County, March 27, 1782, died at Waterford, N. Y., March 20, 1853, son of Henry Bailey and Margaret Losee.

290   x GEORGE WRAY, baptized December 23, 1781; died November 21, 1816; unmarried.

291   xi WESSEL, born September 23, 1783; died January 19, 1784.

14

SAMUEL TEN BROECK (135).

Samuel, the eldest child of Dirck Wesselse Ten Broeck
(68), was born at the Roelof Jansen Kil homestead on
the twenty-seventh of September, 1745; his paternal
grandparents were sponsors at his baptism, as recorded
in the family Bible. On the leaves of the same record
is found his own entry of his marriage on the twelfth of
August, 1768, to "Emitie Van Alsteyn."

He was in the full vigor of manhood when the clouds
of war with England settled over the colonies, and at
once he appeared as a representative of his district. He
assisted in the choice of the delegate from Albany
County to the Provincial Congress, which met in New
York in May, 1775, and when the commissions were issued in October following, he was appointed Second
Major of Colonel Peter R. Livingston's Regiment, the
Tenth of the New York Militia.[81]

He was commissary for his district, and superintended
the sending of supplies furnished by the farmers to
Barrytown, at which point they were available for shipment.

In this section there was established a system of vigi-
lance known as "The Night Watch," for protection
against the Tories and secret enemies of the colonists.
The following account is taken from the fragment of an
old book which contained a journal of their proceedings:[82]

That the night watch shall consist of eighty-four men, to be
divided into seven sub-divisions. That twelve men be the guard

GENERAL SAMUEL TEN BROECK.
From the Oil-Portrait of 1832.

for each night, exclusive of the officers. That the night watch be kept at Samuel Ten Broeck's, and shall consist of twenty-eight men, which number is to be divided into seven companies.

We are thus shown how his home became the center of interest as well as a place of defense.

After the close of the war, the laws of the State provided for a National Guard. Samuel Ten Broeck was then appointed General of Militia, and was thereafter called by this title. As a citizen he was much esteemed for his benevolence and high character.

He was elected member of Assembly from Albany County in 1781, and for two terms he filled this position with general acceptance.[83]

He built a substantial, handsome house upon land which was part of the original Ten Broeck bouwerie; the time of completion is approximately known by the lettering upon the massive wrought-iron fire-back, which bears the initials of himself and wife in this fashion: The wide hallway customary at this period forms an imposing, spacious room; the slender Colonial balustrade of mahogany and the stairway are of unique style; but the most curious and interesting are the heavy oaken timbers and beams which support the hipped-roof.

1773
E.
S. T. B.

Within a few years after building, General Henry Livingstone purchased this place and gave it the name of "Calendar House," after family estates in Scotland, which name it still bears. Samuel Ten Broeck then returned to the homestead on the Roelof Jansen Kil.

His portrait, painted in 1832, together with the cane,

is in possession of his grand-niece, Mrs. Albertina S. Mynderse, of Schenectady, N. Y. The sword shown, crossed with the cane, was the one used by the General during the Revolution. His seal is owned by his grand-nephew, Mr. Walter T. L. Ten Broeck, Rhinebeck, N. Y.

General Ten Broeck had no descendants. His wife lived until their married years had numbered sixty-six. The inscription which marks her resting-place reads:

In memory of Emma Ten Broeck, who died June 24, 1834,
aged 84 years, 8 mos. and 13 days.

In faith she died, in dust she lies;
But faith foresees that dust shall rise
When Christ, with His Almighty word,
Calls his dead saints to meet their Lord.

Seven years later her husband was buried by her side in the Ten Broeck family lot, and the stone marking the spot bears the story of his life in these words:

In memory of Samuel Ten Broeck, who died May 30, 1841,
aged 95 years, 7 months and 22 days.

His usefulness in Church and State
Was early known to men.
Blest with an active life till late
And happy in his end.

LEONARD TEN BROECK (137).

He was one of the foremost men among the Ten Broecks of the Livingston Manor district to bear arms in the struggle for Independence.

"CALENDAR HOUSE"

Built by General Samuel Ten Broeck about 1773.

In the earliest arrangement of troops Leonard Ten Broeck was a First Lieutenant in the Albany County Regiment. In October, 1775, his commission confirmed this rank, placing him in command of the First Company. The regiment was then called the Tenth of the New York Militia.[81] In the report of the Committee on Arrangement of Regiments in 1777, he was reported and approved as still serving in the same rank.

He fought bravely throughout the perilous days, and his gallantry at the taking of Burgoyne is a matter of history.

It appears that threads of love were woven in this strand of patriotism, for on the seventh of March, 1776, was issued his marriage license with Gertrude, the daughter of Jacob Schermerhorn. Four sons and four daughters were born to them.

Leonard Ten Broeck was a man who commanded high respect and confidence, and as his life rounded out to more than four-score years, he seemed by reason of his age to be the connecting link between two centuries of history.

His death occurred two years before that of his wife. They were laid side by side in the little burying-ground at the Ten Broeck homestead on Roelof Jansen's Kil, where others of the family had been interred before.

His memorial was written thus :

Leonard Ten Broeck,
who died November 11, 1836, aged 84 years and 1 day.

This spot contains the ashes of the just,
Who sought no honours and betray'd no trust.
This truth he prov'd in every path he trod,
" An honest man 's the noblest work of God."

The lettering on his wife's stone reads,

In memory of Gertrude Ten Broeck, wife of Leonard Ten
Broeck,
Who died September 2, 1838,
aged 82 years 10 months and 19 days.

Mourn not as those whose hopes expire
When death has quenched the vital fire;
For life immortal from the grave
Shall spring through Him who died to save.

Children of Leonard Ten Broeck (137) and Gertrude Schermerhorn.

292　ı DIRCK WESSELS, baptized at Red Hook September
14, 1777; died unmarried, 1827.

293　ıı MARIA MAGDALENA, baptized at Rhinebeck March
19, 1780, married Thomas Duncan.

294　ııı JACOB, baptized at Johnstown September 21, 1782;
married Prudence Chapman.

295　ıv SAMUEL L., born June 10, 1785; died June 17, 1824;
married at St. Peter's, Rhinebeck, October 1,
1809, Polly Miller.

296　v CATHARINA, born January 3, 1788; died October 4,
1859; married first, August, 1807, Conrad Salpaugh, died January, 1816, son of Jacob Salpaugh, of Germantown, N. Y.; married second,
December 27, 1818, John Pitcher, born August
15, 1774, died May 27, 1851, son of William
Pitcher and Anna Smith, of Red Hook, N. Y.

297　vı ELBERTINA, baptized at Johnstown July 25, 1790;
died young.

298　vıı DOROTHY, born September 30, 1792; died young.

ALBERTINA TEN BROECK (SANDERS).
From the Oil-Portrait of 1832.

299 VIII LEONARD WILLIAM, born February 14, 1797; died January 24, 1852; married October 11, 1820, Helen, born May 3, 1796, died September 21, 1855, daughter of Walter Tryon Livingston and his first wife, Eliza Platner.

ALBERTINA TEN BROECK (140).

Albertina was born at the bouwerie, on the Roelof Jansen Kil, on November the twenty-third, 1760, and was married there in 1799.

The former date suggests that she was born before the house erected by Major Dirck Wesselse Ten Broeck (3) had given place to the present one, which was built by his grandson. This suggestion seems to meet with confirmation from the fact that Albertina executed two silhouettes of the place (see pages 26 and 66) in which the houses differed, although the scene was similar.

Together with the pictures have descended their traditional titles. According to these, the one with the cornucopia represents the house of Major Ten Broeck, built in the early days of the eighteenth century; the other gives the family arms for the center, and below are the house and barns built by her father, in 1762, and familiar to Albertina as she grew into womanhood.

Underneath the second silhouette can be read the words, "Welcome every Friendly Guest," which set forth the spirit of hospitality for which the name of Ten Broeck has always stood synonymous.

It is said Albertina Ten Broeck injured her eyesight in making these pictures, which are cut with the most minute care.

She married John Sanders, of Scotia. He had served
among the Minute Men of 1777, when, under command of Captain Fonda, they compelled the surrender
of "Johnson Hall." He was Senator under the first
Constitution of New York, from 1799 till 1802, inclu-
sive; a member of the Council of Correspondence in
1800, and also a member of the convention to form the
second Constitution, adopted in 1822.[83]

Judge Sanders was a gentleman of the old school. In
his dress he adhered to the customs of the last century
— small-clothes, silk stockings, and shoes with silver
buckles. His was a manner full of kindliness and hos-
pitable friendliness, but he was withal noted for his
dignity, resolution, and courage.

Scotia was the title of the estates of the family. By
the marriage of John Sanders, Senior, to Deborah Glen,
in 1739, this large estate, belonging until then to the
Glens, was merged into the Sanders name, and the joint
Glen and Sanders line.

The house at Scotia, to which John Sanders, Junior,
took his bride, Albertina Ten Broeck, had been built by
John A. Glen in 1713, on the left bank of the Mohawk
River, about three quarters of a mile above Schenectady. It had been rendered defensible during the French
wars, and must have been in the path of many stirring
and warlike expeditions.

Albertina and John Sanders passed the happy years
of a long married life here, and are buried almost within
its shadow, in the Sanders family burial-place. Their
descendants still own and occupy the mansion.

Their portraits, painted by Phillips in 1832, are owned

JUDGE JOHN SANDERS
From the Oil-Portrait of 1832

by a grandson, Judge W. T. L. Sanders, of Schenectady. The silhouettes belong to Mrs. Harold Wilson, of Clermont, New York.

Children of Albertina Ten Broeck (140) and John Sanders.

300   I JOHN, born at Scotia, Schenectady County, December 27, 1802; died May 21, 1883; married October 2, 1826, Jane, born September 4, 1804, died October 27, 1871, daughter of Walter Tryon Livingston and his second wife, Elizabeth McKinstry.

301   II DIRCK (THEODORE) WESSELS, born at Scotia October 20, 1804; died at Albany September 20, 1884; married 1st, at Bethlehem, Albany County, N. Y., January 20, 1829, Margaret Nicoll, born July 5, 1809, died October 18, 1862, daughter of William Nicoll Sill and Margaret Mather; married 2d, January 9, 1867, Rachel B. Winne, daughter of Gerrit Van Santen Bleecker and Jane Shepard.

ANTHONY TEN BROECK (148).

Anthony Ten Broeck, of Claverack, married first, on the thirteenth of October, 1782, his second cousin, Christina Ten Broeck (197). His family of eleven children are by this alliance. Six years after the death of Christina, he married for his second wife Mrs. Maria Heermance, who outlived him many years.

Anthony died on October the twelfth, 1832. His will bears the date of the same year as his death, and is recorded at Hudson, New York.

15

Children of Anthony Ten Broeck (148) and Christina Ten Broeck (197).

302   I ANNATJE, born at Claverack September 28, 1783;
    died young.

303   II CATHARINA, born at Claverack November 12, 1785;
    died February 1, 1834; married April 18, 1811,
    Rev. Moses Burt, of Amsterdam, N. Y., born
    February 2, 1779, died May 30, 1837.

304   III HENRY ANTHONY, born at Claverack March 25,
    1787; died at Newark, N. J., April 18, 1845;
    married 1st, December 10, 1810, Rhoda Green,
    born March 6, 1793, died May 21, 1833, daugh-
    ter of Elisha Brown and Amy ——; married
    2d, September 30, 1835, Delia Maria, born
    January 14, 1799, died October 3, 1882, daugh-
    ter of George Gorham Coffin and Sarah Nixon.

305   IV CORNELIUS PETER, born at Claverack April 3, 1789;
    died December 23, 1817; unmarried.

306   V ANNATJE, born October 28, 1790; died November
    17, 1861; married January 1, 1816, Robert
    Hendrick Van Rensselaer, of Claverack, born
    November 15, 1779, died February 4, 1835,
    son of Hendrick J. Van Rensselaer and Rachel
    Douw.

307   VI ANTHONY, born August 22, 1792; died March 10,
    1814; unmarried; buried at Claverack.

308   VII JOHN ANTHONY, born April 4, 1794; died August
    29, 1855; buried at Claverack; married June
    20, 1827, Hannah Everts, born January 10,
    1795, died March 22, 1875.

309   VIII MARY, born July 17, 1796; died April 25, 1860, un-
    married.

310   IX WILLIAM C., born June 6, 1798; died May 10, 1880;
       married November 25, 1824, Christina Van
       Deusen, died March 16, 1885, aged 76.1.18.

311   X CHRISTINA, born August 14, 1800; died June 10,
       1883; married April 7, 1829, Abraham Adam
       Ten Broeck (344), born July 22, 1803, died No-
       vember 1, 1869, son of Adam Ten Broeck and
       Lydia Monson.

312   XI CORNELIA RUTSEN, born August 1, 1804; died with-
       out children, February 22, 1880; married June
       27, 1838, George H. Mitchell, M. D., died
       December 4, 1876.

Children of Hendrick Ten Broeck (151) and Martha Comstock.

313   I HENRY, born February 21, 1798; died August 18,
       1868; married Maria Van Vechten.

314   II SAMUEL, born August 23, 1800; died at Waterford,
       N. Y., March 31, 1856.

SAMUEL J. TEN BROECK (153).

Samuel, the son of Johannes Ten Broeck (72), of Hudson, N. Y., married his first cousin Maria, the daughter
of Jeremias Ten Broeck (73). In his father's will he is
called Samuel, but in that of his father-in-law his name
is written Samuel J. (which probably referred to his
father's name, Johannes, as was the prevalent custom),
and he himself added this initial when witnessing a deed
in 1806, thus proving it his legal signature.

He was among the men of this district who enlisted
for the Revolutionary service, and was commissioned
Captain in the Tenth Regiment of the New York Militia

on October the twentieth, 1775.[86]   The year following
he was made Second Lieutenant-Colonel.

He belonged to one of the old families of Hudson,
where his descendants still reside.   He made his will
on the third of May, 1834, and it was recorded in August, 1836, one year after his death.

Children of Samuel J. Ten Broeck (153) and Maria Ten Broeck (161).

315   i JOHANNES, born March 8, 1789; died August 9,
          1819; unmarried.

316   ii DIRCK WESSEL, born July 16, 1792; died April 29,
          1817; buried at Claverack; married at St.
          John's, Red Hook, October 12, 1815, Margaret
          Benner. There were no children.

317   iii NICHOLAS, born January 31, 1796; died May 29,
          1858, unmarried. He met his death by an acci-
          dental shot. Buried at Claverack.

318   iv MARIA S., born November 17, 1799; died February
          21, 1869; married December 17, 1828, William
          E. Heermance, born February 14, 1802, died
          April 29, 1854, son of Philip Heermance, M. D.,
          and Anna Van Välkenburgh.

Children of Maria Ten Broeck (155) and Peter Van Rensselaer.

319   i ELIZABETH, born at Claverack April 5, 1783; mar-
          ried December 18, 1814, Wessel Ten Broeck
          (333), born at Claverack August 27, 1787, son
          of Samuel J. Ten Broeck and Christina Ten
          Broeck.

320   ii HENRY, born August 20, 1791; died young.

321 III HENRY PETER, born at Claverack October 8, 1794;
married Maria Fort, died November 5, 1869,
aged 72.

322 IV MARIA HOFFMAN, born April 13, 1797; died young.

323 V MARIA, born at Claverack November 30, 1799; died
unmarried.

Children of Niclaes Ten Broeck (157) and Maria Schuyler.

324 I MARIA HOFFMAN, born April 27, 1801; died October 13, 1853; married September 10, 1829,
Peter Quidor Schuyler, born April 21, 1801,
died 1860, son of John H. Schuyler (170) and
Annatje Fort.

325 II HARMANUS SCHUYLER, born November 3, 1802;
died February 15, 1803.

326 III DAVID VAN RENSSELAER, born February 25, 1804;
died November 30, 1873; buried at Claverack;
married 1st, in 1826, Jane Doane, died May
31, 1851, aged 43 years and 8 months; married
2d, in 1856, Mrs. Sarah Heermance.

327 IV JOHN JEREMIAH, born August 18, 1806; married
November 26, 1833, Helen (585), born at Germantown, N. Y., March 14, 1815, died January
21, 1884, daughter of Seth Ten Broeck and
Polly Schepmoes.

328 V CHRISTINA JANE ELSIE, born February 4, 1809;
died January 11, 1831; married September 8,
1830, Philip H. Knickerbacker, M. D. There
were no children.

329 VI CORNELIA CATHERINE, born September 30, 1811;
died September 21, 1856; unmarried.

330 VII ANN CATHARINE, born March 17, 1812; died August 24, 1814.

Children of Niclaes Ten Broeck (157) and Cornelia Hoffman.

331 I JANE MARIA, born October 1, 1818; died November 2, 1820.

332 II NICHOLAS EDWIN, born August 17, 1825. A merchant of New York City.

SAMUEL J. TEN BROECK (159).

Samuel, the eldest of the seven children of Jeremiah Ten Broeck (73), was born the twenty-eighth of March, 1757. He, like his cousin Samuel (153), married one bearing the family name—his second cousin, Christina Ten Broeck (262).

He resided at Claverack, and when the young men of this section responded to the call to arms, although not of age, he entered the Ninth Company of the Livingston Manor Regiment—probably as Ensign. In the promotions of 1776 he was made Second Lieutenant.[87]

He was entitled, according to the usage prevalent among those of Dutch ancestry, to adopt his father's initial J. for his own middle letter; accordingly, we find his will, which is recorded at Hudson, New York, and bears date of May the tenth, 1826, is written over his name as Samuel J. Ten Broeck, of Claverack. He died the twenty-fifth of April, 1830, and was buried at Claverack. In conformity with the act of February the second, 1848, Christina Ten Broeck received the pension accorded the widow of a lieutenant in the Revolutionary war. She died probably in 1850.

Children of Samuel J. Ten Broeck (159) and Christina Ten Broeck (262).

333   I WESSEL, born August 27, 1787, at Claverack ; married
            December 18, 1814, Elizabeth (319), born at
            Claverack April 5, 1783, daughter of Peter Van
            Rensselaer and Maria Ten Broeck.

334   II JEREMIAH, born June 11, 1790 ; died January 11, 1826;
            buried at Claverack ; unmarried.

335   III WILLIAM, born 1792 ; died August 18, 1836, aged 44 ;
            married November 28, 1813, Margaret Becker,
            born November 7, 1795.

ADAM TEN BROECK (160).

Adam, the second son of Jeremiah Ten Broeck (73),
was born on July the twenty-fourth, 1759.   Before he
reached the age of manhood the spirit of the times drew
him into active military service.   Among the men of his
own town he was chosen to bear the standard for the
Fourth Company, Eighth Regiment of the First Claverack Battalion.   He received his appointment as Ensign
February the twenty-fifth, 1778, under Robert Van Rensselaer, Colonel Commandant.[88]

He was a member, for a time, of Colonel Goosen Van
Schaick's Regiment, the First of the New York line.
After Independence was achieved he received a grant of
land in recognition of his services.

He was an original member of the Society of the Cincinnati.[89]

He married twice : first at Claverack, on May the thirtieth, 1784, to Lydia Maria Monson.   By this alliance
there were nine children.   His second marriage was on

the twenty-eighth of January, 1807, to Hannah Morrison, and five children were born to them.

Adam Ten Broeck died the thirtieth of May, 1826, in the sixty-seventh year of his age. His second wife, who was more than twenty years his junior, outlived him for a period of forty-four years. She died on April the seventeenth, 1870, at the age of ninety.

Children of Adam Ten Broeck (160) and Lydia Maria Monson.

336   I JEREMIAH, born at Claverack October 28, 1785; died young.

337   II JEREMIAH, born at Claverack February 13, 1787; married May 28, 1810, Alida, born November 9, 1784, daughter of Peter Cole and Tabitha Roorback. They lived at Middleburg, New York.

338   III JOHN VAN RENSSELAER, born September 11, 1789; died August 5, 1832; married 1st, November 8, 1812, Elizabeth, born April 3, 1791, died November 15, 1815, daughter of David Van Ness and Annatje Van Buren; married 2d, August 1, 1820, Emmeline Pamela, born April 3, 1804, died March 2, 1885, daughter of Rev. Daniel Parker and Anna Fenn.

Twins. {

339   IV SETH, born at Johnstown, Columbia County, September 11, 1789; died July 12, 1845; married at Germantown, N. Y., September 17, 1812, Marytje (278), baptized November 25, 1787, died February 13, 1830, daughter of William Schepmoes and Lena Ten Broeck.

340   V AUSTIN MONSON, born September 27, 1791; died May 21, 1875; married March 26, 1815, Margaret, born December 14, 1793, died February 12,

"SCOTIA."

The Glen-Sanders Residence.   Built in 1713.

1873, daughter of Abraham Van Hoesen and
Geertruy Everson.

341   vi Dirck Wessel, born February 5, 1796; married ——
      Bronk.   No children.

342   vii Anna Maria, born June 2, 1798; died April 3, 1865;
      married Abram Henry Race.

343   viii Samuel, born August 10, 1800.

344   ix Abraham Adam, born at Claverack July 22, 1803;
      died November 1, 1869; married April 7, 1829,
      Christina (311), born August 14, 1800, died June
      10, 1883, daughter of Antony Ten Broeck and
      Christina Ten Broeck.

Children of Adam Ten Broeck (160) and his second wife, Hannah
Morrison.

345   i Eliza Alida, born August 27, 1808; died single. She
      resided at Chatham, N. Y.

346   ii Catharine, born August 25, 1810; died February 8,
      1874; married December 24, 1835, William T.
      Van Deusen, born May 28, 1810, died February
      18, 1884.

347   iii Jane, born June 18, 1813; died March 13, 1837;
      buried at Claverack; unmarried.

348   iv Lydia M., born June 26, 1815; died May 25, 1860;
      married December 7, 1843, Conrad W. Melius.

349   v James Adam, born June 22, 1819; married February
      29, 1844, Sarah M. Herder, born March 8, 1820.

Children of Johannes Ten Broeck (162) and Sophia Miller.

350   i Sartje, born at Claverack March 13, 1787.

351   ii Maria, born at Claverack November 6, 1788.

16

352   III JEREMIAH, born at Claverack December 13, 1790.

353   IV ANNATJE, born August 11, 1798.

Children of Jeremias Ten Broeck (165) and Jane Ten Broeck (265).

354   I JANE, born at Claverack September 7, 1797; died
       February 3, 1813.

355   II ABRAHAM, born June 17, 1799; married February 18,
       1821, Lavina Becker, died January 31, 1877,
       aged 77.2.17.

356   III WESSEL, born November 27, 1802; died August 1,
       1859.

357   IV MARIA, born September 24, 1805; died December 12,
       1835; unmarried.

358   V JACOB SAMUEL, born April 21, 1808; died December
       1, 1873; married January 24, 1832, Caroline
       Hover, born November 19, 1813, died February
       10, 1883.

359   VI CHRISTINA CATHARINE, born September 28, 1810;
       died without children; married May 10, 1836,
       Nicholas Bogart Van Rensselaer, born March
       27, 1808, son of Robert S. Van Rensselaer and
       Catherine Nicholas Bogart.

Children of William Ten Broeck (186) and Sarah Harvey.

360   I ELIZA HARVEY, died at Flatbush, L. I., December 30,
       1866; married 1st, October 29, 1809, Ralph
       Voorhees Beckman, born December 17, 1785,
       died January 30, 1833; married 2d, Michael
       Schoonmaker, born June 21, 1772, died Novem-
       ber 14, 1845, son of Rev. Martinus Schoon-
       maker and his second wife, Mary Bassett. There
       were no children by either marriage.

361   II JOHN W., died at New Brunswick, N. J., October 5, 1821, aged 33; unmarried.

JOHN TEN BROECK (189).

Born at Raritan Landing on the tenth of September, 1757, he married Mary Ladner, who, at the age of fourteen, had become the wife of John Webster, and was now a widow of twenty-five, with two daughters, Sarah (*vide* 191) and Mary Webster.

John Ten Broeck brought his bride to the home of his youth, for the responsibility of the homestead rested largely upon him at this time. Three years later, upon the death of his father — in 1790 — he became part owner of the property, and by purchase and deed from each of the other heirs, he kept it intact, and resided there until his death.[90]

He died in the prime of life, shortly before reaching the age of forty-one, and was buried in the family lot on the place. The stone marking the spot bears the date of his death, August the eighteenth, 1798.

By his will, recorded in Trenton, N. J., Book 38, he devised the Ten Broeck homestead to his son John.

Children of John Ten Broeck (189) and Mary Ladner Webster.

362   I JOHN, born November 13, 1787; died January 30, 1825; buried at Raritan Landing; married Sarah Edgar.

363   II CATHARINE, born July 6, 1792 : died April 5, 1872; married March 27, 1809, David Gulick, born December 8, 1785, died November 19, 1834.

364 III GEORGE; probably died unmarried.

365 IV JANE, died June 16, 1843, in her forty-sixth year; married July 26, 1815, Rev^d. Henry V. Garretson, born September 13, 1793, died June 9, 1839.

PETER TEN BROECK (190).

He was born at the Ten Broeck homestead, at Raritan Landing, on the fourth of September, 1760, and baptized in the Dutch Church of New Brunswick the seventh of December following.

Peter Ten Broeck was a lad of sixteen at the date of the battle of Trenton, and the frightful sounds of the artillery were among his most vivid recollections of that memorable time.

He crossed the line from Middlesex to Hunterdon County to find his bride, Ame (Emma), the daughter of Joseph Chamberlain, a man prominent in matters of both church and state in the township of Alexandria. They were married on the fourth of July, 1782. Very soon they went to Readington, in Hunterdon County, and purchased the property opposite the Dutch Church.

This church had been erected in 1738, although the congregation had been organized as early as 1717. In 1787 Rev. Peter Studdiford was called to the pastorate. During all the previous period the people had heard "the gospel undefiled in Holland Dutch," and although Dominie Studdiford did not understand the language, yet, upon accepting, he had engaged to study it sufficiently to preach in the Dutch tongue, occasionally, for the edification of the older people. This he essayed to do, but found it too difficult, and, to his relief, the Consistory kindly changed the terms of the "call."

Some of the congregation were very much displeased with this course, and one Sunday morning, having obtained possession of the key, locked the church door against the dominie. Peter Ten Broeck, who was a warm friend of the pastor, hearing that the church was locked against him, soon came up with an axe, and said to the malcontents, "If you do not open that door I will!" The door was opened, and the sermon was preached in English. The excitement soon died away, and the trouble about not preaching in Dutch was ended."[1]

"Emmy" Chamberlain Ten Broeck became a member of this church by certificate from the Presbyterian congregation at Alexandria. She died at Readington, but was buried with her father's family in the Alexandria churchyard. On the top of a flat table stone is this inscription:

Sacred to the memory of Emma,
Wife of Peter Ten Broeck, who departed this life December 5,
1805, in the 49th year of her age.

In life religion was her stay.
She in her dying hour,
By its triumphant power,
Hailed with joy the realms of day.

Peter Ten Broeck married again, on May the thirty-first, 1812, Catharine Emmons, of Readington, a woman of remarkable beauty. There were seven children by this second marriage, and Peter Ten Broeck lost his second wife two years before his death, which occurred on the twentieth of July, 1840. They were both buried under the shadow of the church. Their home is still owned by a descendant.

Letters of administration on his estate were granted to John Runk, a son-in-law, on the fifth of August, 1840.

Peter had outlived his brother Rensselaer (191), co-executor of the estate of their father, Captain John Ten Broeck (78), and a large store of family papers had come into his possession. These he guarded with most zealous care throughout his life, but unfortunately, during the "improvement" of the house which was made after his death they became scattered, and traces of few of them can be found. Doubtless, had these been preserved, many difficult questions, interesting alike to the family and to the public, might have been solved.

Children of Peter Ten Broeck (190) and Emma Chamberlain.

366   I MARY, born July 20, 1783, at Readington, N. J.; died July 14, 1836; married 1st, Abraham A. Van Fleet, born September 14, 1779, died August 20, 1822, son of Abraham Van Fleet and Ann Lowe; married 2d, Edward E. Cox.

367   II EMMA, born August 29, 1787; died November 25, 1848; buried at Rosemont, N. J.; married December, 1811, John Runk, born July 3, 1791, died September 22, 1872, son of Samuel Runk and Margaret Snyder; he married second, November 1, 1855, Amy M., born July 6, 1812, died July 22, 1896, daughter of Jeremiah Gary and Rebecca Servis, widow of Abraham S. Skillman.

368   Twins { III JOHN VAN RENSSELAER, born August 26, 1791;
                died young.
369   { IV ELIZABETH. She died February 7, 1792.

Children of Peter Ten Broeck (190) and his second wife, Catharine
Emmons.

370   I JOHN P., born August 1, 1813; died July 2, 1846;
           married July 16, 1836, Elizabeth, born May 7,
           1818, died March 23, 1838, daughter of James
           Waterhouse and Mary Matlack.

371   II ELIZABETH, born October 24, 1816; married January
           16, 1836, George Washington Waterhouse, born
           January 4, 1815, died September 17, 1861, son
           of James Waterhouse and Mary Matlack.

372   III CATHARINE VAN FLEET, born January 27, 1819;
           married April 20, 1839, Cornelius Van Derveer
           Nevius, born November 18, 1816, died Septem-
           ber 23, 1858, son of Minna Nevius and Jo-
           hanna Stothoff.

373   IV PETER QUICK, born August 5, 1821; married Feb-
           ruary 24, 1841, Sarah Kinney, born October 15,
           1819, daughter of Henry Shurts and Mary
           Kinney.

374   V JANE GARRETSON, born June 11, 1824; died June 6,
           1895, married October 26, 1842, John Vorhees
           Schomp, born June 7, 1821, died November 11,
           1893, son of Peter Schomp, of Readington, and
           Willimpe Voorhees.

375   VI SARAH FORMAN, born November 10, 1826; married
           1st, February 27, 1851, Joseph Trimmer, born
           April 14, 1819, died September 5, 1857, son of
           Samuel Trimmer and Deborah Pegg; married
           2d, July 30, 1870, William C. Van Doren, born

October 13, 1813, died December 28, 1889, son
of Christopher Van Doren and Esther Lan-
ning.

376 VII MARGARETTA, born November 13, 1830; died November 14, 1831.

Children of Van Rensselaer Ten Broeck (191) and Sarah Webster.

377   I SARAH WEBSTER, born October 7, 1793; died April
7, 1885; married at New Brunswick, N. J., July
6, 1814, John Forman, born March 16, 1792,
died April 5, 1872.

378   II MARY W., born August 13, 1795; died May 16,
1837; unmarried.

379   III JOHN VAN RENSSELAER, born November 21, 1797;
died March 29, 1866; married 1st, August 5,
1822, Ida McIntire; married 2d, May 9, 1842,
Sarah, born April 16, 1809, died April 30, 1878,
daughter of Herman Tremper and Sarah Hall,
and widow of Barzillia Hopkins.

380   IV EMMA CHAMBERLAIN, born December 7, 1799; died
March 1, 1877; married March 11, 1821, James
V. Spader, born September 14, 1799, died Feb-
ruary 28, 1871, son of William Spader and
Catharine Van Derveer.

381   V RICHARD KROESEN, born April 13, 1803; died in Savannah, Ga.; married April 9, 1826, Caroline
Lucia, born February 21, 1812, died November
21, 1866, daughter of John Fletcher, of Savannah, Ga., and Martha Edwards.

382   VI JANE GARRETSON, born April 8, 1807; died December 12, 1880; married April 13, 1826, Isaac
Voorhees, born March 8, 1807, died September
11, 1880, son of Peter Voorhees.

383 VII PETER VAN RENSSELAER, born June 30, 1809; died
March 12, 1870; married January 1, 1833, Ann
Eliza Arnold, daughter of —— Arnold and
Elizabeth Dunn.

SAMUEL TEN BROECK (193).

The youngest child of Captain John Ten Broeck (78)
studied medicine, and as a young man went to Shrewsbury, N. J., where he practised his profession throughout his life. His bright, genial manner made him a
general favorite, and he was the trusted friend, as well
as physician, of many families.

He became the possessor of much real estate, and his
homestead is still to be seen on the beautiful avenue of
that charming village.

He married on the fourth of June, 1797, Mary, the
daughter of Edmund Williams — a family whose connec-
tions were among the best in Monmouth County. Seven
children were born to them, but of the four sons only
one lived until the age of manhood, and he also died,
unmarried, in his twenty-second year.

Dr. Ten Broeck made his will in February, 1826.
Three months later his wife, Mary, died, and before the
end of the year following, the youngest daughter and
eldest son were both taken from him by death. In-
fluenced by these changes, on the eighth of January,
1828, he disposed of all his real estate by deed to his
remaining children, share and share alike, with the confidence that they would " provide the grantor with every
necessary convenience " as long as he should live.

17

Within a few months, on August the twenty-fourth, 1828, his own end came. He was buried in the ground of the Presbyterian churchyard at Shrewsbury, where also rest all his family, excepting the two eldest daughters.

The will and deeds disposing of the property are recorded at Freehold, N. J.

Children of Samuel Ten Broeck (193) and Mary Williams.

384   I JANE GARRETSON, born June 2, 1798; died at Albany, N. Y., December 6, 1857; buried in Albany Rural Cemetery; married Rev. James W. Woodward, died about 1861. There were no children. He was a member of New Brunswick Presbytery until 1840, but sometime of Alden, Presbytery of Buffalo, N. Y.

385   II MARY, born August 4, 1799; died at Albany, April, 1857; married William F. Maywell, of New York, who died in Albany, April, 1857; they are both buried in Albany Rural Cemetery.

386   III ELIZABETH HARVEY, born April 16, 1803; died at Shrewsbury, May 22, 1827; married by banns, November 14, 1824, John P. Corlies, born February 27, 1801, died March 1, 1879.

387   IV SAMUEL W., born March 24, 1807; died December 2, 1827.

388   V EDMUND WILLIAMS, born October 26, 1810; died July 19, 1832.

389   VI JOHN T., born September 14, 1815; died August 29, 1816.

390   VII WILLIAM, born April 21, 1818; died June 26, 1819.

JOHN C. TEN BROECK (194).

He was the eldest child of Cornelis Ten Broeck (83) and Maria Bodyn. Born in Claverack the fifteenth of March, 1755, he was almost immediately taken to New Jersey, where his baptism is recorded in the Readington Dutch Church April the thirteenth. When he was about nine years of age his parents returned to the place of his birth, and there he grew up, and received the best education possible in those unsettled and exciting times.

At the breaking out of the war between England and the colonies he enlisted, and was commissioned First Lieutenant of the Sixth Company, First Regiment of the New York Continental line, on November the twenty-first, 1776. The regiment was commanded by his kinsman, Colonel Goosen Van Schaick (*vide* 203), and was composed of the flower of New York.[92]

He distinguished himself as a brave soldier throughout the war, and was promoted to the captaincy June the twenty-ninth, 1781. He received the title of major as a brevet.

Major Ten Broeck was engaged in the battles of Trenton, Brandywine, and Monmouth. He shared the privations of Valley Forge, and it was at Yorktown that he received his only wound, being hit in the shoulder by a shell.

In preparation for the campaign of 1777 the First New York marched to the Mohawk Valley in answer to the summons of Colonel Marinus Willett, but the family tradition is that John C. Ten Broeck was in Fort Stanwix with Colonel Peter Gansevoort, and it is supposed he was specially detailed to attend him there at the time the invasion from Canada was impending.

Major Ten Broeck was an original member of the Society of the Cincinnati, and his place descended to the late Mr. William Ketchum, of Plattsburg, New York.[93]

An ivory miniature of him is in possession of his great-granddaughter, Mrs. James Wilson, of Newark, N. J. This plate has been reproduced from an oil painting, an enlarged copy of the miniature, owned by Mr. Thomas Hillhouse, of New York. The uniform in which he was represented was probably that of some military organization to which he belonged before enlisting in the New York troops.

When peace was assured, Major Ten Broeck returned to the upper Hudson, and on the thirtieth of December, 1784, married his second cousin, Antje Ten Broeck (147). They resided at Hudson, New York.

Lafayette had commanded the division of troops to which Major Ten Broeck belonged, and when he visited the United States in 1825 the Major was very anxious to see his old commander. Learning that Lafayette was to pass from Albany to Troy on the Erie Canal, he took passage on the packet-boat, sought the General's presence, and recounted to him certain incidents of a review at Valley Forge : A party of distinguished Frenchmen had come to call upon their countryman in camp, and the General had ordered his troops to appear, in honor of the occasion. The officers had demurred, feeling they would make but a pitiable show, and begged they might be excused on account of the condition of their uniforms. But Lafayette had refused, saying, " Never mind

MAJOR JOHN C. TEN BROECK.
From the Oil-Painting.

your clothes. When I tell them of the battles you have fought they will not mind your clothes." To his great pleasure, General Lafayette at once remembered him. The Major delighted in telling the story of this meeting.[11]

After the marriages of their children they finally took up their residence at Walnut Grove, the home of their son-in-law, Thomas Hillhouse, Senior, in the town of Watervliet, Albany County, N. Y. Here Major Ten Broeck died on the tenth of August, 1835, and his wife outlived him less than three years. They were buried in the family vault on the estate, but when the property passed into the hands of strangers their remains were taken to the Hillhouse plot in Albany Rural Cemetery, where they now rest.

Children of John C. Ten Broeck (194) and Antje Ten Broeck (147).

391 I MARIA BOIVN, born at Claverack September 10, 1785; died July 11, 1863; married September 22, 1804. Joseph Ketchum, born March 16, 1781, died March 1, 1863, son of H. Ketchum and Mary Barlow, of Waterford, N. Y.

392 II ANNA VAN SCHAICK, born at Claverack, December 29, 1787; died at Brooklyn, N. Y., February 24, 1865; married October 4, 1812, Thomas Hillhouse, born September 24, 1766, died July 15, 1834, son of William Hillhouse and Sarah Griswold; he had married first Harriet Hosmer, who died October 3, 1811.

393 III CATHARINE H., born June 26, 1790; died November 30, 1864; married May 9, 1825, Rev.d Morris W. Dwight. There were no children.

PETER BODINE TEN BROECK (196).

He was born the sixth of August, 1759, and named for his maternal grandfather. His baptism was by the Rev. Johannes Casparus Fryemoet. Although it is recorded that at times this clergyman went "on errands of strife to the congregation at Readington, New Jersey, and there baptized," yet the fact that the sponsors in this case were Jeremiah Ten Broeck and his wife points strongly to Claverack as the place. There were some of the Kingston branch of Ten Broecks in New Jersey at this time, but the name Jeremiah does not appear in their records.

The data referring to Peter B. Ten Broeck's life are very meagre. In May, 1789, he witnessed a deed, for the conveyance of land from John Van Rensselaer " to John Ten Broeck of the City of Hudson, yeoman."

Although very youthful for military service in the days of '76, he enlisted with the men of Albany County under Col. Robert Van Rensselaer.[115]

A miniature representing him in uniform is owned by his niece in the third generation, Mrs. Henry Seaman Howard, of Stamford, Conn. It will be seen the uniform is similar to that worn by his brother, and probably the same artist painted both pictures.

There is no record of his ever having married.

Children of Gabriel Ten Broeck (198) and Catharine Bodine.

394   i PETER BODINE, baptized at Readington, N. J., November 14, 1791.

395   ii PHŒBE, born April 28, 1796.

396   iii CORNELIUS, born June 2, 1798.

PETER BODINE TEN BROECK
From the Miniature.

MARIA TEN BROECK (203).

Maria was born in New Brunswick, N. J., the thirty-first of July, 1750, and on November the fifteenth, 1770, was married in New York City to Goosen Van Schaick. He was a descendant of the early colonist of Beverwyck, who, with others in 1662, resolved to form an agricultural settlement on the Esopus.

Goosen Van Schaick's first experience as a soldier was when he served under General Amherst in the French War. This was a preparation for the necessity of the Revolutionary days, when he was commissioned Colonel of the Second Regiment of the New York line. He was afterward General in the regular service, and held this rank at the time of his death, which occurred on July fourth, 1789.[96]

Their seven children, with one exception, outlived their father many years, as did also his wife, Maria Ten Broeck Van Schaick, who died at Albany January the fifteenth, 1829.

Children of Maria Ten Broeck (203) and Goosen Van Schaick.

397 I ALIDA, born December 25, 1771; died April 1, 1823; married October 13, 1797, Brandt Schuyler Swets, born September 11, 1772, son of Cornelis Swets and Catharina Schuyler.

398 II JOHANNES, born January 1, 1774; died March 8, 1820; married in 1795 Margaret, born April 30, 1776, died at New York, March 6, 1872, daughter of John N. Bleecker and Margaret Van Deursen.

399   III SYBRANT, born May 19, 1776; died at sea.   He was
        Lieutenant in the United States Navy, and his
        ship, which sailed for Caracas, South America,
        was lost, with all on board.

400   IV TOBIAS, born December 9, 1779; died April 21, 1868;
        married Jane, died April, 1823, daughter of
        Henry Staats and Jane Lot.

401   V MEINARD (MYNDERT), born September 26, 1782; died
        at New York December 1, 1865; married Au-
        gust 9, 1815, Elizabeth, born September 8, 1787,
        died August 20, 1861, daughter of John Howe
        and Joanna Stoutenberg.

402   VI ELIZABETH, born June 11, 1786; died August 18,
        1786.

403   VII ABRAHAM, born July 28, 1787; died August 8, 1827;
        unmarried.

Children of Catryna Ten Broeck (207) and David Fonda.

404   I SUSANNA, born January 11, 1781.

405   II JOHANNES TEN BROECK, born February 15, 1782.

406   III ELIZABETH, born November 7, 1783.

407   IV ISAAC, born August 30, 1785.

408   V TOBIAS, born February 20, 1787.

409   VI JOHANNES, born November 19, 1788.

410   VII MARY, born July 2, 1790.

SIXTH GENERATION.

RICHARD LIVINGSTON (215).

Richard Livingston grew into manhood at the time when young people in all Dutch families were encouraged to avoid the use of their hereditary tongue. In this way his baptismal name Dirck was gradually superseded by the English equivalent, Richard.

Through the removal of his parents to Montreal, in his youth, he made the acquaintance of and married a Canadian lady, Elizabeth Rencour.

He was Lieutenant-Colonel in his brother James's regiment, which first did service in Canada, and later in New York.

He died in March, 1784, and was buried at Stillwater, New York.

Children of Richard Livingston (215) and Elizabeth Rencour.

411   I ELIZABETH; died young.

412   II JOHN; died in the merchant service at Martinico, W. I.; unmarried.

413   iii   Richard Montgomery, born March 13, 1773; married 1st. Mary Barnard; married 2d, Mrs. Charlotte Peck Bush.

414   iv   Stephen, born February 15, 1784; married 1st, Maria Hartshorn, born January 19, 1786, died September 31, 1871; married 2d, Eleanor Niver, daughter of John Niver, of Livingston Manor, and widow of John Buzzard.

JAMES LIVINGSTON (216).

James, the son of John Livingston and Catharine Ten Broeck, was born the twenty-seventh of March, 1747. He married Elizabeth Simpson, of Montreal.

Possessing some influence among the Canadians, he raised a body of men under the standard of the American Congress. As their commander, he marched against Fort Chambly, seized its entire stores and garrison, and afterward accompanied General Montgomery to Quebec.

On the failure of the expedition, Colonel Livingston returned to New York, and in 1776 his men were incorporated by Congress into a regiment called the Canadian Battalion. He was at the battle of Stillwater in 1777, in 1780 was quartered in the Highlands, and served until 1781, when his regiment was reduced.[97]

Children of James Livingston (216) and Elizabeth Simpson.

415   i   Elizabeth, born May 18, 1773; died at Utica, N. Y., August 27, 1818; married Peter Smith, of Peterboro, N. Y.

416   ii   James, born January 5, 1775; died at Jamestown, N. Y.; married Elizabeth Livingston.

417 III JOHN, born May 19, 1777; married Jane Van Vechten.

418 IV MARY, born October 13, 1780; died unmarried.

419 V EDWARD, born May 22, 1783; died at Columbus, Ohio; married Martha Nelson.

420 VI MARGARET CHINN, born February 18, 1785; died September 15, 1871; married July 8, 1801, Daniel Cady, born in Canaan, Columbia County, N. Y., April 29, 1773, died at Johnstown, N. Y., October 31, 1859, son of Eleazer Cady and Tryphena Beebe.

421 VII RICHARD MONTGOMERY, born June 7, 1787; died at Schuylerville, N. Y., March 4, 1838; married Sarah Jacobs.

422 VIII CATHARINE TEN BROECK, born June 23, 1789; married Henry Brevoort Henry, of New York.

423 IX ABRAHAM, born April 7, 1793.

Children of Abraham Livingston (239) and Maria Peoples.

424 I ELIZABETH, born 1785; married Ruggles Hubbard, of Troy, N. Y.

425 II ANGELICA, born 1787; died young.

426 III CATHARINE, born 1789; married Samuel Mather, of Middletown, Conn.

427 IV ROSANNAH, born 1791; married Philip P. Schuyler, of Rhinebeck, N. Y.

428 V JOHN P., born 1793; married Sarah Blood, of Stillwater, N. Y.

429 VI MARIA, born 1795; married James O'Donnell, of Stillwater, N. Y.

430 vii Jane, born 1798 ; married Edwin Williams, of Middletown, Conn.

431 viii Thomas, born 1800 ; drowned when about nine years of age.

CATHARINE TEN BROECK LIVINGSTON (220).

She was born on the second of November, 1755, and baptized twelve days later in the Dutch Church of New York City.

During her childhood the family resided in Montreal, and when they returned to New York, Catharine remained with her married sister Annatje (217), then Mrs. Jacob Jordan, of Montreal, until the completion of her education. Shortly following her return to the family home at Stillwater, she was taken to Boston by a French lady, whose praises are still sung by the descendants, although her name is only a surmise. During this visit, at a ball given in that city in honor of Lafayette, Catharine met young Doctor Willard, whom she afterward married.

Elias Willard was born on the seventeenth of January, 1756, at Harvard, Massachusetts, a small town not far from Concord. His ancestors had been men of note in the early days of New England history.

From his own journal, now the property of a great-granddaughter, one is very fortunate in obtaining glimpses of the epochs in the life and time of Elias Willard as well as of his wife. One of the most vivid pictures is given under date of April, 1775, wherein is described his pilgrimage to the battle-field of Lexington on the day following the contest. He was then studying medicine, and when his course was completed he was appointed surgeon in the army, and served throughout the war. Part of the time he was stationed at the Boston Hospital, and doubtless it was at that period the young people first met. In regard to his marriage he writes: "In the year 1778, July the eighth, I was married to Catharine Ten Broeck Livingston, and immediately thereafter visited Albany and the country to the northward."

It seems probable Catharine remained near her paternal home, as her husband purchased an estate at Stillwater and resided there after the close of the war, for some time. In 1785 they moved to Canada for a while, and at this period is written the following:

"The time of our arrival in Montreal was June the seventeenth, 1785. A melancholy accident deprived us of one of our children, named Sarah Ten Eyck, about four years old. Depression of spirits, occasioned by this and several other circumstances, rendered my wife inconsolable, and she wished much to return to Stillwater."

They removed finally to Albany, retaining the place at Stillwater as a summer residence, and Doctor Willard makes this note of the change: "In the year 1790 I purchased the place I now live upon from General Abraham Ten Broeck for three thousand dollars." The house is situated on Broadway, next to the Fourth Presbyterian Church. North Pearl Street was not then opened through.

Catharine Ten Broeck Willard died here on the twenty-sixth of January, 1827, and the death of her husband followed in less than two months, on the twentieth of March. They are buried in Albany Rural Cemetery, where children and children's children rest near them.

An ivory miniature of Doctor Willard is owned by a descendant, Mrs. Augustus Gillinder, of New York.

Children of Catharine T. B. Livingston (220) and Elias Willard.

432   I RENETTE MCCARTY, born in Boston May 19, 1779; married at Stillwater on Sunday, June 10, 1798, Thomas W. Ford.

433   II JOHN, born March 10, 1781; died in 1860; married in 1813, Mary Ann Jenkins.

434   III SARAH TEN EYCK, born June 20, 1783; died November 22, 1787.

435   IV MARGARET CHINN, born August 22, 1785; died May 15, 1866; married at Albany, September 3, 1811, Major Israel Smith, born September 15, 1776, died June 3, 1853, son of Samuel Smith and Hannah Stringham.

436   V ANNE JORDAN, born in Montreal August 24, 1787; died at Buffalo, N. Y., December 14, 1862; married Judge Estes Horn.

437   VI SARAH TEN EYCK, born May 30, 1790; died October, 1829; married General John Trotter, of Albany.

438   VII EDWARD CHINN, born June 30, 1792; died September 8, 1826; married Mary Buckmaster.

439   VIII MARIA LIVINGSTON, born November 19, 1794; died November 15, 1840; unmarried.

440   IX CATHARINE LIVINGSTON, born November 27, 1797;
      died April 5, 1872; married June 16, 1827,
      William Clark Young, born November 25, 1799,
      died December 22, 1893.

441   X ELIZABETH SCHUYLER, born October 20, 1800; died
      April, 1830; married September 5, 1826, Walter
      Rutherford Morris.

Children of Philip Philip Livingston (222) and Sarah Johnson.

442   I PHILIP HENRY, born at Jamaica, W. I., October 30,
      1769; died at Red Hook, N. Y., in 1831; mar-
      ried May 8, 1788, Maria Livingston, died at
      New York August, 1828, daughter of Walter
      Livingston and Maria Schuyler.

443   II GEORGE, born at Jamaica, W. I., October 14, 1771;
      died unmarried.

444   III CATHARINE, born at Jamaica, W. I., October 13,
      1772; died at Jamaica, March 20, 1819; married
      at New York, October 13, 1796, John Saunders,
      died at Jamaica December, 1818. No children.

445   IV CHRISTINA, born in New York September 26, 1774;
      died August 24, 1841; married March 29, 1797,
      John Marane McComb.

446   V SARAH, born at Jamaica February 29, 1776; died at
      New York April 12, 1797; unmarried.

447   VI HENRY, born at Jamaica May 13, 1777; died at the
      age of four.

448   VII EDWARD PHILIP, born at Jamaica November 24,
      1779; died November 3, 1843. He was Lieu-
      tenant-Governor of New York in 1830, United
      States Senator from 1808–12, 1823–24, and
      1838–39. He married 1st, at Clermont, N. Y.,

November, 1799, Elizabeth Stevens Livingston, born May 5, 1780, died June 10, 1829, daughter of Robert R. Livingston and Elizabeth Stevens; married 2d, Mary C. Broome.

449 VIII JASPAR HALL, born at Jamaica December 3, 1780; died 1835; married at New York July 4, 1802, Eliza Livingstone, daughter of Brockholst Livingston and Catharine Keteltas.

450   IX WASHINGTON, born at Jamaica July 6, 1783; died aged about ten months.

451   X MARIA MARGARET, born at New York December 30, 1787; died September 3, 1791.

CATHARINE LIVINGSTON (224).

Baptized the twenty-fifth of August, 1745. She married in her nineteenth year Stephen Van Rensselaer, the seventh Patroon of Rensselaerwyck and proprietor of the manor.

They had been married less than six years when Stephen Van Rensselaer died, leaving his wife with three children. His will, made on September the seventh, 1769, was recorded the following year in the New York office.

Catharine, after having duplicated the years of her wedded life in widowhood, married for her second husband Dominic Eilardus Westerlo. He was a native of Holland, but was called when only twenty-two years of age to the Dutch Church in Albany, where his ministry was one of unusual ability and success.

Catharine lived to see her children occupy positions of wide influence and trust. She died the seventeenth of April, 1810.

Children of Catharine Livingston (224) and Stephen Van Rensselaer.

452 ı STEPHEN, born November 1, 1764; died January 26,
1839; married 1st, June 6, 1783, Margarita
Schuyler, baptized September 24, 1758, died
March, 1801, daughter of Philip Schuyler and
Catharine Van Rensselaer; married 2d, May
17, 1802, Cornelia Paterson, born June 4, 1780,
died August 6, 1844, daughter of William Paterson, the second Governor of New Jersey.

453 ıı PHILIP S., born 1767; died September 25, 1824;
married in 1787, Anne de Peyster Van Cortlandt. There were no children.

·454 ııı ELIZABETH, born 1768; died 1841; married 1st, September 18, 1787, John Bradstreet Schuyler, baptized July 23, 1765, son of Philip Schuyler and
Catharine Van Rensselaer; married 2d, November 17, 1800, John Bleecker, born in Albany,
1766, son of John Rutger Bleecker and Elizabeth Staats.

Children of Sarah Livingston (227) and John Henry Livingston.

455 ı HENRY ALEXANDER, born August 26, 1777; died
June 4, 1849; married 1st, Elizabeth Beekman,
daughter of James Beekman and Sarah Lefferts;
married 2d, Frederica Sayres, born in Bath,
England, died April, 1870.

DIRCK TEN BROECK (245).

Dirck, the eldest child and only son of General Abraham Ten Broeck, was born on the third of November,
1765. He married, at the age of twenty, Cornelia Stuy-

19

vesant, who was three years younger — the daughter of
Petrus Stuyvesant and Margaret Livingston.

He had the good fortune to belong to the first generation of patriots, with their enthusiasm not to a province,
but to a nation.   His social and political position was
well assured, both by the family name he bore and the
confidence which his father continued to merit.   Thus
his life opened with every promise.

He had studied law, and in 1796 was elected Member
of Assembly from Albany County.[98]   In 1798 he was
appointed Speaker of the House of Assembly, and for
three sessions his polished diction and eloquent power
were felt in the deliberations of that body.   When Mrs.'
Margaret Stuyvesant Gibson (457) died at Waterford,
N. Y., on the twenty-second of December, 1873, the
Troy *Whig* published the following:

> Her father, Dirck Ten Broeck. was speaker of the Assembly
> when John Jay was Governor, in 1796, 1798, and 1800.   Some
> of the old residents of Albany yet well remember when Speaker
> Ten Broeck rode to the capitol in his coach-and-four, with as
> much dignity as the Chancellor of England.

A lithograph, or copper-plate, was executed at this
period, which represents the men foremost in the State
government of those days.   A copy is bound with the
fourth volume of the "Documentary History of New
York," and there is also a facsimile print of the group
in the State Library at Albany.   The plate of Dirck Ten
Broeck here given is reproduced from this.

Under the will of his father, in 1810, he received
lands that had continued in the Ten Broeck family for

THE HON. DIRCK TEN BROECK.
Speaker of New York House of Assembly, 1798–1800.

several generations, but his circumstances made it a necessity for him to practise law, which he did in New York City. Owing to financial difficulties, it had been necessary to part with some personal property, and a set of very handsome china, bearing the entwined monogram of himself and wife, is still prized by those who are not descendants.

His great-granddaughter, Miss Gibson, of New York, possesses his seal. It is of silver, oval in shape, and in size about an inch by three-quarters of an inch. On one side the initials "D. T. B." are surmounted by a horse's head unbridled, and the reverse is the coat-of-arms and crest, with the motto, "Sustineo." Mrs. Edward Ten Broeck, of Chicago, owns some very interesting relics belonging to this branch of the family.

The family of children born to Dirck Ten Broeck and his wife was an unusually large one; in the record below are given the names of twelve, and to this must be added five more, who died in earliest infancy.

Cornelia Stuyvesant Ten Broeck died at Trenton, N. J., the twenty-fourth of February, 1825; her husband survived her more than seven years, and died in December, 1832.

Children of Dirck Ten Broeck (245) and Cornelia Stuyvesant.

456   I ABRAHAM, born at Albany July 13, 1788; died December 18, 1810; unmarried.

457   II MARGARET STUYVESANT, born at Albany, July 24, 1790; died December 22, 1873; married June 11, 1818, Rev^d. Robert Gibson, son of Robert Gibson, of Charleston, S. C.

458   III PETRUS STUYVESANT, born at Albany January 26,
         1792; died at Danvers, Mass., January 21,
         1849; married August 10, 1819, Lucretia Lor-
         ing Cutter, died at Clinton, Iowa, October 12,
         1861, daughter of Levi Cutter, of Portland,
         Maine, and Lucretia Mitchell.   A clergyman.

459   IV STEPHEN VAN RENSSELAER, born at Albany May
         23, 1793; died May 26, 1793.

460   V DIRCK, born at Albany April 22, 1794; died April
         23, 1794.

461   VI ELIZABETH MARIA, born at Albany May 20, 1795;
         died October 19, 1795.

462   VII CORNELIA, born at Watervliet, N. Y., April 23, 1798;
         died May 5, 1798.

463   VIII DIRCK WESSELS, born at Albany April 5, 1800; died
         April 6, 1800.

464   IX STEPHEN PHILIP VAN RENSSELAER, born at Bouwery
         House, New York, December 21, 1802; died
         August 2, 1866; married September 1, 1825,
         Mary Nielson, daughter of William Nielson, of
         New York.   There were no children.   A physi-
         cian.

465   X NICHOLAS WILLIAM, born in New York, September
         14, 1805; died September 25, 1805.

466   XI ELIZABETH, born April 10, 1810; died April 30, 1810.

467   XII ELIZABETH VAN RENSSELAER, born May 20, 1813;
         died June 2, 1813.

Children of Catharina Ten Broeck (263) and William Van Orden.

468   I WESSEL TEN BROECK, born September 16, 1788;
         died at New Baltimore, Greene County, N. Y.,
         January 13, 1871; married Maria Schuhmacher,

born June 8, 1796, died May 7, 1872, daughter
of Tjerck Schuhmacher and Jane Breestede.

469   ii HENRY, born September 14, 1790; died July 13,
1863; married February 20, 1822, Temperance
De Witt, born April 29, 1800, died July 22,
1888, daughter of Henry De Witt and Catharine Dumond.

470   iii WILLIAM, born April 3, 1793; baptized at Linlithgo
Church, May 20, 1793; died young.

471   iv WILLIAM, born October 16, 1794; died July 28, 1839;
unmarried.

472   v JANE ANN, born February 13, 1799; died July 12,
1828; married at Kaatsbaan August 23, 1817,
Benjamin Van Orden, born July 3, 1790, died
April 26, 1873, son of Benjamin Van Orden
and Elizabeth Vandenburg.   No children.

JACOB TEN BROECK (264).

The Will of Jacob Ten Broeck, made at Clermont
(now Germantown), under date of February the third,
1829, and proved at Hudson, N. Y., June the eleventh,
the same year, adds one more link to the interest that
must always center in the ancient Bible of Wessel Ten
Broeck, and the portrait of the ancestor, Jacob Ten
Broeck (see plates on page 39 and 61), the prized heir-
looms of generations, in the direct line from son to son.

An extract from the Will best shows the value then
placed upon them :

Item.   I give and bequeath unto my grandson, Jacob Wessel . . . the old Bible.   It is my particular request that

my daughter, Helen, shall have it in care until my grandson, Jacob Wessel, shall attain the age of twenty-one years.

He then devises the portrait of his grandfather to the same grandson, and adds, " It is my particular request that my son Jacob shall have it in care for my grandson, Jacob Wessel, until he attain the age of twenty-one years." By this provision Jacob Wessel Ten Broeck (770) became the owner.

There perhaps were times when the full value of the book and its records was only partly appreciated; as it is said by one of the family, he recalls the time when the heavy volume was placed upon his tiny dress-skirt, that he might not wander far from under the maternal hand.

The book needs only to be weighed in the hands one moment to realize what a restraining factor it must have been !

Children of Jacob Ten Broeck (264) and Christina Schepmoes (274).

473   i   JANE, born March 15, 1795; died May 10, 1811.

474   ii   WILLIAM SCHEPMOES, born May 1, 1798; died October 5, 1822; unmarried.

475   iii   JACOB, born May 13, 1800; died March 24, 1883; married at St. John's, Red Hook, November 6, 1821, Anna Benner, born November 15, 1797, died March 26, 1879. daughter of Henry Benner and Catharine Pitcher.

476   iv   LENA (HELEN), born at Germantown September 8, 1803; died at Clermont July 10, 1840; married September 20, 1836, Rev^d. Thomas K.

THE BIBLE OF WESSEL TEN BROECK (6).
Printed at Dordrecht, Holland, 1682.

Lape. of Athens, N. Y., born November 2, 1801,
died January 2, 1879; he married 2d, July 20,
1841, Caroline Rossman, of Claverack.

477   v CATHARINE MARIA, born at Germantown July 26,
1805; died March 27, 1896; married November 1, 1826, William Henry De Witt, born May
27, 1804, died March 25, 1886, son of John I.
De Witt and Maria Breasted.

478   vi CHRISTINA, born at Germantown September 25,
1807; died January 17, 1811.

479   vii SARAH. ——

Children of Anna Ten Broeck (273) and James Kortz.

480   i ANNA CATHARINE, born April 14, 1799; died December 6, 1873; married Rev. A. B. Chittenden.

481   ii MARIA, born at Kaatsbaan, N. Y., July 3, 1801; died
March 23, 1877; married —— Gilmor.

482   iii JACOB, born at Kaatsbaan September 22, 1803.

483   iv ELIZA (or ELIZABETH), born at Kaatsbaan November
26, 1804; died June 30, 1868; unmarried.

484   v CATHARINE, born at Kaatsbaan April 11, 1807; died
August 22, 1878; unmarried.

485   vi JANE, born at Kaatsbaan July 29, 1809; died December 4, 1883; unmarried.

486   vii JAMES WILLIAM, born March 14, 1812; died at Catskill, N. Y., August 21, 1887; married June 4,
1856, Martha J. Millard, born November 29,
1824, died April 9, 1872, daughter of James
Millard.

Children of Leendert (Leonard) Ten Broeck (287) and Sarah Doll.

487   I SARAH MAGDALENA, born August 27, 1803; died February 18, 1857; married John Vanderwerken.

488   II LEONARD DOLL, born August 29, 1805; died December, 1839; married Marietta Veadenburg.

489   III JOHN HERMAN, born September 3, 1807; died March 28, 1879; married November 9, 1854, Letitia Amalia Younglove, daughter of John Younglove and Melissa Clemens.

490   IV SUSANNA CHRISTINA, born September 4, 1809; died unmarried.

491   V CORNELIUS, born October 19, 1811; died October 7, 1874; married May 28, 1833, Georgina Pearson, born January 11, 1814, died at Albany February 18, 1888, daughter of George Pearson and Judith Van Vechten.

Children of Catharina Ten Broeck (289) and Isaac Bailey.

492   I SARAH MARIA, born at Waterford, N. Y., May 29, 1817; died August 6, 1882; married September, 1840, Jeremiah Green.

493   II ELIZABETH HART, born at Waterford October 2, 1821; married July 5, 1843, John Patrick.

Children of Jacob Ten Broeck (294) and Prudence Chapman.

494   I ALBERTINA, born October 9, 1819; died January 22, 1865; married March 26, 1837, David Evans, born February 1, 1811, died September 28, 1879, son of Freeman Evans and Aurelia Tryon.

495 II EMMA, born August 4, 1821; died April 6, 1896; married January 23, 1840, Addison W. Potter, born September 3, 1817, died February 11, 1885, son of Peleg Potter and Sophia Hodge.

496 III GERTRUDE ANN, born October 17, 1824, died August 27, 1877; married October 20, 1841, Isaac H. Smith, born December 9, 1819, died April 17, 1885, son of Jacob Smith and Esther Ann Hodge.

497 IV THEODORE, born January 18, 1827; died March 6, 1865; married June 9, 1856, Lucetta Salisbury, born August 22, 1834, daughter of Daniel E. Salisbury and Apphia Keach.

498 V DORCAS, born January 1, 1832; died April 8, 1854; unmarried.

Children of Samuel L. Ten Broeck (295) and Polly Miller.

499 I SAMUEL, born at Clermont, N. Y., September 9, 1813; married March 20, 1836, Maria Parks, born at Claverack October 1, 1816, died at Rhinebeck, N. Y., April 7, 1881.

500 II CATHARINE, born May 11, 1816; baptized at Linlithgo Church June 16, 1816.

501 III LEONARD, born June 26, 1819; baptized at Linlithgo Church July 26, 1819.

Children of Catharina Ten Broeck (296) and her first husband, Conrad Salpaugh.

502 I JACOB, born May 15, 1808; died in 1866; unmarried.

503 II ALBERTINA MARIA, born June 25, 1810; died February, 1885; married May 2, 1835, Cornelius Bortle.

20

504   III LEONARD DIRCK, born February 3, 1814; died
          young.

505   IV GERTRUDE ELIZA, born at Johnstown, Columbia
          County, December 17, 1815; died March 25,
          1889; married March 28, 1841, John Conaro,
          died December 2, 1858. There were no chil-
          dren.

Children of Catharine Ten Broeck (Salpaugh) (296) and her second husband, John Pitcher.

506   I WILLIAM L., born April 14, 1820; married August
          31, 1843, Etta G. Hubbard, born February 16,
          1824, daughter of Caleb Hubbard, of Hartford,
          Conn., and Margaret Hann.

507   II EMMA TEN BROECK, born October 1, 1821 ; married
          August 10, 1864, Edward Nelson Barringer,
          born May 5, 1811, died January 6, 1875, son
          of Jacob Barringer and Lydia Terse, of Red
          Hook, N. Y. No children.

508   III HENRY MOFFAT, born May 25, 1823; died September
          12, 1895; married February 22, 1845, Frances
          M. Myers, born December 17, 1821, died Janu-
          ary 5, 1894, daughter of Henry Myers.

509   IV SAMUEL TEN BROECK, born June 8, 1830; married
          October 5, 1855, Matilda Barringer, born in
          1839, daughter of George Barringer and Cathe-
          rine Halsey.

LEONARD WILLIAM TEN BROECK (299).

Leonard William, the youngest of the family of Leonard Ten Broeck (137), was born the fourteenth of February, 1797.

LEONARD W. TEN BROECK.
From the Oil-Portrait of 1832.

From early manhood his interest as a patriot and citizen was shown by his upright and useful life. The confidence he inspired was manifested by the honors put upon him by the people. He belonged to the State Militia, and was advanced to the rank of Major-General. He served as a member of the fifty-fifth session of the Assembly in 1832, from Columbia County, and later was appointed Sheriff of the county.

He married on the eleventh of October, 1820, Helen, the daughter of Walter Tryon Livingston. She was a member of the Dutch Church, and the good Christian lives of both were "clean and blameless amongst men."

The portraits, painted by Phillips in 1832, are owned by their son Mr. W. T. L. Ten Broeck of Rhinebeck, New York.

His death occurred in the prime of life, cutting off a career of great influence. His wife outlived him less than four years. They are buried in the family cemetery at Clermont, and the stones bear these inscriptions:

Leonard W. Ten Broeck.

Died January 24, 1852, aged 54 years, 11 mos. and 10 days.

Thou art gone to the grave, but we will not deplore thee,
'Though sorrow and darkness encompass the tomb;
The Saviour has passed through its portals before thee,
And the lamp of his love is thy guide through the gloom.

Helen,

Wife of Leonard W. Ten Broeck.

Died September 21, 1855.

Aged 59 years, 4 mos. and 18 days.

Children of Leonard W. Ten Broeck (299) and Helen Livingston.

510   I JANE LIVINGSTON, born October 25, 1823; married
September 15, 1846, Charles P. Sanders, born at
Schenectady, November 26, 1824, died March
26, 1891, son of Peter Sanders and Maria
Elmendorf.

511   II SAMUEL, born June 5, 1827; died July 4, 1863; buried
at Clermont; married August 29, 1848, Helen
L. Brooks, died February 1, 1875, daughter of
Thomas Brooks and Helen Labagh. He served
in the Civil War as Captain of Company M,
Fifth Regiment of New York Cavalry.

512   III WALTER TRYON LIVINGSTON, born July 8, 1830;
married August 28, 1855, Helen U. Schultz,
born September 18, 1833, daughter of Peter J.
Schultz, of Rhinebeck, N. Y., and Helen Rowe.

513   IV ALBERTINA SANDERS, born April 23, 1835; married
May 29, 1860, Barent A. Mynderse, M. D., born
June 15, 1829, died October 2, 1887, son of
Aaron Mynderse, of Schenectady, and Anna
Maria Vedder.

Children of John Sanders (300) and Jane Livingston.

514   I ALBERTINA, born December 22, 1828; died November 19, 1834.

515   II WALTER TRYON LIVINGSTON, born September 7,
1830.

516   III EUGENE LIVINGSTON, born at Johnstown, N. Y.,
November 1, 1835; married November 23,
1859, Lizzie A. Passage, born July 23, 1840,
daughter of David Passage and Elizabeth Henderson.

HELEN LIVINGSTON (TEN BROECK).
From the Oil-Portrait of 1832.

517 iv Mary Elizabeth Livingston, born January 8, 1841 ;
married June 25, 1863, Harold Wilson, born
January 7, 1836, son of William H. Wilson, of
Clermont, N. Y., and Anne Hulme, of Philadelphia.

Children of Theodore W. Sanders (301) and Margaret Nicoll Sill.

518 i Elizabeth Nicoll Sill, born December 22, 1829 ;
died February 7, 1831.

519 ii Catharine Mary, born December 7, 1831 ; married
June 17, 1854, William J. Mott, of Great Neck,
L. I., born February 22, 1825, died May 13,
1894, son of James W. Mott and Abigail Jones.

520 iii Margaret Mather, born February 5, 1834 ; died
April 16, 1839.

521 iv Albertina, born April 26, 1836.

522 v William Nicoll Sill, born August 24, 1838 ; married February 3, 1864, Catharine Van Rensselaer Osborn, born February 17, 1843, daughter
of James Henry Osborn and Christina Schuyler
Van Rensselaer.   He served during the Civil
War as Captain of Company F, Third Regiment, of New York Volunteers.

523 vi Alexander Glen, born October 29, 1840 ; died September 29, 1842.

524 vii Lydia Mather, born December 19, 1842.

525 viii Lindsay Glen, born February 23, 1853 ; died April
15, 1853.

Children of Catharina Ten Broeck (303) and Moses Burt (Rev.)

526 i Anthony Edgar, born July 12, 1812 ; died September
9, 1886 ; married November 8, 1846, Laura A.

158   Ten Broeck Family Records

Jarvis, born January 31, 1824, daughter of James
Grant Jarvis and Temperance Frisbee.

527   II WILLIAM A., born November 27, 1815; died January 14, 1856; buried at Claverack; unmarried.

528   III MARY FRANCES, born November 15, 1820; died June
23, 1851; married April 30, 1850, Rev. William
O. Jarvis, born July 1, 1822, son of James
Grant Jarvis and Temperance Frisbee.   No
children.

Child of Henry Anthony Ten Broeck (304) and his first wife, Rhoda Green Brown.

529   I ANTHONY, born January 15, 1815; died September
22, 1880; married 1st, May 2, 1838, Amelia
Stagg, born February 6, 1817, died February
26, 1843, daughter of Jacob Stagg and Sarah
Mesier; married 2d, January 6, 1845, Rhoda
Ann Brown, born February 20. 1823, daughter
of Nathaniel Gorham Brown and Anna Caswell.

Child of Henry Anthony Ten Broeck (304) and his second wife, Delia Maria Coffin.

530   I HENRY H., born July 8, 1840; married November
18, 1867, Louise D. Barber, born October 9,
1846, daughter of Dr. John Barber and Sarah
Langford.

Children of Annatje Ten Broeck (306) and Robert H. Van Rensselaer.

531   I ROBERT HENRY, born June 17, 1817; died March
5, 1888; married October 4, 1843, Joanna
Franchot, daughter of Paschal Stanislaus Franchot and Catharine Hansen.

532 II ANTHONY, born February 9, 1819; died February 23, 1819.

533 III CHRISTINA, born March 8, 1820.

534 IV ANTHONY, born November 25, 1821; married 1st, November 8, 1860, Mary Woodworth, daughter of Joseph W. Woodworth and Susanna Hallett; married 2d, December 6, 1883, Mary J. Thatcher, daughter of Joseph Thatcher and Jane De Golmar, and widow of Jeremiah M. Race.

535 V CAROLINE ANN DE PEYSTER, born November 19, 1823; died August 5, 1896; married May 3, 1848, Edward Livingston, died May 20, 1872, son of Robert Le Roy Livingston and Anna M. Diggs.

536 VI JULIA FRANCES, born November 17, 1825; died April 8, 1890; married September 30, 1852, Ambrose Lockwood, died May 19, 1870, son of Hezekiah Lockwood and Mary Sturgis.

537 VII STEPHEN VAN CORTLANDT, born March 9, 1829; married October 20, 1858, Cornelia Rachel Douw Everts, born January 19, 1837, daughter of John Charles Everts and Christina Van Rensselaer.

Children of John Anthony Ten Broeck (308) and Hannah Everts.

538 I JANE CHRISTINA, born 1828; died October, 1828.

539 II JANE EVERTS, born May 27, 1830; married Samuel G. Waterman.

540 III CHARLES EVERTS, born May 7, 1832; married Anna Newmann.

541   IV Anthony C., born August 15, 1834; married Catharine Waterman.

Children of William C. Ten Broeck (310) and Christina Van Deusen.

542   I Mary Lane, born October 7, 1825; died young.

543   II Cornelia Alida; died young.

544   III Henry Edgar; died young.

545   IV Cornelia Alida, born April 29, 1828; died December 3, 1878; married Isaac Warren Valance.

546   V Christina C., born November 15, 1829; died December 18, 1884; married F. Asbury, Ireland.

547   VI Elizabeth Ann, born July 4, 1831; married Jacob Weatherwax.

548   VII William Mathew, born June 29, 1832; married Kate Merrill.

549   VIII Delia M., born August 1, 1837; married John Van Deusen Ten Broeck, born May 18, 1835, son of David S. Ten Broeck (571), and Alida Van Deusen.

550   IX Cornelius Henry, married Lucy Ann Vandenburg.

551   X Julia F., born November 30, 1839; died October, 1876; married Moses Weatherwax.

Children of Henry Ten Broeck (313) and Maria Van Vechten.

552   I Martha; married Henry Lape.

553   II John Van Vechten; married Mary Potter.

554   III Henry; died unmarried.

555   IV Edward Francis; married Fanny Austen.

556   V Samuel Augustus; married Sarah Walters.

557   VI Mary; died unmarried.

Children of Maria S. Ten Broeck (318) and William E. Heermance.

558   I SAMUEL TEN BROECK, born October 10, 1829; married February 11, 1867, Catharine M. Tobey, born April 2, 1841, daughter of Silas W. Tobey and Alida Staats Miller.

559   II MARY JANE, born February 1, 1832; died November 19, 1896.

560   III CAROLINE, born April 18, 1834; died February 11, 1838.

561   IV WILLIAM T., born April 5, 1837; married September 14, 1864, Jane P. Hood, daughter of Duncan Hood and Mary Neimeyer Van Ness.

562   V CAROLINE ANNA, born December 16, 1842; married February 9, 1871, Lewis M. Herrick, born 1841, died Nov. 18, 1871, son of Castle W. Herrick, of Hudson, N. Y., and Jane H. Heermance.

Children of Maria Hoffman Ten Broeck (324) and Peter Quidor Schuyler.

563   I JOHN EDWIN, born September 16, 1831; married April 27, 1871, Annie E. Stevenson, born January 21, 1842.

564   II NICHOLAS TEN BROECK, born December 4, 1833; married in Johnson County, Ark., September 24, 1871, Martha A. Griffin, born July 25, 1841.

565   III ANNA HOFFMAN, born October 18, 1835; married May 27, 1868, George W. Bodle.

Child of David Van Rensselaer Ten Broeck (326) and his first wife, Jane Doane.

566   I HARMON JAY, born May 18, 1831; married December 15, 1853, Mary C. Fowks.

21

Children of David Van Rensselaer Ten Broeck (326) and his second
wife (Mrs.) Sarah Heermance.

567   I GEORGE EDWIN, born August 21, 1857; died December 22, 1877.

568   II LUCY JANE, born July 6, 1859; died in 1865.

Children of John Jeremiah Ten Broeck (327) and Helen Ten Broeck (583).

569   I JULIA; married William Pease.

570   II FRANCIS FERDINAND; died unmarried.

Children of William Ten Broeck (335) and Margaret Becker.

571   I DAVID S., born December 29, 1814; married May 31, 1834, Alida Van Deusen.

572   II WALTER V., born April 17, 1817; married December 6, 1842, Elizabeth Clum, died August 6, 1885.

573   III PETER VAN RENSSELAER, born April 17, 1817; married January 19, 1842, Mary Jannette Bortle, of Claverack.

574   IV JACOB LAWRENCE, born July 27, 1819; married August 9, 1838, Elizabeth M. Clum, died February 23, 1855.

575   V WILLIAM AMBROSE, born November 20, 1823; married May 29, 1845, Mary Ann Comfort, born December 11, 1824, died January 14, 1866, daughter of Hiram Comfort and Julia L. Ludington.

576   VI JEREMIAH, born March 22, 1826; married at Flatbush November 27, 1851, Maria Keifer, born October 31, 1833, daughter of William Keifer and Ann Osterhout.

Children of John Van Rensselaer Ten Broeck (338) and Elizabeth
Van Ness.

577   ı RENSSELAER, born January 29, 1814; died April 5,
1884; married Mary Monroe Terry, daughter
of Joseph H. Terry.

578   ıı ELIZABETH, born October 29, 1815. Sister at the
Convent of the Sacred Heart, Honesdale, Pa.

Children of John Van Rensselaer Ten Broeck (338) and his second
wife, Emeline P. Parker.

579   ı GEORGE AUGUSTUS, born October 21, 1821; died
August 20, 1832.

580   ıı ALEXANDER PARKER, born October 24, 1823; died
December 16, 1860; married July 8, 1852, Mary
C. Dempsey, born August 24, 1824, died at
Delhi, N. Y., December 31, 1876, daughter of
Lawrence Dempsey and Anna.

581   ııı AMASA JUNIUS, born September 26, 1825; died at
Delhi, N. Y., February 21, 1852; married July
24, 1848, Josephine Alida Howard, daughter
of Calvin Howard, M. D., and his first wife,
Sarah Gregory. Josephine A. Howard married
2d, Harmon Camp, of Windham.

Children of Seth Ten Broeck (339) and Marytje Schepmoes (278).

582   ı WILLIAM SCHEPMOES, born at Germantown, August
19, 1813; died April 23, 1825.

583   ıı HELEN, born at Germantown March 14, 1815; died
January 21, 1884; married 1st, November 26,
1833, John Jeremiah Ten Broeck (327), born
August 18, 1806, son of Niclaes Ten Broeck
and Maria Schuyler; married 2d, William
Denison, of Brooklyn.

584   III BETSEY, born at Germantown May 19, 1817; died
        young.

585   IV CHRISTINA, born at Germantown, April 30, 1819;
        died October 19, 1838.

586   V ELIZABETH, born at Germantown, October 15, 1820;
        married September 14, 1842, James Calkins, of
        Hudson, N. Y., born in 1819.

587   VI SETH, born at Germantown August 28, 1822; died
        June 15, 1868.

588   VII JOHN A., born June 22, 1823; died February 12,
        1824.

589   VIII EMELINE, born November 15, 1826; died May 13,
        1827.

590   IX SAMUEL ADAM.

Children of Austin M. Ten Broeck (340) and Margaret Van Hoesen.

591   I ABRAHAM, born March 11, 1816; died January 31,
        1819.

592   II CATHARINE ANN, born in Hudson, N. Y., April 30,
        1819; married December 17, 1836, Calvin
        Groat, of Copake, N. Y., born August 24, 1810,
        died July 21, 1892, son of Hon. Dedrick Groat.

593   III JANE CORNELIA, born February 10, 1821; married
        James G. Wheeler.

594   IV CHARLOTTE E., born November 30, 1822; died No-
        vember 5, 1878; married September 10, 1841,
        Peter Oakley, born March 30, 1821, son of
        Isaac Oakley and Catharine Coons.

595   V LYDIA M., born January 14, 1824; died in Michigan
        August 27, 1864; married William Vosburg.

596   VI WALTER B., born February 2, 1827; married January
25, 1855, Marietta Van Deusen, born February
15, 1835, daughter of Seymour Van Deusen and
Caroline M:Arthur.

597   VII ANDREW E., born January 5, 1829; died at Gales-
burg, Mich., August, 1896; married Mary Bul-
lock, of Yates County, N. Y.

598   VIII CHARLES ALEXANDER, born March 14, 1833; died
June 8, 1834.

599   IX JAY DANFORTH, born April 29, 1835, at Copake,
N. Y.; married January 28, 1858, Margaret
Ophelia Ames, born June 10, 1837, daughter
of William Noxon Ames, of Hudson, N. Y., and
Evangeline Best.

600   X RENSSELAER, born September 14, 1838; married September 17, 1867, Phoebe Wilson, born September
11, 1846, daughter of Ira Wilson and Jena Smith.

Children of Abraham Adam Ten Broeck (344) and Christina Ten Broeck (311).

601   I ROBERT HENRY, born October 29, 1832; married
Zilla Meeks.

602   II VIRGINIA, married Daniel Caly; no children.

Child of Catharine Ten Broeck (346) and William T. Van Deusen.

603   I AUGUSTUS, born October 5, 1845; married October 4,
1866, Georgiana Crosby, born August 2, 1850.

Children of Lydia M. Ten Broeck (348) and Conrad W. Melius.

604   I EDWARD; died young.

605   II JENNIE L.; died young.

606   III ANNA MARIA; married Paul R. Brown.

Children of James Adam Ten Broeck (349) and Sarah M. Herder.

607   I EMMA JANE, born December 6, 1844; died unmarried.

608   II THEODORE R., born December 15, 1848.

609   III GEORGE A., born March 17, 1852.

610   IV HARRIET E., born May 11, 1858; died unmarried.

Children of Jacob Samuel Ten Broeck (358) and Caroline Hover.

611   I CATHARINE M., born December 28, 1833; died August 24, 1870.

612   II MARTHA JANE, born April 20, 1836; married June 2, 1851, Edward C. Van Tassel.

613   III LUCINA, born April 6, 1840; married April 8, 1865, George H. Snyder.

614   IV CHRISTINA L., born May 4, 1843.

615   V ALIDA, born March 23, 1846; married February 9, 1881, Jacob Cramer.

616   VI EVA, born February 13, 1849; married January 29, 1878, John Platner.

617   VII HELEN V., born July 4, 1851; died November 10, 1877.

618   VIII JACOB WILLIAM, born October 19, 1854; married June 17, 1879, Adelaide Brooks.

619   IX OVERTON FRANKLIN, born December 10, 1858; died February 4, 1862.

ELIZA H. TEN BROECK (360).

She was the only daughter of William Ten Broeck, of New Brunswick. She married first, in that city on the eighth item of this is as follows:

I give and bequeath to my cousins, Mrs. Jane G. Woodward and Mrs. Sarah W. Forman, the portraits or oil paintings of my great-grand Parents, to be divided by themselves. And I bequeath the family coat-of-arms to my cousin Mrs. Sarah W. Forman.

The portraits and the arms are those reproduced by plates, for this work.

JOHN TEN BROECK (362).

The Ten Broeck farm at Raritan Landing, comprising the homestead and two hundred and twenty-five acres of land, was sold by John Ten Broeck to Edward Stelle

615   v ALIDA, born March 23, 1846; married February 9,
          1881, Jacob Cramer.

616   vi EVA, born February 13, 1849; married January 29,
          1878, John Platner.

617   vii HELEN V., born July 4, 1851; died November 10,
          1877.

618   viii JACOB WILLIAM, born October 19, 1854; married
          June 17, 1879, Adelaide Brooks.

619   ix OVERTON FRANKLIN, born December 10, 1858; died
          February 4, 1862.

ELIZA H. TEN BROECK (360).

She was the only daughter of William Ten Broeck, of
New Brunswick. She married first, in that city on the

twenty-ninth of October, 1809, Ralph Voorhees Beekman. After residing there a number of years, they removed to Flatbush, L. I. Here her husband died on January the thirtieth, 1833; and after a widowhood of a number of years she married into the well-known Schoonmaker family, her husband being Michael, son of the Rev. Martinus Schoonmaker. She outlived her second husband twenty-one years, and died on the thirtieth of December, 1866.

She was preëminently a type of the generation to which she belonged, and although she had no children, she possessed the charm of manner and brightness of mind that attracted to her home the younger members of her own family as well as a wide circle of friends.

Her will, made on March the thirteenth, 1851, was proven at Brooklyn the thirtieth of March, 1867. The eighth item of this is as follows:

I give and bequeath to my cousins, Mrs. Jane G. Woodward and Mrs. Sarah W. Forman, the portraits or oil paintings of my great-grand Parents, to be divided by themselves. And I bequeath the family coat-of-arms to my cousin Mrs. Sarah W. Forman.

The portraits and the arms are those reproduced by plates, for this work.

JOHN TEN BROECK (362).

The Ten Broeck farm at Raritan Landing, comprising the homestead and two hundred and twenty-five acres of land, was sold by John Ten Broeck to Edward Stelle

on the fourteenth of January, 1813. The deed is recorded at New Brunswick in Book 9, page 768.

Children of John Ten Broeck (362) and Sarah Edgar.

620   I MARY SCOTT, baptized at New Brunswick Presbyterian Church May 4, 1811; married June 5,
1833, Marinus W. Warne, of New York. }

621   II SARAH ANN; married —— Storms.

622   III WARNE.

Children of Catharine Ten Broeck (363) and David Gulick.

623   I ELIZA WEBSTER, born February 27, 1811; died Feb-
ruary 21, 1890; married May 7, 1834, the Rev.
Enoch Van Aken, born July 21, 1808, died
January 2, 1885, son of John E. Van Aken and
Rachel Van Vliet, of Esopus, N. Y.

624   II ALEXANDER, born April 9, 1814; married Maria
Louisa Coons, who died in 1894. He was a
clergyman.

625   III MARY SCOTT, born March 29, 1818; died August 6,
1854; unmarried.

626   IV JANE GARRETSON, born September 17, 1822; died
March 18, 1889; married April 3, 1851, John
Van Aken, born May 7, 1825, died December
14, 1894, son of William Van Aken and his first
wife, Polly Van Benschoten.

627   V NANCY SCOTT, born March 8, 1826; died February
13, 1897; married Frederick Frelinghuysen
Elmendorf, who died October 11, 1885; no
children.

628   VI JAMES; died in infancy.

Children of Jane Ten Broeck (365) and Rev. Henry V. Garretson.

629   I REMSEN; died February 6, 1843, aged 26.

630   II JOHN; married Sarah Jones.

631   III ROBERT; died unmarried.

632   IV HENRY; died unmarried.

633   V DAVID GULICK; married Margaret Turner.

634   VI ELIZA SCOTT; married William C. Wile, M. D.

Children of Mary (Polly) Ten Broeck (366) and Abraham A. Van Fleet.

635   I PETER TEN BROECK; born September 8, 1802.

636   II CORNELIUS WYKOFF, born May 4, 1804; died April 12, 1866; unmarried.

637   III SAMUEL W., born July 25, 1806; died August 12, 1878; married Mary M. Moore, born August 8, 1815, died June 30, 1893.

638   IV ABRAHAM, born May 10, 1814; died May 19, 1814.

639   V WILLIAM GEARY, born December 5, 1818; married May 13, 1840, Rebecca Voorhees, born December 29, 1815, died August 11, 1887, daughter of John Voorhees and Helen Thompson.

Children of Mary Ten Broeck (366) and her second husband, Edward E. Cox.

640   I CLARISSA S., born April, 1825; died June 14, 1825.

641   II ARTHUR SUTPHIN, born February 12, 1828.

EMMA TEN BROECK (367).

Emma, the second daughter of Peter Ten Broeck, of Readington (190), married in her twenty-fifth year John, the son of Samuel Runk, and Margaret Snyder.

22

At the time of her marriage she went to Kingwood, in the upper part of Hunterdon County, New Jersey, where her husband's family resided. Here the public life of John Runk commenced, when he was made a member of the Board of Chosen Freeholders in 1825, which position he held for eight years. He was elected sheriff of the county in 1836, and served three years. In 1844 he was elected member of Congress, and four years later, in the position of presidential elector, he cast his vote for General Zachary Taylor for President. In 1850 he was nominated for Governor of New Jersey, but failed to be elected owing to a small adverse majority.

On the twenty-fifth of November, 1848, Emma Ten Broeck Runk died at Kingwood, leaving a family of seven sons and three daughters. She had been their ideal, and the harmony and beauty of her daily life were a legacy to each of them in all the years to come.

In 1854 Hon. John Runk removed to Lambertville, New Jersey. He was here elected a member of the Board of Chosen Freeholders, and was the Director for two years. He was a charter member of the Society of Free Masons, and filled the position of Treasurer for many years.

He was a man of fine physique, eminently endowed with social qualities. His knowledge of men, generous hospitality, and above all true nobility of character caused him to be highly esteemed by the community at large.

His death occurred at Lambertville on the twenty-second of September, 1872.

Children of Emma Ten Broeck (367) and John Runk.

642   I MARGARETTA SNYDER, born March 16, 1813; died August 4, 1892; married June 26, 1844, William G. Mentz, born February 17, 1808, died September 18, 1881, son of George W. Mentz, of Philadelphia, and Hannah.

643   II WILLIAM, born November 9, 1814; died in Brooklyn, L. I., November 29, 1871; married March 23, 1848, Ann Rebecca Halsey Seymour, born October 24, 1829, died July 23, 1872, daughter of William N. Seymour and Ann R. G. Halsey.

644   III MARY ANN, born November 11, 1816; died in Philadelphia October 10, 1895; married December 14, 1853 (his second wife), Stacy B. Barcroft, born January 29, 1795, died March 19, 1870, son of Ambrose Barcroft, Sr., and his third wife, Francena Opdycke, widow of John Hoagland.

645   IV PETER TEN BROECK, born April 15, 1818; died at Elderton, Pa., March 31, 1860; married June 4, 1845, Fanny Barcroft, born August 26, 1821, daughter of Ambrose Barcroft, Jr., and Anna Woolverton.

646   V CANDACE, born September 17, 1819; died October 29, 1819.

647   VI SAMUEL, born December 9, 1820; died September 16, 1892; married April 13, 1865, Lucy Lind, born May 13, 1841, daughter of Joseph Lind and Sarah McCammon, and widow of Joseph H. Ingersoll.

648   VII LEWIS WATERHOUSE, born March 14, 1823; died at Readington, N. J., December 27, 1882.

649 VIII GEORGE ALEXANDER, born August 24, 1825; died
July 25, 1887; married March 24, 1877, Letitia
Roberson, born January 27, 1826, died March
23, 1888, daughter of William Roberson and
Sarah West.

650 IX JANE CORYELL, born November 12, 1827.

651 X DE WITT CLINTON, born January 8, 1830.

652 XI JOHN, born January 10, 1833.

Child of John P. Ten Broeck (370) and Elizabeth Waterhouse.

653 I PATIENCE GERTRUDE, born March 12, 1838; married
at Rochelle, Ill., January 14, 1858, Albert G.
Hoadley, born January 26, 1836, son of Enoch
Hoadley and Samanthe Flagg.

Children of Elizabeth Ten Broeck (371) and George W. Waterhouse.

654 I MARY L., born December 10, 1836; died May 24,
1846.

655 II SAMUEL R., born December 23, 1838; died April
5, 1871.

656 III CATHARINE TEN BROECK, born July 1, 1841; married
June 16, 1864, Jacob Whiteman, born August
20, 1837, son of Jacob Whiteman and Caroline
Spangenburg.

657 IV SARAH TEN BROECK, born July 29, 1843; died January 19, 1866.

658 V JANE L., born October 8, 1845; died February 5,
1868.

659 VI ANNA M., born May 29, 1848; died March 24, 1873.

660 VII PETER TEN BROECK, born February 12, 1851; died
May 27, 1857.

661 VIII SIDNEY H., born October 4, 1853; died February 6,
1864.

662 IX MINERVA T., born December 24, 1857.

Child of Catharine V. F. Ten Broeck (372) and Cornelius V. D. Nevius.

663 I PETER TEN BROECK, born November 13, 1840; died
at Plainfield, N. J., September 13, 1894; married November 3, 1869, Mary E. Sharpe, born
April 19, 1848, daughter of Wessel Ten Broeck
Sharpe and Mary Ann Myer.

Children of Peter Q. Ten Broeck (373) and Sarah K. Shurts.

664 I CATHARINE M., born January 26, 1843; married 1st,
January, 1866, William F. Rowland, of Brook-
lyn, L. I., born 1838, died at Elizabeth, N. J.,
August 9, 1876, son of William Rowland and
Mary Whareham; married 2d, October 20, 1879,
John C. Joralemon, born at Belleville, N. J.,
December, 1830, son of Christopher Joralemon
and Catharine Van Iderstine.

665 II HENRY SHURTS, born January 26, 1845; died July
1, 1863.

666 III JANE ELIZABETH, born November 26, 1847; married
July 19, 1869, William Henry Hill, born No-
vember 15, 1845, son of William Hill and Eliza
Hackett Lowe.

667 IV THEODORE, born October 16, 1849; died January 11,
1850.

668 V SARAH ALLETTA, born February 14, 1852; married
1870, John Pierson.

669   vi MARY EMMA, born July 1, 1855; died November 13, 1856.

670   vii FRANK LA RUE, born February 8, 1857; married January 14, 1879, Minnie Newell Smith, born January 11, 1861, daughter of Joseph Smith and Harriet De Jonks.

671   viii GEORGE WASHINGTON, born February 17, 1861; died April 21, 1861.

Children of Jane G. Ten Broeck (374) and John Voorhees Schomp.

672   i PETER J., born August 28, 1843; married December 28, 1864, Lucretia Ann Griggs, born June 6, 1847, daughter of Abram Prall Griggs and Sarah Herder.

673   ii WILHELMINA, born March 7, 1846; married April 16, 1868, John Schomp, born June 2, 1843, died September 14, 1896, son of Jacob G. Schomp and Eliza Van Fleet.

674   iii JOHN TEN BROECK, born January 12, 1849; married February 9, 1870, Lydia Conover Polhemus, born April 29, 1854, daughter of Theodore Polhemus and Ellen Ten Eyck.

675   iv LEWIS RUNK, born July 28, 1853; died August 10, 1853.

Children of Sarah F. Ten Broeck (375) and Joseph Trimmer.

676   i ANNIE JOSEPHINE, born December 19, 1851; died January 28, 1853.

677   ii SAMUEL TEN BROECK, born September 4, 1853.

678   iii EDWARD CROSIER, born February 10, 1857.

Children of Sarah Ten Broeck (377) and John Forman.

679   I JANE TEN BROECK, born August 27, 1815; died February 9, 1885; unmarried.

680   II WILLIAM VAN RENSSELAER.

681   III HENRIETTA H.; married Henry Hughes.

682   IV ELIZA HARVEY BEEKMAN.

683   V SAMUEL HARVEY; died young.

684   VI MARY MATILDA; died young.

Child of John V. R. Ten Broeck (379) and his first wife, Ida McIntire.

685   I VAN RENSSELAER; killed during the late Civil War.

Children of John V. R. Ten Broeck (379) and his second wife, Sarah Tremper Hopkins.

686   I JANE, born May 9, 1843; died November 9. 1843.

687   II ARINTHA, born August 9, 1845; married November, 1874, William A. Robinson.

688   III WOODHULL KROSEN, born March 14, 1851; married February 3, 1871, Carrie E. Lasher.

Children of Emma C. Ten Broeck (380) and James V. Spader.

689   I KROSEN TEN BROECK, born October 18, 1822; married April 4, 1855, Mary E. Franken, daughter of Mourents E. Franken, of Curaçao, W. I., and Maria J. Brion.

690   II ISAAC VOORHEES, born August 7, 1827; died January 29, 1857; married September 17. 1851, Elizabeth Hicks, born September 14, 1827, died March 9. 1865, daughter of John Hicks and Mary Dunn.

691 III WILLIAM VAN DERVEER, born November 21, 1831;
died May 19, 1853; unmarried.

Children of Richard Krosen Ten Broeck (381) and Caroline L. Fletcher.

692 I JOHN DENNIS, born November 27, 1827; died at
Savannah, Ga., April 17, 1886; married July
13, 1853, Emily Bliss, born July 14, 1832,
daughter of James Burt Bliss and Eliza Smith.

693 II JAMES BOND READ, born March 6, 1830; died July
10, 1830.

Children of Jane G. Ten Broeck (382) and Isaac Voorhees.

694 I AUGUSTUS, born September 28, 1828; married January 28, 1851, Maria Voorhees, born December
14, 1826, died May 26, 1876.

695 II TERRESSA, born Jan. 13, 1830; died Sept. 9, 1837.

696 III SARAH F., born November 13, 1833; died January
27, 1894; married September 10, 1856, Rev.
John Martin Wagner, born at Flonheim, Ger-
many, July 8, 1826, died January 21, 1894, in
Brooklyn, L. I. Graduated from Rutgers, 1853,
and New Brunswick Theo. Sem., 1856.

697 IV JANE, born Sept. 19, 1836; died Oct. 28, 1841.

698 V TERRESSA, born May 6, 1839; died Oct. 26, 1841.

699 VI JANE, born June 13, 1842; died Aug. 17, 1842.

700 VII CORNELIA, born April 16, 1844; married September
18, 1867, Gilbert S. Van Pelt, son of Gilbert
S. Van Pelt, of New Brunswick, N. J., and
Margaret Chambers Davidson.

Children of Peter V. R. Ten Broeck (383) and Ann Eliza Arnold.

701   I MARTHA S., married Lewis Campbell, of Metuchen, N. J.

702   II JANE, unmarried.

Child of Mary Ten Broeck (385) and William F. Mayell.

703   I HENRY, born May 12, 1824; died in Albany, August 18, 1890; married December 24, 1845, Elizabeth Northrop, born April 3, 1825, died June 22, 1893, daughter of Isaac M. Northrop and Nancy Stiles.

ELIZABETH H. TEN BROECK (386).

Elizabeth was the youngest daughter of Dr. Samuel W. Ten Broeck (193), and her entire life was spent at Shrewsbury, N. J.

She was married to John P. Corlies by banns, published in Christ Church on the fourteenth of November, 1824. She died when her only child was four months old, and was buried with her father's family, in the Presbyterian churchyard. The inscription on the stone is at least curious. It reads:

> Sacred to the memory of
> Elizabeth H., wife of John P. Corlies,
> who departed this life May 22, 1827,
> aged 24 years, one month and six days.

Husband, child, and parents, too,
Relatives, friends, and world, adieu.
Dearest Lord, thou hast called me to an interview,
Therefore cheerfully give up all for you.

23

Child of Elizabeth H. Ten Broeck (386) and John P. Corlies.

704   I MARY JANE, born January 17, 1827; died August 14, 1827.

Children of Maria Bodyn Ten Broeck (391) and Joseph Ketchum.

705   I JOHN TEN BROECK, born June 6, 1805; died February 10, 1832; married 1st, November 30, 1830, Caroline Elizabeth Cargill; married 2d, January 25, 1836, at Plattsburg, N. Y., Lucy Ann Swetland, born September 11, 1817, daughter of William Swetland and —— Meyers.

706   II SAMUEL, born July 27, 1807; died 1826.

707   III MARY LANE, born March 9, 1810; died January 6, 1877; unmarried.

708   IV CHARLES, born May 15, 1812; died June 3, 1812.

709   V JOSEPH, born October 16, 1813; died November 23, 1883; married in Brooklyn, January 3, 1839, Sarah Hannah Keeler, born at Norwalk, Conn., March 9, 1824, daughter of Joseph Keeler and Hannah Hoyt.

710   VI ANNA CATHARINE, born September 20, 1824; died May 1, 1878; unmarried.

Children of Anna Van Schaick Ten Broeck (392) and Thomas Hillhouse.

711   I SARAH ANN, born July 8, 1813; died at Ithaca, N. Y., July 26, 1890; married April 17, 1838 (his second wife), Amos Stone Perry, born at Sherborn, Mass., December 1, 1801, died January 9, 1888, son of West Perry and Mary Stone.

712   ii THOMAS, born March 10, 1816; married December 11, 1844, Harriet Prouty, born May 28, 1823, daughter of Phineas Prouty, of Geneva, N. Y., and Margaret Matilda Van Vranken.

713   iii JOHN, born December 17, 1817; died March 29, 1882; married May 26, 1847, Catharine Mynderse Van Vranken, born July 23, 1825, died October 15, 1880, daughter of Nicholas Van Vranken and Janet McClelland.

714   iv WILLIAM (M. D.), born November 22, 1820; married 1st, June 25, 1845, Cornelia Lawrence Hillhouse, born November 19, 1825, died June 26, 1851, daughter of James Abraham Hillhouse and Cornelia Ann Lawrence, of New Haven, Conn.; there were no children. He married, 2d, January 18, 1854, Frances J. Betts, born November 27, 1823, daughter of Samuel R. Betts and Caroline A. Dewey.

SEVENTH GENERATION.

❧

Children of Richard M. Livingston (413) and his first wife, Mary
Barnard.

715   I JOHN, born June 23, 1799; married in 1835, Nancy
Standing.

716   II STEPHEN, born August 22, 1803; married September
13, 1826, Annie Belcher, died October 6, 1843.

717   III RICHARD M., born January 20, 1806; married October 20, 1829, Eunice Humphrey.

718   IV HENRIETTA E., born April 3, 1813; unmarried.

719   V PERMELIA, born July 27, 1815; married June 6, 1849,
Otis Searles.

720   VI MARIETTA (or MARGARET), born November 2, 1820;
married October 3, 1848, Wilson Phelps.

721   VII EDMUND, born September 30, 1822; married September 28, 1847, Adaline Stoddard.

722   VIII EDWARD, born September 30, 1822; died September
12, 1894; married September 6, 1849, Phoebe
Amanda Curtis, born February 8, 1829, daughter of Henry Curtis and Hannah Lyman.

Children of Stephen Livingston (414) and his first wife, Maria Hartshorn.

723   I RENSSELAER, born in 1806; married Catharine Cronk.

724   II ELIZA, born January 12, 1808; died July 7, 1864; married Charles W. Lynde of Brooklyn.

725   III MARGARET C., born July 4, 1809; married John H. Murray of Johnstown, Montgomery Co., N. Y.

726   IV JANE AUGUSTA, born April 12, 1811; died May 23, 1848; married July 21, 1834, Edward Hezekiah Owen of New York, born December 10, 1807, died September 21, 1876.

727   V JOHN STEPHEN, born March 20, 1813; married Julia Waterbury.

728   VI MARIA, born May 15, 1814; died February 14, 1872 married Edward Wells, of Johnstown, N. Y.

729   VII WILLIAM HENRY, born November 20, 1816; married Mary Beckley.

730   VIII ALFRED, born January 3, 1819; married Martha Gillesbré of New York.

731   IX DANIEL CADY, born November 26, 1820; married Sarah Margaret Stewart of Johnstown, N. Y.

732   X EDWARD WILLARD, born October 20, 1823.

733   XI SELAH OTIS, born September 30, 1826.

734   XII CHARLES MONTGOMERY, born October 28, 1828.

Children of Margaret Chinn Livingston (420) and Daniel Cady.

735   I HARRIET, born November 9, 1802; died March 3, 1810.

736   II TRYPHENA, born September 11, 1804; died in 1892;
married May 21, 1827, Edward Bayard, son of
James Bayard. No children.

737   III ELEAZER LIVINGSTON, born May 26, 1806; died
August 16, 1826; unmarried.

738   IV JAMES LIVINGSTON, born October 14, 1808; died
August 5, 1809.

739   V HARRIET ELIZA, born October 5, 1810; died March
11, 1894; married Daniel Cady Eaton, died
in Paris, France, June 11, 1855, son of Professor
Ames Eaton of Troy, N. Y.

740   VI DANIEL, born June 24, 1814; died October 27, 1814.

741   VII ELIZABETH, born November 12, 1815; married May
1, 1840, Henry Brewster Stanton, born June 27,
1805, died January 14, 1887, son of Joseph
Stanton and Susan M. Brewster.

742   VIII MARGARET CHINN, born December 9, 1817; married
September 5, 1842, Duncan Mac Martin, born
February 24, 1817, died July 6, 1894, son of
Peter Mac Martin and Flora McIntyre.

743   IX CATHARINE HENRY, born January 7, 1820; married
at Johnstown, Montgomery Co., N. Y., June
14, 1841, Samuel Wilkeson, born May 9, 1817,
died at New York, December 2, 1889, son of
Samuel Wilkeson of Buffalo, N. Y., and Jane
Oram.

744   X ELEAZER LIVINGSTON, born January 28, 1827; died
September 24, 1829.

Child of Stephen Van Rensselaer (452) and his first wife, Margarita
Schuyler.

745   i Stephen, born 1789; died 1868; married, 1817, Harriet Bayard.

Children of Stephen Van Rensselaer (452) and his second wife, Cornelia
Paterson.

746   i Catharine, born 1803; died 1874; married 1830,
Gouverneur Wilkins.   No children.

747   ii William, born 1805; died, 1872.

748   iii Philip S., born October 14, 1806; died June 1, 1871;
married October 17, 1839, Mary Rebecca Tall-
madge, born May 16, 1817, died August 3,
1872, daughter of James and Laura Tallmadge.

749   iv Cortlandt, born May 26, 1808; died July 25, 1860;
married September 13, 1836, Catharine Ledyard
Cogswell, born September 22, 1811, died December 24, 1882, daughter of Mason Fitch
Cogswell and Mary Ledyard.

750   v Henry, born May 14, 1810; died March 23, 1864;
married August 22, 1833, Elizabeth Ray King,
born August 17, 1815, daughter of John Alsop
King and Mary Ray.

751   vi Cornelia Paterson, born July 8, 1812; died Jan-
uary 16, 1890; married February 16, 1847,
Robert J. Turnbull of Charleston, S. C., born
October 3, 1807, died June 4, 1854.

752   vii Alexander, born 1814; died 1878; married 1st,
1851, Mary Howland; married 2d, 1864, Louisa
Barnewall.

753 VIII EUPHEMIA WHITE, born, 1816; died, 1888; married
1843, John Church Cruger of New York City.

754 IX WESTERLO, born 1820; died 1844; unmarried.

Children of Elizabeth Van Rensselaer (454) and her first husband, John
Bradstreet Schuyler.

755 I PHILIP, born October 26, 1788; died in Pelham,
N. Y., February 12, 1865; married September
12, 1811, Grace Hunter, born May 10, 1790,
died in Pelham, December 23, 1855, daughter
of Robert Hunter of New York and Ruth Brick.

756 II STEPHEN VAN RENSSELAER, born May 4, 1790;
died young.

Children of Elizabeth Van Rensselaer (454) and her second husband,
John Bleecker.

757 I STEPHEN VAN RENSSELAER, died April 26, 1826;
unmarried.

758 II JOHN RUTGER, died July 19, 1832; unmarried.

759 III CATHARINE WESTERLO, born October 1, 1809; died
September 12, 1886; married October 31, 1826,
Cornelius Glen Van Rensselaer of Greenbush,
N. Y.

Children of Margaret Stuyvesant Ten Broeck (457) and Rev. Robert
Gibson.

760 I ROBERT PHILLIPS, born April 3, 1819; died at New
York, December 27, 1890; married July 1, 1845,
Susanna Moser, born January 7, 1822, daugh-
ter of George Moser and Sarah Graeff of Lan-
caster, Pa. (Princeton, Class of 1845; New
York College of Medicine, 1855.)

ANNA BENNER (TEN BROECK) (475).
From the Oil-Portrait of 1834

761   II CORNELIA STUYVESANT, born April, 1821; died August 31, 1883; married Joseph B. Enos of Waterford, N. Y.   No children.

762   III JOHN BRECKENRIDGE (D. D.), born 1823; died at Williams Bridge, N. Y., June 7, 1896; married May 13, 1847, Fanny P. Wood of New York.

Children of Rev. Peter Stuyvesant Ten Broeck (458) and Lucretia Loring Cutter.

763   I PETER GERARD STUYVESANT (M. D.), born October 8, 1822; died December 19, 1867; married August 8, 1864, Mary Octavia Woodbury, born April 1, 1834, daughter of William White Woodbury and Octavia Kidder.   No children.

764   II WILLIAM CUTTER, born January 14, 1829; died December 28, 1865; unmarried.   (Bowdoin College, 1849.)

765   III EDWARD PAYSON, born January 1, 1839; died at Chicago, Ill., July 22, 1892; married December 11, 1860, Mary Augusta Deane, born January 5, 1839, daughter of Ebenezer Furbish Deane and Emily Lord.

766   IV CORNELIA STUYVESANT, born June 26, 1820; died January 18, 1892; married May 30, 1853, George Edwin Bartol Jackson, born August 14, 1829, died at Portland, Me., October 19, 1891, son of Henry Jackson and Elizabeth Durgin.

767   V LUCRETIA MITCHELL, born July 7, 1824; married May 10, 1843, Nathaniel Bradley Baker, born September 29, 1818, died September 13, 1876, son of Abel Baker and Nancy Bradley.

24

768   VI HARRIET CUTTER, born September 11, 1833; mar-
        ried September 20, 1854, Francis Bolles Pea-
        body, born October 27, 1827, son of Stephen
        Peabody and Jerusha Pride Bolles.

769   VII HELENA LOUISA, born October 31, 1835; died May
        26, 1891; married May 23, 1860, Thomas
        Franklin, born May 6, 1828, died November
        15, 1886, son of Walter Simonds Franklin and
        Sarah Buel.   No children.

JACOB TEN BROECK (475).

He was born in Clermont (now Germantown), Columbia County, N. Y., on the thirteenth of May, 1800.
Here he grew to the age of manhood, and remained
until 1844, when he removed to the town of Greenport,
in the same county.   After living there for two years he
gave the farm to one of his sons, and took up his residence in the city of Hudson.

He at once became active in the affairs of the city.   He
was a charter-director of the Farmers' National Bank of
Hudson, and outlived all those with whom he was so associated, serving continuously in the capacity of director
throughout his life.

In 1862 he represented the First Assembly District of
the County of Columbia in the State Legislature.   In
1863 and 1864 he was mayor of Hudson, and owing to
the Civil War had an unusually responsible and laborious
administration, the duties of which he performed with
the ability and honor that always characterized him as
a public official.[98]

JACOB TEN BROECK (1175)
From the Oil-Portrait of 1834

He had, throughout his life, been industrious and en-
terprising, and by the application of these qualities to
business, he secured an honorable reputation and a
competency.

From early manhood he was an exemplary Christian.
At Clermont his home was the center for ministerial
hospitality — an open house for every good cause. He
ever maintained the same spirit of charity, and was a
constant contributor to the Reformed Dutch Church, of
which he was a loyal son. He served as elder, both in
Germantown and Hudson, as long as his strength permitted.

About 1840 he was captain of militia in Clermont,
and the "general training days," with their bright military trappings, were festive and memorable occasions.

Jacob Ten Broeck died in Hudson, on the twenty-
fourth of March, 1883. He had married at St. John's,
Red Hook, on the sixth of November, 1821, Anna, the
daughter of Henry Benner and Catharine Pitcher. The
Benner family were of ancient lineage in Upper Bavaria,
honored for brave deeds in the days of the crusades.

The portraits of Jacob Ten Broeck and his wife, painted
by Phillips in 1834, are owned by their daughter, Miss
Christina Catharine Ten Broeck of Hudson.

This branch of the family represents one of the rare
instances in our country in which the name "homestead" stands for the property that has been continuously in the line, from father to son, for eight generations.
Part of the tract of six hundred acres purchased of Robert Livingston by Dirck Wesselse Ten Broeck (3), while
a merchant of Albany, is now the home of Jacob Ten

Broeck's grandson. Unfortunately, part of the original purchase was taken from the lawful owners, in those troublous times when Great Britain demanded taxes from a people who purposed to govern themselves.

Children of Jacob Ten Broeck (475) and Anna Benner.

770   I JACOB WESSEL, born April 22, 1823; died March 22, 1896; married May 24, 1848, Sarah Ann Evarts, born August 6, 1827, died October 6, 1886, daughter of Jacob Evarts and Gertrude De Lamater.

771   II WILLIAM HENRY, born April 22, 1823; died February 23, 1888; married February 24, 1847, Mary Jane Evarts, born August 6, 1827, daughter of Jacob Evarts and Gertrude De Lamater.

Twins.

772   III CHRISTINA CATHARINE, born May 1, 1825.

773   IV HELEN MARIA, born October 21, 1827; married September 26, 1854, Abraham S. Bogardus, born August 6, 1826, died February 6, 1885.

774   V JANE ANN, born at Germantown, April 22, 1830; married September 27, 1848, William Rowe Moore, born August 22, 1826, son of Garret Moore and Lanah (Helen) Rowe.

775   VI ANDREW JACKSON, born August 5, 1832; died October 31, 1850; unmarried.

776   VII MARY ELIZABETH, born May 13, 1836; died February 4, 1874; married June 11, 1868, Refine Latong Rossman; no children.

777   VIII MARGARET, born May 27, 1839; died January 29, 1841.

CATHARINE M. TEN BROECK (DE WITT).
From the Oil-Portrait of 1834.

LENA (HELEN) TEN BROECK (476).

Helen Ten Broeck was born at Germantown, New York, on September the eighth, 1803. On the twentieth of September, 1836, she became the wife of Rev. Thomas K. Lape, then pastor of the Lutheran Church at Athens. She died in less than four years afterward, and left no children. Her portrait, painted by Phillips in 1834,—two years before her marriage,—is still in the home of her childhood at North Germantown, New York.

CATHARINE MARIA TEN BROECK (477).

Born on the twenty-sixth of July, 1805, she married on November the first, 1826, William Henry De Witt, the fourth son of John I. De Witt, of "The Embocht," Greene County, New York, whose ancestors had been eminent in public affairs in Holland.

William H. De Witt's early life was spent upon his father's farm, and he attended the schools nearest at hand. Possessed of great mental aptitude, his parents sent him to Rutgers College, New Jersey. After the college course he entered upon the study of law, but not finding this congenial he relinquished it, and returned to the farm.

Shortly after, he married Catharine M. Ten Broeck. She was a woman of good judgment, amiable, unselfish, and conscientious — one who had friends in every circle. In 1830 they purchased the Seth Ten Broeck farm at Germantown, adjoining that of Jacob Ten Broeck (475).

Possessed of a keen intellect and of untiring energy,

William H. De Witt was upright and fearless. He was
politically active, and was regarded as a wise party
leader, but was never induced to accept any public office
of importance. He was a close and trusted friend of
Martin Van Buren, De Witt Clinton (who was also a
relative), and others prominent in affairs of the State.

He died on the twenty-fifth of March, 1886. After
his death, Catharine Ten Broeck De Witt frequently
spent the winters with her daughter, Mrs. Isaac Carhart,
in Brooklyn, and her death occurred there on the twenty-
seventh of March, 1896. They are both buried in the
hallowed ground of the old churchyard at Germantown,
New York.

The portraits painted in 1834 by Phillips are now in
possession of their daughter, Mrs. Charles H. Hover, of
Germantown.

Children of Catharine M. Ten Broeck (477) and William H. De Witt.

778   I JACOB TEN BROECK, born May 29, 1828; died at
Milwaukee, Wis., February 3, 1876; married
in Brooklyn, N. Y., October 23, 1851, Juliet
Louise May, born May 8, 1831, drowned by
the foundering of the "Ironsides" off Grand
Haven, Mich., September 15, 1873.

779   II MARY JANE, born at Catskill, N. Y., March 22, 1830 ;
married at Germantown, N. Y., October 27,
1851, Benjamin Townsend Hoogland, born
March 25, 1829, died at Brooklyn, September
15, 1890, son of Col. Benjamin R. Hoogland
and Eliza Van Alst. He was a descendant of
Sarah Rapalje, the first white child born in New
Netherlands, June 9, 1625.

WILLIAM H. DE WITT.
From the Oil-Portrait of 1834.

780 III JOHN, born August 14, 1832; died August 23, 1834.

781 IV MARTIN VAN BUREN, born April 17, 1835; married December 2, 1864, Jane C. Hover, born at Germantown, N. Y., August 27, 1840, daughter of Jonas Hover and Ann Sturges.

782 V HELEN CHRISTINA, born at Germantown, N. Y., April 9, 1838; married April 29, 1858, Everlin Beckley Hamlin, born at Hudson, Ohio, August 14, 1836, son of Charles Rogers Hamlin and Sarah D. Beckley. No children.

783 VI CATHARINE ANN, born April 3, 1841; married September 9, 1873, Isaac Carhart, born at Middletown, N. J., March 14, 1815, son of George Carhart and Mary Herbert. No children.

784 VII ADA TEN BROECK, born January 23, 1843; married February 1, 1883, Charles H. Hover, son of Chauncey Hover and Julia Elmendorf.

785 VIII EUGENE, born July 12, 1846; married July 24, 1870, Barbara R. Lasher, daughter of George I. Lasher and Hannah Barringer.

Child of Leonard Doll Ten Broeck (488) and Marietta Veadenburg.

786 I JOHN H.

Child of John Herman Ten Broeck (489) and Letitia A. Younglove.

787 I A daughter; married Herbert W. Grindal.

Children of Cornelius Ten Broeck (491) and Georgina Pearson.

788 I GEORGE PEARSON, born July 31, 1834; died May 20, 1871; unmarried.

789　II SARAH ANNA, born February 1, 1842; died April 6, 1886; married March 10, 1864, Nathan Brewster Morse, Jr.; died February 21, 1879.

790　III EDWARD BRINCKERHOFF, born November 20, 1845; married in Albany, June 15, 1881, Lydia Sanford Ransom.

791　IV ELIZABETH, born July 7, 1851; died March 1, 1883; unmarried.

Children of Albertina Ten Broeck (494) and David Evans.

792　I JACOB LEONARD, born September 15, 1838; married 1st, July 21, 1864, Melissa A. Yoemans, born April 7, 1844, died November 18, 1881, daughter of Calvin Yoemans and Elsie Warner; married 2nd, January 8, 1883, Jennie Ashton.

793　II MARTIN VAN BUREN, born February 29, 1840; married April 4, 1871, Lilian C. Chamberlain, born April 5, 1850, daughter of Aaron Chamberlain and Nancy Pellet.

794　III JANE, born March 4, 1842; died February 4, 1848.

795　IV ELLA, born February 2, 1844; married April 4, 1870, Luke Collins, born at Brighton, England, March 5, 1809, died November 11, 1893, son of James Collins.

796　V ALICE ELIZABETH, born January 8, 1848.

797　VI FRANK, born March 29, 1850; died February 15, 1854.

798　VII D. EVADORE, born May 11, 1852; died August 17, 1855.

799 viii Lafayette, born October 27, 1855; married August
25, 1883, Rose Elizabeth Redhead, born February 25, 1861, daughter of William Redhead
and Ann Ralph.

800 ix Spencer, born January 26, 1857; died March 18,
1864.

Children of Emma Ten Broeck (495) and Addison W. Potter.

801 i Anna Eliza, born September 22, 1844; married
Charles N. Moore.

802 ii Peleg A., born March 15, 1847; married Martha
St. Barnard.

Children of Gertrude Ann Ten Broeck (496) and Isaac H. Smith.

803 i George W., born April 8, 1843; married May 19,
1868, Sophia Koons, born September 14, 1844,
daughter of William P. Koons and Mary M.
Kastendike.

804 ii Emma Ten Broeck, born August 24, 1844; married
December 16, 1873, Alexander Scott.

Children of Theodore Ten Broeck (497) and Lucetta Salisbury.

805 i Jennie, born March 28, 1857; died young.

806 ii Theodore, born August 20, 1859; of Syracuse, N. Y.

Children of Samuel Ten Broeck (499) and Maria Parks.

807 i Elizabeth, born December 31, 1836, at Livingston;
married John A. Traver of Rhinebeck.

808 ii Samuel P., born March 20, 1839; married October
25, 1876, Adaline Monfort of Wappingers, N. Y.

25

809   III JANE, born May 9, 1841 ; married December 4, 1867,
         William Haines of Rhinebeck.

810   IV LORENZO, born October 1, 1843 ; married October
         25, 1876, Susan Nelson of Rhinebeck.

811   V MARY, born March 10, 1846, at Rhinebeck.

812   VI CHARLES, born December 21, 1849.

813 VII DERRICK WESSEL, born August 12, 1852 ; died Jan-
         uary 12, 1857.

814 VIII KATE, born April 1, 1854 ; died March 27, 1874.

Children of Albertina M. Salpaugh (503) and Cornelius Bortle.

815   I HELEN, born October 20, 1836 ; married June, 1857,
         William H. Hedges, died about 1884.

816   II CORNELIA, born September 30, 1838 ; married 1st,
         February 22, 1858, Stephen Bachman, died
         April, 1863; married 2nd, July, 1874, Henry B.
         Van Vleck.

817 III CATHARINE ; died young.

818   IV EMMA ; died young.

819   V WILLIAM, born April, 1843 ; died 1877 ; unmarried.

820   VI KATE, born April 13, 1845 ; married September 3,
         1867, Madison Miller of Hudson, born October
         9, 1841.

821 VII FRANK, born 1848 ; married January 18, 1876, Ruth
         Goodrich.

Children of William Leonard Pitcher (506) and Etta Hubbard.

822   I MARGARET CATHARINE, born at Livingston, October
         27, 1844.

823   ii Leonard William, born October 14, 1846 ; married 1st, April 15, 1868, Jerusha B. Hall, died September 15, 1873 ; married 2nd, May 23, 1878, Anna D. Reynolds, died January 8, 1892 ; married 3d, August 19, 1893, Anna Elizabeth Sheak.

824   iii Mary Etta, born at Livingston, November 12, 1848 ; married January 4, 1871, at "Queechy Place," Esek Finch, of Canaan, N. Y., born April, 1847, son of David Finch and Catharine M. Sedgwick.

825   iv Emma Jane, born at Hudson, September 9, 1851.

826   v Elizabeth Ann, born April 13, 1854 ; died July 5, 1860.

Children of Henry Moffat Pitcher (508) and Frances M. Myers.

827   i Mary Catharine, born April, 1846 ; married November 4, 1878, Frederick Pells of Rhinebeck, son of David Pells and Abby Louise Shaffer.

828   ii Albertina, born July 18, 1848.

829   iii Gertrude, born August 28, 1850 ; married October, 1876, William H. Cramer of Rhinebeck, son of Charles J. Cramer and Evanna Van Steenburg.

830   iv John H., born April, 1853 ; married August, 1878, Mina Haws.

831   v Walter Ten Broeck, born January 31, 1856 ; married February, 1885, Anna Lent, daughter of Henry Lent.

832   vi Helen Francis, born April 23, 1858.

Children of Samuel Ten Broeck Pitcher (509) and Matilda Barringer.

833   I MARY, born October, 1856; married, probably 1880, Arthur Rifenburgh.

834   II LOUISE, born 1858; married, probably 1886, Horace Shedd.

835   III BEULAH, born 1868.

836   IV OLIVER, born February, 1875.

Children of Jane Livingston Ten Broeck (510) and Charles P. Sanders.

837   I ALEXANDER LINDSAY, born June 25, 1847; died October 29, 1847.

838   II LEONARD TEN BROECK, born at Scotia, N. Y., October 12, 1848.

839   III MARIA, born September 9, 1851; died September 24, 1851.

840   IV CHARLES PETER (Jr.), born November 16, 1856; married February 22, 1882, Anna Maria Beekman Lee, born January 29, 1860, daughter of William H. B. Lee and Rebecca P. De Graff.

841   V LIVINGSTON, born at Scotia, July 10, 1867.

Children of Samuel Ten Broeck (511) and Helen L. Brooks.

842   I LEONARD WILLIAM, born June 5, 1850; married 1st, November 16, 1882, Helen M. Pangburn, died November 25, 1883, widow of Abraham Lansing; married 2nd, Melissa Van Eps, widow of William Slover.

843   II MARIA LABAGH, born July 30, 1852; married Charles Bradt.

Children of Walter Tryon Livingston Ten Broeck (512) and Helen U. Schultz.

844   ɪ DIRCK WESSEL, born July 30, 1856; married at Cleveland, Ohio, March 8, 1897, Lula Gregory, born February 28, 1870, daughter of John Fisher Gregory and Blanche Lawrence.

845   ɪɪ PETER J. SCHULTZ, born October 14, 1857; died April 19, 1866.

846   ɪɪɪ HELEN ROWE, born August 3, 1860; married December 22, 1885, Wallace Traver, born March 5, 1857, son of Alexander S. Traver and Elizabeth S. Hughan.

847   ɪᴠ JANE LIVINGSTON, born June 19, 1862; died December 29, 1886.

848   ᴠ ALBERTINA SANDERS, born May 27, 1864.

849   ᴠɪ MARY ELIZABETH, born May 2, 1866.

850   ᴠɪɪ LUCY SCHULTZ, born November 29, 1867.

851   ᴠɪɪɪ WALTER TRYON LIVINGSTON, born January 16, 1872; married October 18, 1893, Clare Newell Fortney, born December 20, 1874, daughter of Rev. George W. Fortney and Anna L. Gunn.

Children of Albertina Sanders Ten Broeck (513) and Barent A. Mynderse, M. D.

852   ɪ HERMAN VEDDER (M. D.), born at Schenectady, May 29, 1861.

853   ɪɪ HELEN LIVINGSTON, born September 13, 1867.

854   ɪɪɪ WILLIAM TEN BROECK, born August 1, 1871.

Children of Eugene Livingston Sanders (516) and Lizzie A. Passage.

855   I CATHARINE MARY COX, born November 7, 1860; died December 9, 1864.

856   II DAVID PASSAGE, born March 3, 1863; married May 5, 1891, Susan Vanderpoel Tabb of Gloucester County, Va.

857   III JOHN, born October 2, 1869.

858   IV WALTER TRYON LIVINGSTON, born January 16, 1871.

Children of Mary Elizabeth Livingston Sanders (517) and Harold Wilson.

859   I ANNE HULME, born January 22, 1867.

860   II JANE LIVINGSTON, born April 24, 1870.

861   III SARAH HULME, born May 12, 1871.

862   IV WILLIAM HENRY, born December 26, 1875.

863   V HAROLD, born November 6, 1881.

Children of Catharine M. Sanders (519) and William J. Mott.

864   I JAMES WILLIS, born August 23, 1855.

865   II WILLIAM SANDERS, born February 19, 1865; married June 6, 1895, Annie Lloyd Moore of Virginia.

Children of William N. S. Sanders (522) and Catharine V. R. Osborn.

866   I HENRY OSBORN, born October 23, 1864.

867   II FRANCIS NICOLL, born October 1, 1870.

868   III EUGENE LIVINGSTON, born September 3, 1878; died October 12, 1895.

ANTHONY EDGAR BURT (526).

Anthony E. Burt was the son of Catharine Ten Broeck of Claverack, and the Rev. Moses Burt, a churchman of more than usual ability. He was born at Claverack, New York, on the twelfth of July, 1812, and in November, 1846, married Laura A. Jarvis.

He had chosen the ministry as his vocation, but his health failing, he was obliged to abandon it. He then went to Rensselaerville, N. Y., where for many years he conducted a school, well known for its high character and thoroughness. By example and precept, he stimulated his pupils to do their best.

He died on the ninth of September, 1886, and was buried from the Episcopal Church, of which he had been a communicant for more than half a century.

Child of Anthony E. Burt (526) and Laura A. Jarvis.

869   1 MARY FRANCES, born January 29, 1854.

ANTHONY TEN BROECK (529).

The Rev. Anthony Ten Broeck, D. D., was a presbyter in the Episcopal Church, some time rector of Grace Church, Newark, the Church of St. James the Less, Philadelphia, and finally of Eatontown, N. J.; but he was, above all, an educator. Early in his ministry he commenced a boys' school in Orange, N. J. He was for a time the head of Burlington College, and was the founder of the Bishop Bowman Institute for Young Ladies, in Pittsburg.

He was a man of strong will and firm purpose, of fine literary tastes and a wide range of study.

The last few years of his life were spent quietly in the small parish near the sea. He died on the twenty-second of September, 1880, and within the walls of St. Luke's Church, New York, where he had received ordination, he was buried in the family vault.

Children of Anthony Ten Broeck (529) and his first wife, Amelia Stagg.

870   I HENRY HOBART (Rev.), born July 8, 1839.

871   II WILLIAM PRAY (Rev.), born June 13, 1841 ; married February 3, 1864, Mary Elizabeth Yundt, born April 30, 1840, daughter of Joseph Yundt of Lafayette, Ind., and Mary Carpenter.

Children of Anthony Ten Broeck (529) and his second wife, Rhoda A. Brown.

872   I RHODA CATHARINE, born April 7, 1846.

873   II MARY, born July 29, 1848.

Children of Henry H. Ten Broeck (530) and Louise D. Barber.

874   I ANNIE L., born March 14, 1869.

875   II JOHN HENRY, born June 12, 1871 ; died August 13, 1872.

876   III SARAH MAY, born October 24, 1876.

877   IV MARSHALL HEBER, born December 4, 1878; died March 6, 1879.

878   V EDITH M., born December 8, 1881.

Children of Jane Everts Ten Broeck (539) and Samuel G. Waterman.

879   I ANNA.

880   II CLARA.

Child of Anthony C. Ten Broeck (541) and Catharine Waterman.

881   I CHARLES OSCAR, married Mary Warner.

Children of Cornelia A. Ten Broeck (545) and Isaac Warren Valence.

882   I ANNA CORNELIA, married David Ritchie.

883   II MARTHA, married Horace G. Nelson.

884   III UNA L.

Children of Christina C. Ten Broeck (546) and F. Asbury Ireland.

885   I WILLIAM TEN BROECK, married Julia Vandenburg, died October, 1876, aged 29.

886   II FRANCES JOSEPHINE, married James McD. Latham.

887   III JAMES MATHEW, married May Zella Pollock.

888   IV CORA CHRISTINA.

889   V ZILLA ASBURY.

Child of Elizabeth A. Ten Broeck (547) and Jacob Wetherwax.

890   I JEFFERSON.

Children of William M. Ten Broeck (548) and Kate Merrill.

891   I ERNEST MERRILL.

892   II LILIAN MARGARET.

893   III WILLIAM MATHEW.

894   IV RAY MELVIN.

26

Children of Delia M. Ten Broeck (549) and John Van Deusen Ten
Broeck (918).

895   I CULVER HALL, married Ella Johnson.

896   II SABINE, married Josephine Mitchell.

897   III ELLA MAUD.

898   IV LENA MAY.

Children of Cornelius Henry Ten Broeck (550) and Lucy A.
Vandenburg.

899   I LOTTIE A., married B. F. Vandenburg.

900   II MARTHA MALVINA.

Children of Julia F. Ten Broeck (551) and Moses Wetherwax.

901   I CHRISTINA FRANCES, married Levinus Fort.

902   II GEORGE ELMER.

903   III EDGAR.

Child of Samuel Ten Broeck Heermance (558) and Catharine M. Tobey.

904   I EMMA WARREN, born March 21, 1869.

Child of William T. Heermance (561) and Jane P. Hood.

905   I EDMUND VAN NESS, born December 3, 1868.

Children of Nicholas Ten Broeck Schuyler (564) and Martha A. Griffin.

906   I BENJAMIN G., born June 27, 1872.

907   II ANNA L., born January 28, 1874; married in Ore-
gon, December 28, 1893, J. E. Young.

908   III LUCY A., born October 20, 1875; died young.

909   IV MARTHA E., born May 6, 1877.

910   v HENRIETTA, born October 23, 1879.
911   vi MARY ALICE, born March 10, 1882.
912   vii EDITH MAY, born March 24, 1885,

Child of Anna H. Schuyler (565) and George W. Bodle.

913   i EDWIN S., born May 26, 1876.

Children of Harmon Jay Ten Broeck (566) and Mary C. Fowks.

914   i HARMON VAN LOAN, born February 18, 1855; died April 28, 1870.
915   ii RACHEL JANE, born March 14, 1868; died August 20, 1868.
916   iii ADA GRACE, born June 10, 1869; married July 21, 1892, Alexander Morris, of Greenbush, N. Y.
917   iv JOHN HENRY, born June 5, 1872.

Children of David S. Ten Broeck (571) and Alida Van Deusen.

918   i JOHN VAN DEUSEN, born May 18, 1835; married Delia M. Ten Broeck (549), born August 1, 1837, daughter of William C. Ten Broeck and Christina Van Deusen.
919   ii CORNELIA CHRISTINA, born November 26, 1841.
919a   iii WESSEL.
919b   iv MATHEW.

Children of Walter V. Ten Broeck (572) and Elizabeth Clum.

920   i WILLIAM EDGAR, born October 17, 1843; died September 27, 1872, married December 24, 1867, Mary F. Miller of Niverville, N. Y.

921   II Philip Clum, born November 11, 1848; married November 6, 1872, Ida D. Crocheron of Hudson, N. Y., born August 9, 1849, daughter of Philip Crocheron and Mary E. Best.

Children of Jacob L. Ten Broeck (574) and Elizabeth M. Clum.

922   I WILLIAM HENRY, born July 2, 1839; married March 14, 1865, Martha L. Niles, born August 13, 1843.

923   II CHRISTINA E., born July 27, 1841; died April 7, 1863.

924   III JOHN H., born August 31, 1843.

925   IV EDWARD AMBROSE, born March 27, 1846; married October 10, 1865, Anna Disbrow, born October 23, 1850.

926   V CHAUNCEY ALLEN, born April 3, 1849.

927   VI STANTON S., born April 16, 1852; died September 28, 1866.

928   VII MARY KATHERINE, born January 1, 1855; died October 1, 1860.

Children of William Ambrose Ten Broeck (575) and Mary Ann Comfort.

929   I CHARLES CORNWALL, born May 7, 1846; married May 7, 1873, Martha Godkins, born May 3, 1846, daughter of Frederick Godkins and Jemima Van Wagonen.

930   II WILLIAM BOWEN, born March 15, 1849.

931   III HELEN JOSEPHINE, born September 4, 1854; died May 24, 1889; married February 26, 1879, W. H. Swart, of Heath, Ulster Co., N. Y.

932   IV HENRY HILL, born October 2, 1856; married October 24, 1878, Ella C. Wilson, died February 7, 1894.

Children of Alexander Parker Ten Broeck (580) and Mary C. Dempsey.

933   I EDGAR PARKER, born September 24, 1853; died June 16, 1861.

934   II MARY EMELINE, born April 19, 1856.

Children of Amasa Junius Ten Broeck (581) and Josephine A. Howard.

935   I ARTHUR HOWARD, born July 26, 1849; married December 27, 1883, Ella M. Madden, born May 12, 1858, daughter of Edward M. Madden and Eudosia Robinson.

936   II MARY JOSEPHINE, born August 2, 1851; married December 13, 1877, Abram O. Whipple.

Child of Catharine A. Ten Broeck (592) and Calvin Groat.

937   I GEORGIANA, born September 17, 1837; married October 2, 1866, Alexander Kelsey, born July 21, 1834, died June 10, 1890.

Child of Charlotte E. Ten Broeck (594) and Peter Oakley.

938   I WALTER E., born November 10, 1842; married December 15, 1863, Emma J. Scofield, born September 22, 1844, died March 16, 1877, daughter of Hiram and Almira Scofield of Benton, N. Y.

Children of Walter B. Ten Broeck (596) and Marietta Van Deusen.

939   I VANDELL, born June 16, 1856.

940   II ALICE, born April 17, 1859; died July 4, 1861.

941   III JAY W., born August 24, 1861.

942   IV CAROLINE, born January 20, 1863.

Children of Jay Danforth Ten Broeck (599) and Margaret O. Ames.

943   I EVA, born November 6, 1860.

944   II MARGARET, born October 16, 1862 ; married October 24, 1888, Frederick Bellenden Walrath.

945   III ELLA, born January 12, 1869; married January 24, 1894, George Alexander King.

946   IV CHARLOTTE OAKLEY, born September 18, 1871.

Children of Rensselaer Ten Broeck (600) and Phoebe Wilson.

947   I CHARLES WARREN, born August 11, 1868; married June 1, 1893, Ella De Milt, daughter of H. R. De Milt of New York.

948   II NELLIE EDNA, born July 17, 1875; married John P. Stevens.

949   III JENA; died young.

Children of Robert Henry Ten Broeck (601) and Zilla Meeks.

950   I ZILLA; died young.

951   II WILLIAM.

952   III ROBERT.

953   IV MORRIS.

Child of Eliza W. Gulick (623) and Rev. Enoch Van Aken.

954   I GULICK, born April 22, 1840; died October 20, 1872; married December 1, 1863, Elizabeth Janette Kearney.

Children of Alexander Gulick (624) and Maria Louisa Coons.

955   i CATHARINE LOCKWOOD, married Philip L. Tipp.

956   ii EDWARD.

Children of Jane Garretson Gulick (626) and John Van Aken.

957   i ALEXANDER GULICK, born January 26, 1852.

958   ii ENOCH, born April, 1854; married January, 1878, Mary Farr, daughter of Francis Farr and Jemima Pierson.

959   iii FREDERIKA ELMENDORF, born October 23, 1857; married May 28, 1885, Josiah Tice, born May 1, 1856, son of John R. Tice of New Brunswick, and Rebecca P. Campbell.

Children of John Garretson (630) and Sarah Jones.

960   i ANNA.

961   ii SYRENA.

Children of David Gulick Garretson (633) and Margaret Turner.

962   i CHARLES.

963   ii EMMA.

964   iii GEORGE.

965   iv ELIZA.

966   v ISABELLE.

967   vi FRANK.

Children of William G. Van Fleet (639) and Rebecca Voorhees.

968   i CORNELIUS W., born May 30, 1845.

969   ii EDWARD H., born September 27, 1854.

Child of Margaretta S. Runk (642) and William G. Mentz.

970   I EMMA TEN BROECK, born April 2, 1850; married
September 3, 1877, Walter Erben, born March
3, 1854, son of Peter Cress Erben and Mary
Davis of Philadelphia.

Children of William Runk (643) and Ann Rebecca H. Seymour.

971   I ELLA SEYMOUR, born August 25, 1849; married
April 30, 1873, Abram Brevoort Odell, born
March 21, 1836, son of Jacob de Lancy Odell
and Ann Elizabeth Devoe.

972   II WILLIAM LITTELL, born June 1, 1852; died July 25,
1863.

973   III EVELYN TEN BROECK, born November 3, 1854;
married June 3, 1886, William M. Runk (982),
born October 11, 1846, died October 5, 1892,
son of Peter Ten Broeck Runk and Fanny
Barcroft.

974   IV WALTER SEYMOUR, born June 20, 1857.

975   V ISABEL HALSEY, born September 27, 1859; married
at Yonkers, N. Y., October 30, 1884, George
Herbert Warren, born June 29, 1852, son of
George Warren and Elizabeth Hedge.

976   VI SARAH BARKER, born December 15, 1861; married
October 15, 1890, Edward Hurst Brown, born
January 4, 1859, son of Philip Sidney Brown
and Natalie Josepha Wescott.

977   VII EDITH HALSEY, born August 30, 1863; died November 8, 1869.

978   VIII GEORGE SEYMOUR, born October 25, 1865; died
March 20, 1868.

PETER TEN BROECK RUNK
1853.

979 IX WILLIAM NORTH SEYMOUR, born March 13, 1867;
married at Germantown, Pa., June 3, 1896,
Annie Roberts Wriggins, born November 12,
1872, daughter of William Howard Wriggins
and Lizzie Roberts.

980 X MARY BARCROFT, born January 11, 1869.

981 XI JENNIE CORYELL, born September 28, 1870; died
July 29, 1872.

PETER TEN BROECK RUNK (645).

He was born in Kingwood, N. J., on the sixteenth of
April, 1818. His early manhood was passed in helping
forward the various industries on the family property,
which were quite extensive, and included mills as well as
farm lands.

Ten Broeck Runk, as he was familiarly called, married
on June the fourth, 1845, Fanny Barcroft, the eldest
daughter of Ambrose Barcroft, Jr. In the spring of 1850
they removed to Armstrong County, Pa., where they
resided until the death of Peter Ten Broeck Runk, which
occurred March thirty-first, 1860. This plate is copied
from a daguerreotype which was taken in March, 1853.

He was never prominent in public affairs, but was
deeply interested in the American, or " Know-Nothing "
party, which advocated the control of the Government
by native citizens.

Children of Peter Ten Broeck Runk (645) and Fanny Barcroft.

982 I WILLIAM M., born October 11, 1846; died October
5, 1892; married 1st, Jan. 11, 1872, Elizabeth

27

Cogswell Hill, born November 5, 1850, died March 1, 1885, daughter of Marshall Hill and Harriet S. Field of Philadelphia; married 2nd, June 3, 1886, Evelyn Ten Broeck Runk (973), born November 3, 1854, daughter of William Runk and Ann Rebecca H. Seymour of Brooklyn.

983   II EMMA TEN BROECK, born October 27, 1849.

984   III HARRY BARCROFT, born November 3, 1853; died at Philadelphia, September 25, 1873.

Children of Samuel Runk (647) and Lucy Lind (Ingersoll.)

985   I STACY BARCROFT, born May 30, 1866; married at Cincinnati, Ohio, December 21, 1892, Ivy Pearl Arnold, born May 27, 1874, daughter of William G. Arnold and Mary Bacon.

986   II MARTHA MINOR, born September 17, 1870.

987   III JENNIE LIND, born December 22, 1874.

988   IV NELLIE STEWART, born February 2, 1878.

Children of Patience G. Ten Broeck (653) and Albert G. Hoadley.

989   I JULIA P., born January 21, 1859; died February 17, 1859.

990   II WILLARD C., born August 15, 1860; died August 12, 1895.

991   III HARRY TEN BROECK, born March 11, 1862.

992   IV ALBERT N., born April 26, 1864.

993   V JENNIE E., born December 25, 1865.

994   VI JESSICA M., born November 19, 1867.

995   VII NELSON V. D., born May 30, 1869.

9⁰6 VIII VERNON B., born October 7, 1872.

997 IX FRANK K., born February 19, 1876.

998 X ARCHIE B., born January 9, 1878.

999 XI CHARLES E., born August 23, 1880.

Children of Catharine Ten Broeck Waterhouse (656) and Jacob Whiteman.

1000 I CAROLINE B., born November 13, 1865.

1001 II ELIZABETH W., born May 18, 1867.

1002 III FLORENCE M., born February 12, 1868.

1003 IV ANNIE V. H., born November 1, 1871.

1004 V JENNIE R., born May 26, 1874.

1005 VI GRACE E., born November 29, 1877.

1006 VII EDITH F., born August 26, 1881.

1007 VIII GEORGE W., born March 31, 1884.

Children of Peter Ten Broeck Nevius (663) and Mary E. Sharpe.

1008 I GRACE MYER, born October 11, 1871.

1009 II MARIAN BARCROFT, born April 11, 1873.

1010 III GUERNSEY VAN DERVEER, born October 2, 1876.

1011 IV KATHERINE VAN RENSSELAER, born October 16, 1879.

Child of Katherine M. Ten Broeck (664) and William F. Rowland.

1012 I JANETTE ELIZABETH, born December 30, 1867.

Children of Jane Elizabeth Ten Broeck (666) and William Henry Hill.

1013 I LILLIE MAY, born May 11, 1870; married at Pasadena, Cal., August 21, 1895, Frederick Elmer

Hutchins, born February 25, 1869, son of Julius
C. Hutchins and Mary Fisher.

1014   II HOWARD MILLER, born March 12, 1872; died October 19, 1891.

1015   III FRANK NEVIUS, born September 14, 1873; died January 4, 1874.

1016   IV KATHERINE FLORENCE, born June 13, 1880.

1017   V FREDERICK GARFIELD, born December 17, 1881.

Children of Sarah Alletta Ten Broeck (668) and John Pierson.

1018   I FRANK.

1019   II LULU.

Children of Frank L. Ten Broeck (670) and Minnie Newell Smith.

1020   I JOSEPHINE SIMPSON, born November 25, 1879.

1021   II ESTHER FRANCES, born July 12, 1881.

1022   III PETER QUICK, born October 15, 1883.

1023   IV FRANK LA RUE, born July 1, 1885.

1024   V JOSEPH SMITH, born June 22, 1887.

1025   VI HELEN MURPHY, born June 29, 1891.

1026   VII AGNES HAMILTON, born July 29, 1893.

1027   VIII DOROTHEA ADA, born August 7, 1895.

Children of Peter J. Schomp (672) and Lucretia Ann Griggs.

1028   I WILHELMINA, born October 15, 1865; died March 26, 1891; married October 12, 1887, Robert Mahon Smythe.

1029   II ESTELLE, born December 20, 1866.

1030   III SARAH, born November 14, 1868; married September 12, 1894, Charles Theodore Unterkircher.

Child of Wilhelmina Schomp (673) and John Schomp.

1031   I JOHN TEN BROECK, born October 31, 1871; married October 31, 1895, Mary Chester Dilley, born July 3, 1874, daughter of Chester Van Syckel Dilley and Anna Besson Thatcher.

Children of John Ten Broeck Schomp (674) and Lydia C. Polhemus.

1032   I JOHN V., born January 21, 1871.

1033   II ELLA TEN EYCK, born May 29, 1872.

1034   III THEODORE POLHEMUS, born February 15, 1874; died June 21, 1888.

1035   IV LILLIE MAY, born November 17, 1876.

1036   V JENNIE MAY, born November 17, 1876; died February 1, 1879.

Twins

1037   VI MARY BELLE, born May 10, 1880; died August 15, 1880.

Children of Arintha Ten Broeck (687) and William A. Robinson.

1037a   I JOSEPH W., born at New Brunswick, N. J., May 5, 1870.

1037b   II SARAH ARINTHA, born September 25, 1872.

1037c   III ARISTROPPE WOODHULL, born November 4, 1884.

Children of Krosen Ten Broeck Spader (689) and Mary E. Franken.

1038   I PIERRE LOUIS, born May 13, 1856; died in early infancy.

1039   II WILLIAM V., born December 18, 1857; married in
       New Brunswick, November 17, 1880, Florence
       Isabel Towle, born September 26, 1855, died
       April 7, 1883, daughter of Henry Towle.

Child of Isaac V. Spader (690) and Elizabeth Hicks.

1040   I EMMA C., born July 1, 1852.

Children of John Dennis Ten Broeck (692) and Emily Bliss.

1041   I CHARLES, born March 10, 1856; died June 21, 1863.

1042   II JOHN, born March 3, 1858; died June 20, 1863.

1043   III FLORENCE, born June 26, 1860; died Jan. 20, 1863.

1044   IV ERMA, born October 28, 1862; died November 28,
       1885; married in Savannah, Ga., June 9, 1885,
       Frederick Grimke Fraser of Charleston, S. C.

1045   V FLORENCE, born January 17, 1865; married May
       10, 1887, Jesse Denham Sinkins of Florida.

Children of Augustus Voorhees (694) and Maria Voorhees.

1046   I ISAAC, born August 28, 1852; died March 7, 1873.

1047   II CATHARINE, born April 16, 1855; died Jan. 20, 1856.

1048   III SARAH WAGNER, born November 4, 1856; married
       November 4, 1879, James Edward Terhune,
       born March 21, 1845, son of Albert Terhune
       and Eleanor Fitzgerald.

1049   IV JOHN A., born May 13, 1859; died April 26, 1883.

1050   V FANNIE STEELE, born August 16, 1864; married
       July 3, 1883, William M. Krumscheid, born Sep-
       tember 15, 1859.

1051   VI ABRAHAM A., born November 5, 1868; died May
       28, 1873.

Children of Sarah F. Voorhees (696) and Rev. John M. Wagner.

1052   i JENNIE G., born February 17, 1858; married March 18, 1885, Frederick Eugene Farrell, born September 25, 1860, son of John Farrell and Harriet Decker.

1053   ii CORNELIA VOORHEES, born August 18, 1860; died October 3, 1880.

1054   iii CONRAD ISAAC FREDERICK, born December 3, 1861; married May 23, 1888, Leah W. De Esterre, born June 23, 1865, daughter of James Francis De Esterre and Esther Gallayher.

1055   iv CALVIN MARTIN, born March 22, 1863; married March 22, 1887, Mary Esther Ormsbee, born April 28, 1863, daughter of John Perry Ormsbee and Mary Jane Lord.

Children of Henry Mayell (703) and Elizabeth Northrop.

1056   i JANE WOODWARD, born June 4, 1847; died at Albany February 12, 1873; married John B. Robbins.

1057   ii TEN BROECK B., born September 2, 1851.

1058   iii JAMES H., born February 5, 1855.

1059   iv SARAH E., born July 22, 1857; died February 5, 1890; married September 8, 1881, William H. Van Derzee, M. D., son of Henry Van Derzee of Albany, N. Y.

1060   v MARY FORD, born October 10, 1860; died March 14, 1869.

1061   vi HATTIE CURTIS, born December 6, 1862; died February 7, 1878.

1062   VII BELLA THOMPSON, born November 25, 1864; married, September 6, 1887, George Paddock, of Newark, N. J.

Child of John Ten Broeck Ketchum (705) and his first wife, Caroline Elizabeth Cargill.

1063   I WILLIAM CARGILL; died 1833.

Children of John Ten Broeck Ketchum (705) and his second wife, Lucy Ann Swetland.

1064   I ANNA MARY, born January 25, 1837; married at Plattsburg, N. Y., September 11, 1867, John Ross, born August 12, 1836, son of Judge Henry H. Ross and Susanna Blanchard.

1065   II WILLIAM SWETLAND, born September 15, 1841; died at Plattsburg, N. Y., April 3. 1896; married April 21, 1868, Sarah Buell Weed, daughter of Roswell A. Weed and Sarah Ann Mead.

Children of Joseph Ketchum (709) and Sarah Hannah Keeler.

1066   I SARAH AUGUSTA, born in Brooklyn, December 2, 1839; married June 27, 1865, at Stamford, Conn., Captain Edward Geer Bush, U. S. A., died July 4, 1893; no children.

1067   II CAROLINE MARIA, born in Brooklyn, July 31, 1843; married at Stamford, Conn., June 20, 1866, Robert Dunscomb Swartwout, born February 17, 1844, died September 29, 1883, son of Robert Swartwout and Sarah Satterlee; no children.

1068   III MARY LANE, born June 30. 1849; died at Rock Island Arsenal, December 5, 1873; married

June 25, 1867, Lieut. Edward Maxwell Wright,
U. S. A., son of Judge John Wright, and died
at Washington, D. C., April, 1880.

1069   iv Joseph, born September 22, 1850; married in Brooklyn, January 22, 1876, Henrietta Mary Kane,
daughter of John Kane.

1070   v Cornelia Anna, born January 22, 1854; married
September, 1879, Henry Seaman Howard, born
May 14, 1853, son of Rev. Robert Theus How-
ard and Mary Hester Seaman.

1071   vi Samuel, born January 18, 1857; died February 22,
1896; married October 31, 1885, Linda Virgil
Stedman, born April 28, 1860, daughter of
Charles Stedman of Mendham, N. Y., and
Amelia Doty.

1072   vii Catharine Dwight, born July 29, 1859; married
July 5, 1882, Lieut. Lester Warren Cornish, U.
S. A., son of Dr. Theodore Osgood Cornish and
Jerusha L. Roys.

1073   viii Eloise McClellan, born May 11, 1864; married
January 4, 1888, Lieut. Solomon Pervis Vestal,
U. S. A.

1074   ix Charles Henry, born September 30, 1865; died
October 26, 1865.

Children of Sarah A. Hillhouse (711) and Amos S. Perry.

1075   i Thomas Hillhouse; died in infancy.

1076   ii Mary Stone, born October 1, 1840; married December 21, 1860, Estévan A. Fuertes, born at
Porto Rico, W. I., May 10, 1838, son of Estévan Fuertes and Demetria Charbonnier.

28

1077   III JAMES HILLHOUSE, born at Troy, N. Y., August 31, 1842; married February 6, 1883, at Norfolk, Va., Ella Brooke, born at Brooke's Bank, Va., May 12, 1854, daughter of William Hill Brooke and Clarissa Lawrence.

1078   IV ANNA VIRGINIA; died young.

1079   V SARAH HILLHOUSE, born January 9, 1846; married October 4, 1870, James Palmer Wilson, born August 4, 1849, son of John Robert Wilson and Caroline Ball.

1080   VI JOHN SCHOOLCRAFT, died March 29, 1882.

1081   VII EDWARD DELAVAN, born December 20, 1854; married December 27, 1883, Alice May Van Schaick, daughter of Stephen D. Van Schaick of New York City and Lucinda Willson.

Children of Thomas Hillhouse (712) and Harriet Prouty.

1082   I MARGARET PROUTY, born at Watervliet, N. Y., January 5, 1846.

1083   II THOMAS GRISWOLD, born at Geneva, N. Y., January 23, 1848; married at Mount Holly, N. J., June 3, 1874, Julia Ten Eyck, daughter of John C. Ten Eyck and Julia Gadsby.

1084   III PHINEAS PROUTY, born at Albany, July 13, 1850; died at Colorado Springs, Col., September 27, 1878; married at All Souls' Church, St. Marylebone, Eng., November 23, 1876, Caroline Matilda Van Rensselaer, born August 30, 1848, daughter of the Rev. Maunsell Van Rensselaer of New York, and Sarah Ann Taylor.

1085 IV HARRIET AUGUSTA, born March 18, 1853; married May 17, 1882, Walter Wood Adams, son of John Hamilton Adams of Rochester, N. Y., and Sophia Wood.

1086 V ANNA, born Nov. 12, 1858; died Nov. 27, 1860.

1087 VI ADELAIDE, born at Geneva, N. Y.

Children of John Hillhouse (713) and Catharine M. Van Vranken.

1088 I JOHN TEN BROECK, born October 24, 1848; married October 31, 1877, Mary Lindsay Dickinson, born July 23, 1850, daughter of John Dickinson of Fordham, N. Y., and Adelaide C. Jones of New York.

1089 II WILLIAM PERCY, born August 10, 1853; married October 21, 1889, May Beatrice Landon, born September 3, 1866, daughter of Alson Reynolds Landon and Caroline A. Barbour.

1090 III MANSFIELD LOVELL, born February 14, 1858; married August 1, 1886, Elizabeth Page Pearson.

Children of William Hillhouse, M. D. (714) and Frances J. Betts.

1091 I JAMES, born at New Haven, Conn., November 19, 1854; married at Church of the Ascension, New York, October 3, 1894, Hildegarde Speyers, born June 16, 1866, daughter of Albert Speyers and Matilda Livingston Rogers.

1092 II CHARLES BETTS, born November 25, 1856; married November 21, 1888, Georgiana Delprat Remsen, born June 26, 1862, daughter of Robert G. Remsen and Margaret Delprat.

1093 III FRANCIS, born September 12, 1859.

RICHARD TEN BROECK (*vide* page 99).

It seems proper that the name and sketch of Richard Ten Broeck, the noted Kentuckian, should find a place in the records of the family and generation to which he belongs.

It has, so far, proved impossible to trace his continuous line of descent, although he wrote thus of himself:

My maternal grandfather, Henry Bicker of Philadelphia, was an officer with Washington during the Revolution, while my paternal grandfather, Col. Dirck Ten Broeck, was likewise a Revolutionary officer, although not attached to Washington's staff. I was born in Albany, N. Y., where my early boyhood was passed and I received my education. In 1829 I became a cadet at West Point. After leaving there I spent several years in the South, where my racing career began, which continued, with occasional breaks, until 1877, when I retired entirely.

The family trait of love for and pride in fine horses reached an unusual development in his case. From boyhood to old age, his ambitions were bound up in the events of the turf. His name was well known in Canada and England, as well as throughout the United States.

Late in life he married the widow of H. D. Newcomb of Louisville, Ky., but an unfortunate temperament separated them. He then built himself a home at Menlo Park, N. J., which he named "The Hermitage." Here he died in the summer of 1892, in probably the eighty-fifth year of his age.[100]

THE EIGHTH GENERATION.

❧

Children of Edward Livingston (722) and Phoebe A. Curtis.

1094   I FLORENCE ELLA, born June 18, 1850; married June
21, 1871, James Hopkins, born December 22,
1848, son of John P. Hopkins and Louisa Bird
of Brooklyn.

1095   II KATHERINE, born March 18, 1852; married December 1, 1873, Dennis Eagan, born in Ireland
February 4, 1844.

1096   III CHARLES, born August 20, 1854; died 1887.

Children of Harriet E. Cady (739) and Daniel C. Eaton.

1097   I HARRIET CADY, born August 4, 1835; died at Baltimore, Md., January 31, 1893; married October 15, 1857, (General) George Stuart Brown of
Baltimore, Md.

1098   II DANIEL CADY, born June 16, 1837; married December 18, 1861, Alice Young, daughter of
Henry Young and Anna Mason.

Children of Elizabeth Cady (741) and Henry B. Stanton.

1099   I DANIEL CADY, born March 2, 1842.

1100   II HENRY, born March 15, 1844; married November 5, 1892, Mary O'Shea.

1101   III GERRIT SMITH, born September, 1845; married Augusta Hazelton.

1102   IV THEODORE, born February 10, 1851; married May 19, 1881, Margaret de Barri.

1103   V MARGARET LIVINGSTON, born October 20, 1852; married October 2, 1878, Frank Lawrence.

1104   VI HARRIET O., born January 20, 1855; married November, 1882, Henry Blatch.

1105   VII ROBERT LIVINGSTON, born March 13, 1858.

Children of Margaret C. Cady (742) and Duncan MacMartin.

1106   I FLORA, born June 17, 1843; married October 28, 1869, William Pelham Wright.

1107   II ELISABETH CADY, born February 8, 1846; married February 4, 1874, Charles Hume Baldwin, M. D., son of Chauncy Baldwin and Harriet Hume.

1108   III ARCHIBALD McINTYRE, born August 16, 1847; married November 10, 1869, Harriet A. Smith.

1109   IV DANIEL CADY, born February 12, 1853; died August 10, 1895; married November 16, 1882, Mary Cole.

1110   V ANNIE, born August 11, 1850; died October, 1855.

Children of Catharine Henry Cady (743) and Samuel Wilkeson II.

1111   I MARGARET LIVINGSTON, born July 8, 1842 ; married
         November 20, 1866, Elwood M. Corson, M. D.,
         of Norristown, Pa.

1112   II BAYARD, born May 17, 1844 ; killed at the battle of
         Gettysburg, Pa., July 1, 1863.

1113   III SAMUEL, born July 18, 1846 ; married Isabel Evans
         of Olympia, Wash.

1114   IV FRANK, born March 8, 1848 ; married Mary Crouse
         of Johnstown, Pa.

1115   V MARY, born August 28, 1851 ; died October 29,
         1851.

Children of Philip S. Van Rensselaer (748) and Mary Rebecca
Tallmadge.

1116   I JAMES TALLMADGE, born February 3, 1842.

1117   II CORNELIA PATERSON, born October 6, 1843 ; died
         December 30, 1857.

1118   III PHILIP STEPHEN, born November 11, 1844 ; died
         March 22, 1882 ; married September 5, 1872,
         Edith Biddle, daughter of Edward Biddle of
         Philadelphia.

1119   IV CLINTON, born April 29, 1846 ; died April 24, 1851.

1120   V FRANKLIN, born May 26, 1852 ; died April 29, 1853.

Children of Cortlandt Van Rensselaer (749) and Catharine Ledyard
Cogswell.

1121   I CORTLANDT, born January 5, 1838 ; died October 7,
         1864.

1122   II PHILIP LIVINGSTON, born November 24, 1839; died March 10, 1873; married Annie Whittemore, daughter of Charles O. Whittemore of Boston and Lovice Ayres.

1123   III CHARLES CHAUNCEY, born January 16, 1842; died May 17, 1843.

1124   IV LEDYARD (M. D.), born November 20, 1843; died March 24, 1892.

1125   V ALICE COGSWELL, born March 19, 1846; died April 13, 1879; married May 7, 1868, Edward Blanchard Hodge (D. D.), born February 5, 1841, son of Hugh Hodge, M. D., and Margaret Elizabeth Aspinwall.

1126   VI ELIZABETH WADSWORTH, born February 22, 1848; died April 27, 1886; married 1868 (General) Edward Burd Grubb.

1127   VII ALEXANDER, born October 1, 1850.

Children of Henry Van Rensselaer (750) and Elizabeth Ray King.

1128   I MARY, born 1834; married 1873, John Henry Screven.

1129   II CORNELIA, born 1836; died 1864; married 1859, James Lenox Kennedy, died 1864.

1130   III STEPHEN, born 1838; married 1863, Matilda Heckscher.

1131   IV EUPHEMIA, born 1842; a Sister of Charity.

1132   V ELIZABETH, born 1845; married 1872, George Waddington of New York.

1133   VI JOHN KING, born 1847; married 1871, Mary Duer King.

1134 VII KATHARINE, born 1849; married 1870, Francis Delafield, M. D.

1135 VIII HENRY, born 1851, a priest of the Society of Jesus.

1136 IX WESTERLO, born 1853; died 1857.

Children of Cornelia P. Van Rensselaer (751) and Robert J. Turnbull.

1137　I CORNELIA VAN RENSSELAER, born December, 1848; died June, 1850.

1138　II KATHERINE EUPHEMIA, born March 6, 1851.

Children of Philip Schuyler (755) and Grace Hunter.

1139　I RUTH, born April 10, 1813; married August, 1836, Thomas W. Ogden of New York.

1140　II ELIZABETH VAN RENSSELAER, born August 15, 1815; died October 26, 1889, at Astoria, L. I.; married April, 1839, Richard H. Ogden of New York.

1141　III GRACE, born April 21, 1818; died in Pelham, N. Y., April 17, 1895; unmarried.

1142　IV KATHARINE, born December 7, 1820; died November 27, 1887; married June, 1848, Rev. John Bolton of Pelham, N. Y.

1143　V HARRIET, born October 26, 1823; died in Pelham, November 22, 1877; unmarried.

1144　VI LETITIA HUNTER, born August 8, 1825; married November 16, 1854, Charles H. de Suze.

1145　VII FANNY, born July 24, 1827.

1146　VIII JOHN, born August 14, 1829; died in Pelham, August 19, 1895; unmarried.

1147　IX MARY, born November 5, 1831.

29

Children of Catharine W. Bleecker (759) and Cornelius Glen
Van Rensselaer.

1148   I JOHN; died young.

1149   II STEPHEN; died young.

1150   III CORNELIA, born March 19, 1831; married September 11, 1856, Rev. Cornelius Winter Bolton of Pelhamville, N. Y.

1151   IV KATHARINE, born October 22, 1834.

1152   V JOHN JEREMIAH (M. D.), born September 12, 1836; married October 20, 1864, Florence Taylor of Baltimore, Md.

1153   VI VISSCHER, born October 13, 1838; married September 5, 1866, Mary Augusta Miller of Schoharie, N. Y.

Children of Jacob Wessel Ten Broeck (770) and Sarah Ann Evarts.

1154   I ANDREW JACKSON, born December 19, 1849; married October 26, 1882, Julia Winans, born January 1, 1852, daughter of David Winans and Elizabeth Hover.

1155   II GERTRUDE, born February 15, 1852; died April 25, 1891, unmarried.

Children of William Henry Ten Broeck (771) and Mary Jane Evarts.

1156   I JACOB HENRY, born April 9, 1848; died December 31, 1862.

1157   II EVARTS HOSEA, born May 5, 1853; married October 10, 1876, Alma C. Gardner, born November 5, 1855, daughter of Peter James Gardner and Elizabeth C. Gardner.

1158   III WESSEL, born June 7, 1864.

HELEN TEN BROECK (LAPE) (476).
From the Oil-Portrait of 1834.

Children of Helen M. Ten Broeck (773) and Abraham S. Bogardus.

1159   I ANNA, born September 21, 1855; married May 16, 1878, James Polhemus Van Wyck, born January 20, 1856, son of Polhemus Van Wyck and Augusta Rowley.

1160   II HELEN ELIZABETH, born May 5, 1858; died September 21, 1862.

1161   III CATHARINE TEN BROECK, born January 20, 1861; died November 25, 1862.

1162   IV JACOB TEN BROECK, born October 17, 1864; married October 30, 1889, Ella M. Gleason, born September 12, 1859, daughter of William H. Gleason and Helen A. Gladwin.

1163   V ABRAM FRANK, born November 25, 1865; married June 3, 1891, Phoebe W. Bussey, born November 5, 1863, daughter of Esek Bussey.

1164   VI ARTHUR NELSON, born November 20, 1867; died August 1, 1868.

Children of Jane Ann Ten Broeck (774) and William Rowe Moore.

1165   I ANNA BENNER.

1166   II WILLIAM TEN BROECK.

1167   III HELEN ROWE, married August 3, 1837, Rev. John Morrison, born December 12, 1859, son of Henry Morrison and Elizabeth Stewart.

1168   IV HARRIET ELIZABETH, died June 11, 1882.

1169   V MARY E.

Children of Jacob Ten Broeck De Witt (778) and Juliet Louise May.

1170   I KATE OSBORNE, born March 3, 1854; died at Albuquerque, N. M., January 19, 1896; married at Milwaukee, Wis., January 4, 1874, Lorin W. Lathrop, of Racine, Wis.

1171   II FRANK HUNTSMAN, born December 17, 1857, at Milwaukee; married at Brooklyn, N. Y., April 3, 1878, Maria F. Kernan, born at Brooklyn, May 6, 1860.

1172   III ADA BELLE, born July 25, 1862; married August 11, 1882, Richard S. Hickey of Geneva, N. Y., born September, 1857.

1173   IV ELIZABETH MAY, born July 27, 1855; died September 11, 1868.

Children of Mary J. De Witt (779) and Benjamin T. Hoogland.

1174   I MARY ELIZABETH, born at Brooklyn, September 21, 1852; died April 16, 1853.

1175   II CHARLES TOWNSEND, born at Brooklyn, June 21, 1854; married at Canandaigua, N. Y., October 27, 1886, Helen Viele Richmond, born at Millport, N. Y., January 31, 1862, daughter of Abel Richmond and Sarah Wescott.

1176   III DE WITT, born June 20, 1857; died December 18, 1892; married February 3, 1886, Verina Bailey of Butler, N. J.

1177   IV HELEN CORNELIA, born October 4, 1859; died May 2, 1860.

1178   V GEORGE, born August 14, 1863; died September 14, 1863.

1179   vi JOHN WILLIAM, born November 25, 1865; married at Patchogue, L. I., April 12, 1893, Mary Alice Vrooman, born September 12, 1866, daughter of Frederick C. Vrooman.

Children of Martin Van Buren De Witt (781) and Jane C. Hover.

1180   i FREDERICK, born in Brooklyn, N. Y., May 14, 1866.

1181   ii MARY, born August 9, 1868.

1182   iii JANE, born November 21, 1871.

1183   iv KATE, born January 18, 1874; died February 12, 1878.

1184   v CORNELIA, born December 1, 1878.

Children of Sarah Ann Ten Broeck (789) and Nathan Brewster Morse.

1185   i TEN BROECK, born January 3, 1868.

1186   ii ELIZA TIFFANY, born February 10, 1869.

1187   iii GERTRUDE LESLIE, born June 15, 1876.

Children of Jacob Leonard Evans (792) and his first wife, Melissa A. Yoemans.

1188   i ELMA C., born May 27, 1865; married November 23, 1882, Nathan J. Dix.

1189   ii DORA D., born May 8, 1866; died April 28, 1876.

1190   iii FRANK ISABELLE, born October 19, 1867; died January 13, 1882.

1191   iv FREDERICK, born September 28, 1869.

1192   v EDNA, born March 15, 1872; died September 13, 1873.

1193   vi ALICE, born March 23, 1874; died April 1, 1874.

1194 VII GUY L., born May 13, 1875.

1195 VIII CALVIN S., born July 16, 1879.

Children of Jacob Leonard Evans (792) and his second wife, Jennie
Ashton.

1196 I EDWARD C., born January 3, 1884 ; died January 5,
1884.

1197 II ROSS LEONARD, born September 26, 1885 ; died July
31, 1886.

1198 III CLARENCE, born December 22, 1887.

1199 IV MYRTLE D., born August 9, 1891.

Children of Martin V. B. Evans (793) and Lillian C. Chamberlain.

1200 I ALICE PAULINE, born March 21, 1872 ; married
June 14, 1892, Douglass J. Hall.

1201 II FREDERICK MARTIN, born February 4, 1878.

1202 III HARRY, born March 20, 1880; died August 1, 1880.

1203 IV HARVEY, born July 3, 1883.

Children of Lafayette Evans (799) and Rose E. Redhead.

1204 I HOWARD DAVID, born March 23, 1888.

1205 II LUKE COLLINS, born March 5, 1890.

1206 III ARNOLD, born March 30, 1892.

1207 IV DONALD, born March 30, 1892.

1208 V MILDRED ANN ELIZABETH, born March 11, 1894.

1209 VI ETHEL MARIE, born August 9, 1895.

Children of Anna Eliza Potter (801) and Charles N. Moore.

1210 I GERTRUDE E., born August 10, 1867 ; married La-
vens A. Catlin.

1211   II Charles F., born May 30, 1871; married Lizzie
       N. Sketon.

Child of Peleg A. Potter (802) and Martha St. Barnard.

1212   I Erie W., born April 21, 1881.

Children of George W. Smith (803) and Sophia Koons.

1213   I Charles Edward, born August 5, 1869.

1214   II Mary Magdalene, born August 7, 1871.

1215   III Caroline Louisa, born August 8, 1875.

1216   IV Grace Evelyn, born May 14, 1880; died November 6, 1890.

Child of Emma T. B. Smith (804) and Alexander Scott.

1217   I Gertrude Ellen, born September 26, 1874.

Children of Elizabeth Ten Broeck (807) and John A. Traver.

1218   I Maria, married March 31, 1892, Frank Wey.

1219   II Eliza, married William Wey.

1220   III Julius, died.

1221   IV Georgiana, died.

1222   V Charles.

1223   VI Jane.

Children of Samuel P. Ten Broeck (808) and Adaline Monfort.

1224   I Kate.

1225   II Samuel.

1226   III Charles.

1227   IV Walter.

Child of Jane Ten Broeck (809) and William Haines.

1228   I SAMUEL, married December 31, 1890, Alice Phillips of Rhinebeck.

Children of Lorenzo Ten Broeck (810) and Susan Nelson.

1229   I NELSON.

1230   II ADELAIDE.

Children of Cornelia Bortle (816) and her first husband, Stephen Bachman.

1231   I JENNIE, born October 20, 1858.

1232   II CORA, born February 14, 1860; died April, 1863.

Child of Cornelia Bortle (816) and her second husband, Henry B. Van Vleck.

1233   I WILLIAM H., born June 19, 1875.

Child of Kate Bortle (820) and Madison Miller.

1234   I ALLIE, born October 24, 1876.

Children of Frank Bortle (821) and Ruth Goodrich.

1235   I ALLIE BELLE, born November 27, 1876.

1236   II FRANK, born August 22, 1880.

1237   III CORNELIUS, born February 17, 1882.

Children of Leonard W. Pitcher (823) and his first wife, Jerusha B. Hall.

1238   I ETTA E., born February 6, 1869.

1239   II ROY LEONARD, born November 24, 1870.

Child of Leonard W. Pitcher (823) and his second wife, Anna D.
Reynolds.

1240   i LEONORA, born November 15, 1879.

Children of Mary Etta Pitcher (824) and Esek Finch.

1241   i WALTER DAVID, born November 16, 1873; died
February 19, 1884.

1242   ii MABEL LOUISA, born March 13, 1875; died May 8,
1890.

1243   iii IRA WALLACE, born April 2, 1886.

Children of Mary C. Pitcher (827) and Frederick Pells.

1244   i ALBERTINA LOUISE, born February, 1881.

1245   ii MARGARET ESTHER, born September, 1882.

1246   iii FRANCES, born November, 1884.

1247   iv HELEN AGNES, born 1890.

Children of Gertrude Pitcher (829) and William H. Cramer.

1248   i WALTER, born April 1, 1880.

1249   ii ANNA DORA, born December 17, 1882.

1250   iii SARAH FULTON, born November, 1885.

1251   iv ELSIE GERTRUDE, born 1889.

Children of John H. Pitcher (830) and Mina Haws.

1252   i ANNA MAY, born September, 1879.

1253   ii BERTHA, born 1882.

30

Children of Walter Ten Broeck Pitcher (831) and Anna Lent.

1254   I   EMMA, born February, 1886.

1255   II   RALPH, born 1890.

1256   III   FLORENCE, born March, 1893.

1257   IV   RUTH GERTRUDE, born July, 1895.

Child of Mary Pitcher (833) and Arthur Rifenburgh.

1258   I   WILLIAM, born 1885.

Children of Charles P. Sanders (840) and Anna Maria Beekman Lee.

1259   I   DOUW LEE, born November 26, 1882.

1260   II   J. GLEN, born July 22, 1892.

Children of Helen Rowe Ten Broeck (846) and Wallace Traver.

1261   I   HORACE, born June 21, 1887.

1262   II   ALBERTINA TEN BROECK, born March 25, 1893.

Children of Walter T. L. Ten Broeck, Jr. (851), and Clare Newell
Fortney.

1263   I   WALTER TRYON LIVINGSTON, born July 28, 1894.

1264   II   CLARE NEWELL, born November 4, 1895.

Children of Rev. William P. Ten Broeck (871) and Mary E. Yundt.

1265   I   WILLIAM HENRY, born January 13, 1865; died July
18, 1865.

1266   II   WALTER FRANCIS, born April 19, 1866; died May
1, 1870.

CANE AND SWORD OF GEN. SAMUEL TEN BROECK (135)
The latter used by him in the Revolution.

1267   III GEORGE HERBERT, born June 25, 1868; married
        June 25, 1895, Charlotte E. Dunn, born June
        25, 1869, daughter of Giles Dunn and Louisa
        Lockwood. Seabury Divinity School, Class of
        1891.

1268   IV MARY YUNDT, born April 6, 1870; died April, 1896.

1269   V JOSEPH ANTHONY, born January 4, 1872. Seabury
        Divinity School, Class of 1895.

1270   VI CATHARINE AMELIA, born October 15, 1873.

1271   VII LOUIS LEONARD, born November 12, 1875.

1272   VIII MARION EDWARD, born November 6, 1877; died
        July 29, 1879.

1273   IX FREDERIC STAGG, born March 25, 1880; died June
        28, 1880.

1274   X ROBERT CARPENTER, born April 21, 1881.

1275   XI ANNA PRAY, born December 4, 1883.

        Child of Ada G. Ten Broeck (916) and Alexander Morris.

1276   I JAMES ALEXANDER, born November 12, 1893.

        Children of Philip Clum Ten Broeck (921) and Ida D. Crocheron.

1277   I WALTER CROCHERON.

1278   II MARY EVA.

1279   III EDNA H.

        Children of Edward A. Ten Broeck (925) and Anna Disbrow.

1280   I WILLIS DISBROW, born September 24, 1867; mar-
        ried April 9, 1890, Anna Hogeboom, born May,
        1870.

1281   II STANTON JACOB (M. D.), born February 21, 1871;
       married October 23, 1895, Grace Palmer.

1282   III PAULINE ELISABETH, born December 7, 1875.

Child of Charles Cornwall Ten Broeck (929) and Martha Godkins.

1283   I FREDDIE, born April 21, 1877; died August 11,
       1877.

Child of Arthur H. Ten Broeck (935) and Ella M. Madden.

1284   I HOWARD ROBINSON, born in California, June 1, 1890.

Children of Georgiana Groat (937) and Alexander Kelsey.

1285   I ANNA E., born February 8, 1872; married July 28,
       1889, William Royce, born December 16, 1867.

1286   II HELEN C., born August 24, 1873.

Children of Walter E. Oakley (938) and Emma J. Scofield.

1287   I KIDA V., born November 19, 1864; died July 9,
       1880.

1288   II ROY S., born August 19, 1871; died October 5,
       1883.

1289   III CLAUD W., born July 22, 1873.

Children of Margaret Ten Broeck (944) Frederick B. Walrath.

1290   I KENNETH TEN BROECK, born August 22, 1889;
       died young.

1291   II PAUL BELLENDEN, born April 24, 1892.

1292   III MARY FRANCIS, born February 26, 1896; died young.

Child of Rev. Gulick Van Aken (954) and Elizabeth Janette Kearney.

1293   I ELIZABETH JANNETTE, born October 16, 1864; died July 6, 1865.

Children of Enoch Van Aken (958) and Mary Farr.

1294   I ENOCH CHESTER.

1295   II HAROLD.

1296   III ETHEL MAY.

1297   IV ELIZA WEBSTER.

1298   V JOHN FRANCIS.

1299   VI GEORGE FARR.

1300   VII NANCY ELMENDORF.

1301   VIII ALEXANDER GULICK.

1302   IX FREDERICK TICE.

Children of Frederika Elmendorf Van Aken (959) and Josiah Tice.

1303   I CATHARINE GULICK, born in New Brunswick, N. J., January 20, 1887.

1304   II BESSIE, born July 18, 1889.

1305   III VIOLA, born May 3, 1891.

1306   IV FREDERIKA, born September 13, 1893.

1307   V REBECCA, born April 6, 1895; died July 22, 1895.

1308   VI MARY FRANKEN, born February 4, 1897.

Children of Emma Ten Broeck Mentz (970) and Walter Erben.

1309   I HELEN TEN BROECK, born at Philadelphia, July 21, 1878.

1310   II AGNES CHRISTINA VAN BUREN, born March 10, 1880.

1311   III WALTER, born August 4, 1887.

1312   IV PHILIP VAN RENSSELAER, born August 24, 1889.

Children of Ella Seymour Runk (971) and Abram B. Odell.

1313   I EVELYN BREVOORT, born at Yonkers, N. Y., August
              10, 1877.

1314   II HERBERT BARCROFT, born March 6, 1881.

Children of Sarah Barker Runk (976) and Edward Hurst Brown.

1315   I ISABEL HALSEY, born October 27, 1892.

1316   II PHILIP SIDNEY, born December 15, 1896.

Children of William M. Runk (982) and his first wife, Elizabeth
Cogswell Hill.

1317   I LOUIS BARCROFT, born at Philadelphia, June 13,
              1873.

1318   II MARSHALL HILL, born October 17, 1875.

1319   III ELIZABETH COGSWELL, born November 12, 1878.

1320   IV WILLIAM TEN BROECK, born May 29, 1880; died
              Wednesday, March 4, 1885.

1321   V FLORENCE LINCOLN, born June 6, 1883; died March
              31, 1885.

Children of William M. Runk (982) and his second wife, Evelyn
Ten Broeck Runk (973).

1322   I HARRY TEN BROECK, born June 18, 1888.

1323   II EVELYN SEYMOUR, born March 29, 1890.

1324   III EDITH HALSEY, born January 1, 1892.

Child of Wilhelmina Schomp (1028) and Robert Mahon Smythe.

1325   I CLIFFORD EARL, born July 4, 1888.

Child of John Ten Broeck Schomp (1031) and Mary Chester Dilley.

1326   I JOHN J., born September 20, 1896.

Child of William V. Spader (1039) and Florence I. Towle.

1327   I PIERRE LOUIS, born April 2, 1883; died in early infancy.

Children of Sarah Wagner Voorhees (1048) and James E. Terhune.

1328   I FLORENCE, born October 19, 1880; died September 3, 1881.

1329   II EDNA LILLIAN, born May 29, 1882; died March 18, 1890.

1330   III GILBERT VAN PELT, born October 23, 1883.

1331   IV MAUD LEE, born November 3, 1886.

Children of Fannie Steele Voorhees (1050) and William M. Krumscheid.

1332   I ANNA, born June 2, 1884; died February 14, 1895.

1333   II ELSA, born July 8, 1886.

1334   III MABEL L., born November 9, 1891.

1335   IV EDNA LOUISE, born November 29, 1893.

Children of Jennie G. Wagner, M. D. (1052), and Frederick E. Farrell.

1336   I FREDERICK EUGENE, born August 23, 1886.

1337   II ALFRED WAGNER, born October 2, 1895.

Children of Conrad I. F. Wagner (1054) and Leah W. De Esterre.

1338   ɪ Martin Francis, born April 26, 1889.

1339   ɪɪ Norman Lester, born December 31, 1890.

1340   ɪɪɪ Charles Wesley, born March 25, 1893.

1341   ɪv Leah Cornelia.

Children of Calvin M. Wagner (1055) and Mary E. Ormsbee.

1342   ɪ Johannes Martin, born May 6, 1890.

1343   ɪɪ William Frederick, born April 20, 1891; died June 23, 1896.

1344   ɪɪɪ Gilbert Eugene, born April 7, 1893.

Children of Anna M. Ketchum (1064) and John Ross.

1345   ɪ Elizabeth Swetland, born July 16, 1868.

1346   ɪɪ Frances Henrietta, born January 1, 1870; married May 20, 1891, George Standish Weed, born February 13, 1862, son of Hon. Smith Mead Weed and Caroline Leslie Standish.

1347   ɪɪɪ Ellen Fairbanks, born November 2, 1872.

1348   ɪv Maria Ten Broeck, born February 18, 1874.

1349   v Constance, born September 15, 1876.

1350   vɪ Anna Mary, born May 31, 1878.

Child of Mary Lane Ketchum (1068) and Lieut. Edward M. Wright.

1351   ɪ Edward Bell, born November 25, 1870.

Children of Joseph Ketchum (1069) and Henrietta M. Kane.

1352   I JOSEPH, born November 2, 1876; died August, 1893.

1353   II REYNOLDS, born May 6, 1879.

Children of Cornelia A. Ketchum (1070) and Henry Seaman Howard.

1354   I CAROLINE KETCHUM, born November 13, 1880.

1355   II TEN BROECK, born February 5, 1882.

Child of Samuel Ketchum (1071) and Linda Virgil Stedman.

1356   I THADDEUS, born November 22, 1887.

Children of Catharine D. Ketchum (1072) and Lieut. Lester W. Cornish.

1357   I LESTER ROYS.

1358   II WARREN DWIGHT, born July 26, 1885.

1359   III THEODORE HOWARD.

1360   IV CATHARINE AUGUSTA.

Children of Eloise McC. Ketchum (1073) and Lieut. Solomon P. Vestal.

1361   I MARION PERVIS, born at Camp Supply, Indian Ter., January, 1889.

1362   II HOWARD, born at Camp Supply, July 4, 1892.

1363   III VAN RENSSELAER, born at Fort Grant, Tex., November 30, 1895.

Children of Mary Stone Perry (1076) and Estévan A. Fuertes.

1364   I FELIX JUAN ESTÉVAN, born in Porto Rico, W. I., November 20, 1861.

31

1365   II JAMES HILLHOUSE, born in Ponce, Porto Rico, August 10, 1863; married January 16, 1895, in Camden, Ark., Mary Hill Cable.

1366   III GEORGE PERRY, born in Brooklyn, N. Y., April 25, 1865; died at Ithaca, N. Y.. October 6, 1878.

1367   IV SARAH DEMETRIA, born at Stamford, Conn., January 6, 1868; married June 22, 1888, Edward Hitchcock, M. D., born September 1, 1854, son of Edward Hitchcock of Amherst, Mass., and Mary L. Judson.

1368   V MARY KATHARINE, born March 16, 1872, at Stamford. Conn.

1369   VI LOUIS AGASSIZ, born at Ithaca, N. Y., February 7, 1874.

Child of James Hillhouse Perry (1077) and Ella Brooke.

1370   I JAMES STONE, born in Brooklyn, N. Y., January 18, 1888.

Children of Sarah Hillhouse Perry (1079) and James P. Wilson.

1371   I ELISABETH RUSSELL, born December 20, 1871.

1372   II ANNA TEN BROECK, born November 9, 1873.

1373   III JOHN ROBERT, born January 24, 1875; died January 5, 1882.

1374   IV MARY PERRY, born October 18, 1881; died March 9, 1887.

1375   V ROBERT CLIFFORD, born March 3, 1883.

1376   VI JAMES PERRY, born August 13, 1889.

Children of Thomas G. Hillhouse (1083) and Julia Ten Eyck.

1377   I THOMAS, born at Orange, N. J., December 16, 1875;
        died at Black Hall, Conn., May 25, 1893.

1378   II AUGUSTA, born at Mt. Holly, N. J., October 24,
        1877, died August 11, 1878.

1379   III JOHN TEN EYCK, born July 3, 1879.

1380   IV HENRY WOLCOTT, born September 28, 1881.

1381   V JULIAN GRISWOLD, born June 13, 1890.

Child of Harriet A. Hillhouse (1085) and Walter W. Adams.

1382   I PHINEAS HILLHOUSE, born in New York May 1,
        1883.

Child of John Ten Broeck Hillhouse (1088) and Mary L. Dickinson.

1383   I ADELAIDE DICKINSON, born December 15, 1881.

Child of William P. Hillhouse (1089) and May Beatrice Landon.

1384   I CAROL TEN BROECK, born at Denver, Col., December 30, 1895.

INDEXES.

INDEX TO REFERENCES.

(Page 5.) [1] Doc. Hist. of New York, O'Callaghan, Vol. II., p. 46.

(Page 8.) [2] N. Y. Gen. and Bio. Record, Vol. XX., p. 106.

(Page 8.) [3] Original Rec. of the Kingston and Albany Dutch Churches. Note.—The relationship of Cornelia Ten Broeck (5), stated on page eight, coincides with the opinion of Mr. C. H. Van Gaasbeek, Jr.; see reference following. The original papers of the legal proceedings of the Kingston Church authorities against Dom. Van den Bosch are still in existence. The contents of these cast a shade of doubt upon this opinion. While these papers establish nothing, yet the inference might be that the wife of Laurentius Van den Bosch was the daughter of Dirck Wesselse Ten Broeck, instead of his sister. In that case the marriage of Cornelia Ten Broeck (9) to Johannes Wynkoop in 1696, was a second alliance.

(Page 9.) [4] N. Y. Gen. and Bio. Record, Vol. XIX., p. 69.

(Page 11.) [5] Notarial Papers, 1660-1676, p. 251. Clerk's Office, Albany, N. Y.

(Page 11.) [6] Wills and Deeds, Book B, p. 402. Clerk's Office, Albany.

(Page 11.) [7] Hist. of New Netherland, O'Callaghan, p. 434.

(Page 11.) [8] Wills and Deeds, Book B, p. 139. Clerk's Office, Albany.

(Page 11.) [9] Coll. on Hist. of Albany, Munsell, Vol. III., p. 464.

(Page 12.) [10] Doc. rel. Col. Hist. N. Y., Vol. III., pp. 569, 570.

(Page 12.) [11] Doc. rel. Col. Hist. N. Y., O'Callaghan, Vol. III., p. 824.

(Page 12.) [12] Hist. of N. Y., Brodhead, Vol. II., p. 430.

(Page 13.) [13] History of Albany, Weise, p. 207.

(Page 14.) [14] Doc. Hist. of N. Y., E. B. O'Callaghan, Vol. II., p. 64.

(Page 15.) [15] History of Albany, Weise, p. 236.

(Page 15.) [16] Doc. Hist. of New York, O'Callaghan, Vol. II., p. 23.

(Page 16.) [17] Doc. Hist. of New York, O'Callaghan, Vol. II., p. 149.

(Page 17.) [18] Doc. rel. Col. Hist. N. Y., O'Callaghan, Vol. III., p. 564.

(Page 18.) [19] Doc. History New York, O'Callaghan, Vol. I., p. 189.

(Page 19.) [20] Doc. rel. Col. Hist. N. Y., O'Callaghan, Vol. IV., pp. 59-63.

(Page 19.) [21] Doc. rel. Col. Hist. N. Y., O'Callaghan, Vol. IV., p. 170.

(Page 20.) [22] Doc. rel. Col. Hist. N. Y., O'Callaghan, Vol. IV., p. 177.

(Page 20.) [23] Doc. rel. Col. Hist. N. Y., O'Callaghan, Vol. IV., pp. 902, 900.

(Page 20.) [24] Doc. rel. Col. Hist. N. Y., O'Callaghan, Vol. IX., p. 665.

(Page 21.) [25] Journal of Legislative Council of N. Y., 1691-1743, p. 404.

(Page 21.) [26] Doc. rel. Col. Hist. N. Y., O'Callaghan, Vol. IV., pp. 194, 811.

(Page 96.) 73 Archives of State of N. Y., Fernow, Vol. I., p. 262.
(Page 96.) 74 History of Albany and Schen. Cos., N. Y., Howell and Tenney, p. 129.
(Page 99) 75 Collections on Hist. of Albany, Munsell, Vol. I., p. 209.
(Page 99.) 76 Calendar of N. Y. Hist. MSS., Rev. Papers, Vol. I., 169; Vol. II., 349.
(Page 100.) 77 Calendar of N. Y. Hist. MSS., Rev. Papers, Vol. I., p. 519.
(Page 104.) 78 Collections on Hist. of Albany, Munsell, Vol. I., p. 257.
(Page 104.) 79 Calendar of N. Y. Hist. MSS., Rev. Papers, Vol. I., pp. 501, 505.
(Page 104.) 80 Hist. of Albany and Schen. Cos., N. Y., Howell & Tenney pp. 354, 418.
(Page 106.) 81 Calendar of N. Y. Hist. MSS., Rev. Papers, Vol. I., p. 173.
(Page 106.) 82 History of Columbia Co., N. Y., Everts & Ensign, p. 29.
(Page 107.) 83 Hist. of Albany and Schen. Cos., N. Y., Howell & Tenney, p. 354.
(Page 109.) 84 Calendar of N. Y. Hist. MSS., Rev. Papers, Vol. I., p. 174; Vol. II., p. 41.
(Page 112.) 85 Early Hist. of Schenectady, Sanders, pp. 212, 214.
(Page 116.) 86 Calendar of N. Y. Hist. MSS., Rev. Papers, Vol. I., p. 174.
(Page 118.) 87 Archives of State of New York, Fernow, Vol. I., p. 269.
(Page 119.) 88 New York in the Revolution, Roberts, p. 98.
(Page 119.) 89 Old New York (April, 1890), Vol. II., p. 200.
(Page 123.) 90 Deed Books 1, 7, and 9, New Brunswick, N. J.
(Page 125.) 91 Hist. of the Reformed Church, Readington, Thompson, p. 78.
(Page 131.) 92 Archives of State of N. Y., Fernow, Vol. I., p. 180.
(Page 132.) 93 Old New York, Vol. II., p. 200.
(Page 133.) 94 Annals of the Van Rensselaers, Van Rensselaer, p. 203.
(Page 134.) 95 New York in the Revolution, Roberts, p. 103.
(Page 135.) 96 Hist. of Albany and Schen. Cos., N. Y., Howell & Tenney, p. 400.
(Page 138.) 97 New York in the Revolution, Roberts, p. 45.
(Page 146.) 98 Hist. of Albany and Schen. Cos., Howell & Tenney, p. 354.
(Page 186.) 99 Hist. of Columbia Co , N. Y., Everts & Ensign, p. 213.
(Page 220.) 100 Turf, Field, and Farm (August, 1892), Vol. LV., p. 155.

NOTE

To find your ancestry in this arrangement of families, refer to the page indicated for your own name. On the head-line of your family will be found your parents' names. Note the number found on this line, and turn back until this appears as a marginal number. Your grandparents' names will then be found on the head-line. Following the same plan you will find the line of ascent. In case the line of descent is being traced, and both parents belong to the Ten Broeck family, the father's line has been made the direct one.

In all cases where the surname has been changed through marriage, the maiden name alone will be found in the index, with the married name in parenthesis following.

Ten Broeck, Charlotte O., 206
  Chauncey A., 204
  Christina (21), 39
  Christina (67), 49
  Christina (80), 52
  Christina (82), 52
  Christina (127), 62
  Christina (192), 81
  Christina (478), 151
  Christina (585), 164
  Christina (Cock), 63, 102
  Christina (Livingston), 59, 88-89, 92
  Christina (Schuyler), 50, 70, 72-74
  Christina (Ten Broeck), (197), 69, 83, 113-114, 121
  Christina (Ten Broeck), (262), 71, 101, 116, 118-119
  Christina (Ten Broeck), (311), 115, 121, 165
  Christina (Van Alen), 31, 36, 40, 45
  Christina (Van Dyck), 40, 60
  Christina (Van Slyck), 54, 83
  Christina C., 187, 188
  Christina C. (Ireland), 160, 201
  Christina C. (Van Rensselaer), 122
  Christina E., 204
  Christina J. E. (Knickerbacker), 117
  Christina L., 166
  Clare Newell, 234
  Cornelia (462), 148
  Cornelia (Wynkoop),31, 35, 42-43
  Cornelia Alida, 160
  Cornelia Alida (Valance), 160, 201
  Cornelia Catharine, 117
  Cornelia Christina, 203
  Cornelia R. (Mitchell), 115
  Cornelia Stuyvesant (Jackson), 185
  Cornelia Wessels (Van den Bosch), 8, 9
  Cornelis (27), 40, 42, 63-64
  Cornelis (83), 53, 69, 81-82, 131
  Cornelius (281), 64, 105
  Cornelius (396), 134
  Cornelius (491), 152, 191
  Cornelius II., 160, 202
  Cornelius P., 114
  Culver II., 202

  David S., 160, 162, 203
  David V. R., 117, 161, 162
  Delia M. (Ten Broeck), 160, 202, 203
  Derrick Wessel (813), 194

Ten Broeck, Dirck (20), 39, 56-58, 86, 87, 88, 98
  Dirck (89), 54
  Dirck (112), 59
  Dirck (113), 58, 60, 86, 98-99
  Dirck (245), 6, 98, 145-147
  Dirck (460), 148
  Dirck Wesselse (Major), 8-35, 48, 50, 51, 53, 55
  Dirck Wesselse (68), 49, 64-67, 83, 106
  Dirck Wesselse (75), 52, 75
  Dirck Wesselse (163), 27
  Dirck Wesselse (195), 82
  Dirck Wessels (292), 110
  Dirck Wessel (316), 116
  Dirck Wessel (341), 121
  Dirck Wessels (403), 148
  Dirck Wessel (844), 197
  Dorcas, 153
  Dorothy, 110
  Dorothea A., 212

  Edgar Parker, 205
  Edith M., 200
  Edmund W., 130
  Edna H., 235
  Edward Ambrose, 204, 235
  Edward Brinckerhoff, 192
  Edward F., 160
  Edward, (Mrs.), 147
  Edward Payson, 185
  Elbertina (297), 110
  Elbertje (136), 67
  Eliza Alida, 121
  Eliza H. (Beekman) (Schoonmaker), 122, 166-167
  Elizabeth (24), 40
  Elizabeth (91), 54
  Elizabeth (205), 84
  Elizabeth (206), 84
  Elizabeth (211), 84
  Elizabeth (212), 84
  Elizabeth (246), 98
  Elizabeth (369), 127
  Elizabeth (466), 148
  Elizabeth (578), 163
  Elizabeth (761), 192
  Elizabeth (Calkins), 164
  Elizabeth (Costar), 31, 36, 46
  Elizabeth (Schuyler), 98
  Elizabeth (Traver), 193, 231
  Elizabeth (Waterhouse), 127, 172
  Elizabeth A. (Wetherwax), 160, 201
  Elizabeth H. (Corlies), 130, 177, 178
  Elizabeth M. (461), 148

Ten Broeck, Elizabeth V. R., 148
Ella (King), 206
Ella Maud, 202
Elsje (Cuyler), 31, 35, 40, 41, 63
Emeline, 164
Emma (Potter), 153, 193
Emma (Runk), 126, 169-171
Emma C. (Spader), 128, 175
Emma Jane, 166
Ephraim (15), 36
Ephraim (79), 52
Ephraim (87), 53
Erma (Fraser), 214
Ernest M., 201
Esther F., 212
Eva (943), 206
Eva (Platner), 166
Evarts H., 226

Florence, 214
Florence (Simkins), 214
Francis F., 162
Frank La Rue (670), 78, 174, 212
Frank La Rue (1023), 212
Freddie, 236
Frederic S., 235

Gabriel, 83, 134
Geertruy (Schuyler), 31, 33, 35, 43-44
George (364), 124
George A. (609), 166
George Augustus (579), 163
George Edwin (567), 162
George Herbert, 235
George P., 101
George Washington, 174
George Wray, 105
Gertrude (257), 101
Gertrude (1155), 226
Gertrude A. (Smith), 153, 193

Harman, 105
Harmanus Schuyler, 117
Harmon Jay, 161, 203
Harmon Van Loan, 203
Harriet C. (Peabody), 186
Harriet E., 166
Helena L. (Franklin), 186
Helen (Lape), 150, 189
Helen (Ten Broeck) (Denison), 117, 162, 163
Helen Josephine (Swart), 204
Helen M., 212
Helen M. (Bogardus), 188, 227
Helen R. (Traver), 197, 234
Helen V., 166
Hendrick (69), 49, 68, 82, 83

Ten Broeck, Hendrick (77), 52
Hendrick (150), 69
Hendrick (151), 69, 115
Hendrick (199), 83
Hendrick (252), 100
Hendrick Wesselse, 8, 9, 10
Henry (313), 115, 160
Henry (354), 160
Henry A. (304), 114, 158
Henry E., 160
Henry H. (530), 158, 200
Henry Hill, 205
Henry Hobart, 200
Henry S., 173
Howard R., 236

Jacob (22), 40
Jacob (26), 40, 45, 60-62, 149
Jacob (131), 63, 102
Jacob (250), 99
Jacob (264), 102, 103, 149-150
Jacob (294), 110, 152
Jacob (475), 150, 186-189
Jacob Henry, 226
Jacob Lawrence, 162, 204
Jacob Samuel, 122, 166
Jacob Wessel, 149, 150, 188, 226
Jacob William, 166
Jacobus, 101
James Adam, 121, 166
James B. R., 176
Jane (188), 80
Jane (347), 121
Jane (354), 122
Jane (473), 150
Jane (686), 175
Jane (702), 177
Jane (Garretson), 124, 169
Jane (Haines), 164, 232
Jane A. (Moore), 188, 227
Jane Christina, 159
Jane C. (Wheeler), 164
Jane E. (Hill), 173, 211
Jane E. (Waterman), 159, 201
Jane G. (Schomp), 127, 174
Jane G. (Voorhees), 128, 176
Jane G. (Woodward), 130, 167
Jane L. (Sanders), 156, 196
Jane Livingston, 197
Jane Maria, 118
Janetje (154), 70
Jannetjen (Ten Broeck), 72, 102, 122
Jay Danforth, 165, 206
Jay W., 206
Jena, 206
Jennie, 193

GENERAL INDEX

33

264 General Index

Hover, Charles H., 191
  Chauncey, 191
  Elizabeth (Winans), 226
  Jane C. (De Witt), 191, 229
  Jonas, 191
  Mrs. Charles H., 190
Howard, Calvin, 163
  Caroline K., 241
  Henry S., 217, 241
  Henry S. (Mrs.), 134
  Josephine A. (Ten Broeck), (Camp), 163, 205
  Robert T., 217
  Ten Broeck, 241
Howe, Elizabeth (Van Schaick), 136
  John, 136
Howland, Mary (Van Rensselaer), 183
Hoyt, Hannah (Keeler), 178
Hubbard, Caleb, 154
  Etta G. (Pitcher), 154, 194
  Ruggles, 139
Hudson, Hendrick, 1
Hughan, Elizabeth S. (Traver), 197
Hughes, Henry, 175
Hulme, Anne (Wilson), 157
Hume, Harriet (Baldwin), 222
Humphrey, Eunice (Livingston), 180
Hunt, Col. Samuel, 78
Hunter, Governor, 21, 27
  Grace (Schuyler), 184, 225
  Robert, 184
Hutchins, Frederick E., 211, 212
  Julius C., 212

Ingersoll, Joseph H., 171
Ireland, Cora C., 201
  F. Asbury, 160, 201
  Frances J. (Latham), 201
  James M., 201
  William T. B., 201
  Zilla A., 201

Jackson, George E. B., 185
  Henry, 185
Jacobs, Sarah (Livingston), 139
James, Duke of York, 3, 4
Jans, Anneke, 11, 26, 48
Jansen, Roelof, 26
Jarvis, James G., 158
  Laura A. (Burt), 157, 199
  William O., 158
Jay, Governor John, 146
Jenkins, Mary A. (Willard), 142
Johanna Catharina (Van Alen), 46
Johnson, Ella (Ten Broeck), 202
  Sarah (Livingston), 89, 143
  Sir William, 64

Jones, Abigail (Mott), 157
  Adelaide C. (Dickinson), 219
  Sarah (Garretson) 169, 207
  Thomas, 90
Jonkman D., 67
Joralemon, Christopher, 173
  John C., 173
Jordan, Jacob, 88
Judson, Mary L. (Hitchcock), 242

Kane, Henrietta M. (Ketchum), 217, 241
  John, 217
Kastendike, Mary M. (Koons), 193
Keach, Apphia (Salisbury), 153
Kearney, Elizabeth J. (Van Aken), 206, 237
Keeler, Joseph, 178
  Sarah H. (Ketchum), 178, 216
Keifer, Maria (Ten Broeck), 162
  William, 162
Kellenaer, Laurentia (Van Gaasbeek) (Chambers) (Ten Broeck), 9
Kelsey, Alexander, 205, 236
  Anna E. (Royce), 236
  Helen C., 236
Kennedy, James L., 224
Kernan, Maria F. (De Witt), 228
Ketchum, Anna C., 178
  Anna M. (Ross), 216, 240
  Caroline M. (Swartwout), 216
  Catharine D. (Cornish), 217, 241
  Charles, 178
  Charles H., 217
  Cornelia A. (Howard), 217, 241
  Eloise McC. (Vestal), 217, 241
  H., 133
  John T. B., 178, 216
  Joseph (391), 133, 178
  Joseph (709), 178, 216
  Joseph (1069), 217, 241
  Joseph (1352), 241
  Mary L., 178
  Mary L. (Wright), 216, 240
  Reynolds, 241
  Samuel (706), 178
  Samuel (1071), 217, 241
  Sarah A. (Bush), 216
  Thaddeus, 241
  William Cargill, 216
  William S., 132, 216
Ketchas, Catharine (Livingston), 144
Kidder, Octavia (Woodbury), 185
King, Elizabeth R. (Van Rensselaer), 183, 224
  George A., 206
  James H., 17
  John Alsop, 183

34

35

www.ingramcontent.com/pod-product-compliance
Lightning Source LLC
Chambersburg PA
CBHW021108270326
41929CB00009B/774